W0081681

Flag Football

by Diana Flores

A Wiley Brand

Flag Football For Dummies®

Published by: **John Wiley & Sons, Inc.,** 111 River Street, Hoboken, NJ 07030-5774, www.wiley.com

For general information on our other products and services, please contact our Customer Care Department within the U.S. at 877-762-2974, outside the U.S. at 317-572-3993, or fax 317-572-4002. For technical support, please visit https://hub.wiley.com/community/support/dummies.

Wiley publishes in a variety of print and electronic formats and by print-on-demand. Some material included with standard print versions of this book may not be included in e-books or in print-on-demand. If this book refers to media that is not included in the version you purchased, you may download this material at http://booksupport.wiley.com. For more information about Wiley products, visit www.wiley.com.

Library of Congress Control Number is available from the publisher.

ISBN 978-1-394-34534-2 (pbk); ISBN 978-1-394-34535-9 (ebk); ISBN 978-1-394-34536-6 (ebk)

Printed and bound by CPI Group (UK) Ltd, Croydon, CR0 4YY

C9781394345342_051225

Table of Contents

INTRODUCTION 1

About This Book 2

Foolish Assumptions 2

Icons Used in This Book 3

Beyond the Book 4

Where to Go from Here 4

PART 1: GETTING STARTED WITH FLAG FOOTBALL 5

CHAPTER 1: Introducing Flag Football 7

Discovering What Flag Football Is — and Isn't 8

Understanding What Makes Flag Football Great 9

Seeing who's playing flag football: A sport for everyone 10

Starting young and growing with the game 11

Tracking flag football's history 12

World Cups 13

Perusing Various Levels of Play 13

Flag football in the NFL 14

International competitions 15

The road to the Olympics (LA 2028) 16

CHAPTER 2: The Wear and Where of Flag Football 17

Where: The Field 17

Playing surface 18

Field dimensions 18

The marks on the field 19

Yard Lines 21

Out of bounds 22

Other marks 22

Down indicator 22

7-yard chain 23

Team areas 23

Wear: Uniforms 23

The jersey 23

Pants 24

Cleats 24

Flags 25

Mouthpiece 25

What is not permitted 26

The Ball 26

CHAPTER 3: **The Who and How of the Game** 29

Looking at Who's Involved in Flag Football 29

Coaches: The beating heart of a team 30

Managers: The team's backbone. 35

Athletic trainers: Keeping players in top shape 35

Referees and officials: The guardians of fair play. 35

The players: The stars of the game. 37

The Big Picture: How the Game Is Played .40

CHAPTER 4: **Regarding the Rules** 41

Remembering the Golden Rule of Flag Football 41

Noting the Ins and Outs of the Game Clock 42

Checking Out the Coin Toss 43

Getting the Gist of Downs and Yards 44

Scoring Points 45

Touchdowns 45

Extra points: One or two points 46

Safeties 46

Recognizing the Roles of the Officials. 46

The referee 47

The field judge 48

The down and side judges 48

Other official responsibilities. 48

Familiarizing yourself with the referees' signals 49

Penalties and other violations 52

PART 2: OFFENSE 55

CHAPTER 5: **The Quarterback** 57

Understanding the Role of the Offense 57

The Quarterback: More Than Just a Strong Throwing Arm. 59

Qualities of a Successful Quarterback: From Mentality

to Precision. 60

Arm strength and release. 61

Accuracy (and timing) 61

Positive leadership 61

Competitiveness 61

Intelligence 62

Strategy. 62

Emotional intelligence. 62

Agility 62

Vision 63

Mastering the Fundamentals. 63

    Stance: Balance starts here 63

    Quick feet 64

    Dropping back 64

    Getting a good grip 64

    Power comes from the hips. 65

    Three keys to a great throw: Timing, accuracy,
    ball positioning. 65

Reading the Defense. 66

    The pre-snap read. 66

    7-second rule 67

    Coverages 68

    Reading in the red zone 75

CHAPTER 6: **The Passing Game** 77

The Anatomy of a Playmaker: Wide Receiver Essentials 78

    Speed and endurance. 78

    Hands 78

    Field awareness. 78

    Competitiveness 79

    Consistency 79

    Timing 79

Wide Receivers. 79

    Lining up 79

    Stance 80

    Release 80

    Motions 80

Center 80

    Stance and snap 80

    Quick release 81

    Field vision and awareness 81

Route Tree 81

Compound Routes 83

Catching the Ball 84

    Eyes on the ball 84

    Hands ready. 85

    Body positioning 85

    Finishing the play. 85

    Beating man-to-man coverage 86

    Gaining yards after catch 86

    Quick feet 87

Hips and dips 87
Field awareness 87
No contact or blocking 87
Thinking Smart: Mastering Game Situations 88

CHAPTER 7: **The Running Game** 89
When Is a Running Play Used? 90
Who Can Run the Ball? 91
Lining Up: Hand-offs and Reverses 92
Variations on Running Formations 93
The Basic Skills for Running the Ball 95
Receiving the hand-off 96
Running at top speed 97
Seeing the field 97
Being agile 97
Evading the clean flag pull 97

PART 3: DEFENSE 99
CHAPTER 8: **The Linebacker** 101
Looking at What the Linebacker Does .102
Filling a hybrid role 102
Playing downfield and backfield 103
Seeing Where the Linebacker Is Positioned 105
Considering the Core Traits of a Dominant Linebacker 106
Quickness 106
Vision 107
Instinct 107
Communication 107
Stance 108
Reading the offense 108

CHAPTER 9: **The Blitzer** 111
Reviewing a Blitzer's Role and Responsibilities 111
Understanding the Core Traits of a Dominant Blitzer 114
Speed 114
Reaction 114
Body control 115
Lining up 115
Stance 116
Studying Blitzer Maneuvers 118
Reading hand-offs 118
Defending a crowded backfield 120
When the blitzer has to cover 121

CHAPTER 10: **The Secondary**. 123

   Reviewing Core Traits of the Secondary Players. 124

      Speed and quickness 124

      Vision. 124

      Hands 124

      Body control (noncontact) and reaction 125

      Flag pulling 125

   Understanding the Game Situation 126

      Knowing the down and distance. 126

      Forcing them to stay in bounds. 127

      Adjusting according to the situation. 127

   Cornerbacks. 127

      What the cornerback does. 128

      Positioning and alignment 129

   Free Safety 130

      What the free safety does 131

      Positioning and alignment 131

   Avoiding Common Mistakes 133

PART 4: BUILDING SKILLS: KEY DRILLS AND PLAYS 135

CHAPTER 11: **Practicing Drills by Position**. 137

   Quarterbacks 138

      Accuracy drills 139

      Throwing on the go 140

      Evading the blitzer. 140

   Wide Receivers and Centers 142

      Catching the ball 142

      Running routes 142

      Agility and footwork 143

   Running Backs 143

      Acceleration and explosiveness 144

      Footwork and agility 144

      Hip agility and fluidity 145

   Cornerbacks and Free Safeties 146

      Defensive footwork. 147

      Attacking the ball. 147

      Pulling flags 148

   Linebackers 149

      Reacting 149

      Pulling flags 150

   Blitzers. 150

      Drill 1: Sprint and redirect flag pull. .151

      Drill 2: Forward blitz, backward drop 151

CHAPTER 12: **Getting into Flag Football Shape**......................153

Understanding the X Factor of Flag Football.....................154
Conditioning by Position 154
Wide receivers, cornerbacks, linebackers, and safeties.........155
Quarterbacks...158
Blitzers..163
Crossing Over: Multi-Sport Advantage 165

CHAPTER 13: **Offensive Plays and Strategies**......................167

Using Strategy to Play to a Team's Strengths 168
Defining the Goals of an Effective Offense 168
1. Consistency 169
2. Efficiency...169
3. Adaptability 169
4. Game control 169
5. Drive 169
Mastering Offensive Formations...............................170
Spread..170
Trips..171
Bunch 172
Beating a Defense 173
Beating man-to-man coverage: Cover 1.....................173
Beating zone coverage 177
Double QB 189
Nailing One- and Two-Point Conversions 191

CHAPTER 14: **Defensive Plays and Strategies** 193

Defining the Goals for Effective Defense Formations 193
Mastering Defensive Formations 195
Game situation..195
Field position 196
Time management 196
Providing Defensive Coverage.................................196
Man versus zone coverages................................197
Man-to-man coverage.....................................197
Cover 2 198
Cover 3 199
Cover 4 201
Cover 31 202
Building the Wall: Core Elements of an Unstoppable Defense......203
Playing Mind Games: Outsmarting the Offense 204

**PART 5: FROM YOUTH LEAGUES TO THE
INTERNATIONAL STAGE**...205

CHAPTER 15: **One Sport, Many Styles**...........................207
    Exploring Varieties of the Game 207
        5-on-5 208
        7-on-7 208
        Beach...209
        Coed (or mixed) 209
    Introducing NFL FLAG Football 210
        Finding where it's played 211
        Understanding the rules...............................211
        Looking at its international intention 212

CHAPTER 16: **Homing in on High School and College
Flag Football**...213
    Becoming a Sanctioned High School Sport in the United States 214
    Exploring Flag Football in College..........................214
        Mexico...215
        United States 216
    Reviewing the Rules 220

CHAPTER 17: **Investigating IFAF International
Competitions**..223
    Citing Continental Championships........................224
        The Americas 224
        Europe...225
        Asia 225
        Africa 225
    Whirling through World Cups 226
    Reviewing World Rankings................................228

CHAPTER 18: **Diving into The World Games**.....................229
    Exploring The World Games History........................229
    Comparing The World Games to the IFAF World
    Championships 231

CHAPTER 19: **Becoming an Olympic Sport: LA 2028** 233
    Dreaming the Dream: From Grassroots to Olympic Bid 233
    Identifying the Power Players: IFAF and NFL's Global Push 235
    Getting on the Road to LA: How Teams Will Qualify 235
    Exploring What This Means for the Sport 236

PART 6: THE PART OF TENS 237

CHAPTER 20: **Ten Essential Skills to Get Started** 239

Listening and Learning 239
Being a Good Teammate 240
Having the Courage to Try (and Try Again) .240
Being Agile 240
Being Fast (If Not the Fastest) 241
Maintaining Coordination and Balance 241
Building Endurance 241
Staying Positive, Even When It's Hard 242
Being Curious About the Game 242
Believing You Belong on the Field 242

CHAPTER 21: **Ten Reasons to Play Flag Football** 243

You'll Build Mental Toughness 243
You'll Find New Opportunities 244
You'll Feel Empowered 244
You'll Find Your Place 244
You'll Discover the Power of Teamwork 245
You'll Have Fun (and It's Easy to Learn) 245
You'll Grow to Believe in Yourself 245
You'll Create Lasting Connections 246
You'll Build Leadership Skills 246
You'll Develop a Healthier Body 246

GLOSSARY 247

INDEX 253

Introduction

I n this book, I want to talk to you about what once was the unthinkable. I want to bring you into a movement that is changing the narrative and making possible what once seemed out of reach.

Flag football has become more than a sport; it's one of the biggest movements in the world of sports today. It has turned from something unrecognized, overlooked, and underestimated into a global force that is breaking barriers, rewriting the narrative, and opening doors for millions.

I want to share with you everything I've learned about this game with the same love and passion that a little 8-year-old girl from Mexico City had when she fell in love with a sport that wasn't "meant" for her. That same girl who played on dust fields with her teammates and paved her own way in a world that once said, "This is not for you," while her heart screamed, "I belong here."

This sport changed my life in ways I never imagined, and I want the same for you. Because if a girl like me can turn her dreams into reality through passion, discipline, and resilience, you can too.

This game is about more than plays and points. It's about building something that matters. Today, you are part of this journey too, a growing, fearless community that dares to dream and dares to act. Together, we're building a dream that belongs to all of us.

This book is for the ones who've ever felt left out. For every girl who was told she was too small, too slow, or just not meant for the game. For every person who thought about giving up. For those who've sat in the bleachers, wondering if they could be the ones on the field. This is your sign: You belong here.

So whether you're picking up a football for the first time or chasing your next championship, welcome. You are part of the movement.

About This Book

Flag Football For Dummies is your go-to playbook for everything flag. I've written this book with one goal: to make it easy, fun, and practical to understand the game from every angle, whether you're stepping on the field for the first time or stepping up as a coach. Here's how it breaks down:

Part 1: Getting Started with Flag Football. Start with the basics: what flag football is, where it comes from, and why it's one of the most inclusive sports on the planet. Learn about the gear, the roles, and the rules that shape the game.

Part 2: Offense. This part dives into the art of moving the ball. From the quarterback's mindset to passing routes and running techniques, you'll learn what it takes to score and how to build chemistry with your team.

Part 3: Defense. Defense brings the fire to the game. It's the side of the ball that turns momentum, makes game-changing plays, and keeps hope alive. In this part, you'll dive into how defensive units operate, how they communicate, react, and attack. You'll learn to anticipate plays, shut down offenses, and bring nonstop energy to every snap. From rusher to safety, every role matters.

Part 4: Building Skills: Key Drills and Plays. Want to improve? This part is packed with drills, routines, and strategy tips for every position. It also breaks down offensive and defensive plays to help you read the field like a pro.

Part 5: From Youth Leagues to the International Stage. Flag football is everywhere, from schoolyards to the World Games. This section explores its global rise, the structure of competitive leagues, and the historic road to the Olympic Games.

Part 6: The Part of Tens. Just for fun and inspiration. Discover fun facts and uncover surprising stories that make this sport so special.

Glossary. This section defines key terms so you can keep up on and off the field.

This book is your guide for how to play, coach, train, and enjoy flag football in the familiar Dummies way: straightforward, engaging, and easy to follow.

Foolish Assumptions

Here's what I'm assuming about you: Maybe you're that girl, like I once was, trying to find her way in this life, willing to discover a new world of possibilities and dreams. Or maybe you're already part of this rising movement of change, using flag football as your platform to grow, to connect, to lead.

You may not know all the rules yet, but you know there's something special about this game, and you sense there's something special about the community around it. You may even sense the power it holds to build confidence, community, and opportunity. Flag football welcomes everyone, and this book was written with you in mind. You're curious about flag football and excited to learn more — whether that means stepping onto the field, coaching a team, or cheering from the sidelines — and you may be asking these questions:

>> How is flag football different from tackle football?

>> What does a quarterback and each player on the field actually do?

>> Why are there so many types of passes and routes?

>> How do teams score, and what makes a good play?

Whether you're new to football or just new to this version of it, this book is here to guide you. No prior experience required, just an open mind and a love for learning something new.

Icons Used in This Book

Throughout this book, icons in the margins highlight certain types of valuable information that call out for your attention. Here are the icons you'll encounter and a brief description of each.

TIP

Here you find quick advice to help you get better results or avoid common mistakes.

REMEMBER

This is key information you'll want to keep top of mind, especially during games.

DIANA SAYS

These are my personal takeaways. In my 10 years of experience playing this sport, I've learned a lot, and I'm sharing things that have helped me grow as an athlete and a leader. I also share personal stories that highlight how special and exciting this sport is.

WARNING

This icon tells you to watch out! It marks important information that may save you headaches.

Beyond the Book

In addition to the abundance of information and guidance related to flag football that I provide in this book, you can find even more help and information online at Dummies.com. Check out this book's online Cheat Sheet: Just go to www.dummies. com and search for "Flag Football For Dummies Cheat Sheet."

Where to Go from Here

This book isn't a rulebook you have to read front to back; it's a field guide that meets you where you are. You can start from the beginning and build a strong foundation, or jump right into the sections that excite you most. If you're brand new to the sport, start with Part 1 to learn the basics. If you already play and want to sharpen your skills, head to Parts 2, 3, or 4 for strategies, drills, and position breakdowns. Curious about the bigger picture? Explore Part 5 and discover how far this sport has come and where it's going.

Whatever path you take, let this moment be your first step, a moment to claim your place in something bigger. No matter where you are in your journey — just starting out, returning after time away, or pushing for the next level — you are ready. Ready to step onto the field with confidence, to bring your spark, your voice, your drive.

So flip the page, lace up your cleats, and lean into the power of what's possible.

1

Getting Started with Flag Football

IN THIS PART . . .

See the game's origins and evolution and why it's so popular.

Find out about fields, uniforms, and equipment.

Get to know the players, coaches, referees, and how the game is played.

Take a tour of flag football rules, according to the International Federation of American Football (IFAF).

Chapter **1**

Introducing Flag Football

Flag football is one of the fastest-growing sports in the world right now, played by more than 10 million people in over 100 countries. It's a noncontact version of American football that showcases speed, agility, and strategy, but more than that, it's an experience. A thrill. A rush. From the moment the ball is snapped, it's go time.

But this isn't just a smaller version of tackle football. It's its own game, and it's electric. Quarterbacks call out plays like field generals. Receivers sprint, cut, and spin their way to open space. Defenders explode into action, eyes locked on the flag, timing their pull just right. Every play feels like a puzzle, and every player has a chance to be the difference-maker.

Flag football is all about fast decisions, sharp movements, and total focus. It's a game that rewards intelligence, creativity, and teamwork. Without the chaos of contact, you get pure strategy and nonstop action. Every player has a role, every move matters, and every game feels like a spark waiting to catch fire. Once you get a taste of it, whether you're playing or watching, it pulls you in. And good luck trying to look away.

This chapter sets the foundation for you to know how to play, coach, train for, and enjoy flag football. I describe what the sport is all about and who plays it, and I introduce the levels of the game — from high school and college competition to World Cups and the Olympics.

DIANA SAYS

Whether you're totally new to the sport or looking to take your game to the next level, what you're about to discover is a sport that's changing lives and redefining what football can be. Take a breath, buckle in, and get ready. Because once you step into the world of flag football, everything changes.

Discovering What Flag Football Is — and Isn't

Some people assume flag football is just "touch football for kids." Others think it's a soft version of tackle. Let's shut that down right now.

Flag football is competitive, strategic, and intense. It's a real sport with its own identity and a growing global community behind it. It has elite athletes, pro-level plays, world-class coaches, and a pathway to the Olympic Games. Flag football is a playground for life. It won't always be easy or fun. You'll fail, fall short, miss flags, and sometimes lose in the final seconds. But just like in life, this game teaches you to rise again, to show up after a loss, to believe in second chances, and to keep pushing until the final whistle. Because sometimes, all it takes is one last play, one Hail Mary with all your heart behind it, to change everything.

So if you're picturing recess at school or a backyard barbecue game, that's cool, but what you're about to discover is something way bigger.

REMEMBER

Yes, flag football shares DNA with tackle football, but it evolved into something different. It's like how beach volleyball isn't the same as indoor volleyball, or how futsal isn't just mini soccer. Flag has its own tempo, tactics, and rules.

What flag football keeps from tackle:

>> The same objective: Move the ball, score touchdowns, and defend your end zone.

>> A wide range of positions and roles.

>> High-level skill, teamwork, and strategy.

What flag football changes:

- ›› No tackling, no helmets, no heavy pads.

- ›› More passing, more movement, more action.

- ›› Everyone can contribute regardless of size or background.

- ›› Flag strips down football to its most exciting core: skill, speed, and smart decision making.

Understanding What Makes Flag Football Great

Flag football is growing like crazy. Over 20 million players across 100-plus countries and counting. With the NFL (National Football League) and IFAF (International Federation of American Football) pushing the sport worldwide, the momentum is real. Schools, federations, and entire countries are investing in the sport.

Can you imagine yourself playing against someone from the other side of the world? It's already happening. China, Japan, Nigeria — countries you may not immediately associate with football — are now proudly part of this global movement. And when you step onto a field at a big international tournament, you'll see players from every continent bringing their own energy, passion, and style. That's the future of the game, and it's already here.

Flag is already played at the World Games, World Cups, and soon . . . the Olympics.

In the following list, I highlight some basic facts about flag football:

- ›› **It's a simple game:** You don't need a stadium, helmets, or a big squad to get started. Grab a ball, belts, and a few friends, and you're ready! It's that simple. Whether you're at a park, a beach, or a gym, flag football is one of the most accessible sports out there.

- ›› **It's a noncontact sport:** Safety is key. In flag, you don't need to worry about tackles or collisions. That makes it ideal for youth development, coed games, and high-level competition. You'll still find intensity, but that intensity is built on technique, not force.

>> **Minimal equipment is needed:** One of the characteristics that has helped this sport to be one of the fastest growing sports in the world is the minimum equipment needed to play the game. This makes flag football an amazing way to introduce people to sports and encourage them to be active, especially for young kids in any corner of the world. Here's what you need:

- A ball
- Flag belts
- Shorts without pockets
- A jersey or shirt
- A mouthguard

That's it. No helmets. No pads. No excuse not to play.

>> **It's a dynamic and fun-to-watch game:** Flag football is full of action. The ball moves constantly, and big plays can happen in an instant. Because of the smaller field and faster pace, fans are always close to the action. No play feels wasted. Every second counts.

Seeing who's playing flag football: A sport for everyone

Flag football breaks stereotypes. No matter who you are, no matter where you're from, or what your strengths are, anybody can find their place on the field. It doesn't matter if you've played sports before or not — flag football meets you where you are and will take you as fast or as slow as you want to go.

The beauty of the game is how simple it is at its core. Because the rules are easy to grasp, it's common to see people who have never played before understanding what's happening within minutes of joining a game. That means the learning curve is gentle, but the ceiling is sky high.

And because the game doesn't rely on physicality or contact, it opens the door for more inclusive formats, like coed teams. This isn't limited to kids or beginners, either. You'll find coed tournaments being played at the adult level, and they're just as competitive and passionate as any other. Personally, I find this part of flag football very exciting and unique. It's something you rarely, if ever, see in other sports, and it shows how this game has the power to connect people beyond the traditional barriers of age, gender, or experience.

It's inclusive by design. Everyone can find their place on the field, and that's part of the magic.

Flag football is for everyone. People of all ages are playing the game right now; from kids in youth leagues to high school teams, college athletes, and adults representing their countries on the international stage. The rising number of opportunities across all levels, as I explore in later chapters, is something truly special. This moment in time is opening doors for athletes of every background to compete, connect, and grow through flag football.

Starting young and growing with the game

More and more kids are picking up flags before they even learn to read plays. Today, you can find flag football leagues for boys and girls as young as five years old, something that would've sounded impossible just a few years back.

More than 10 years ago, when I started playing the game, I never imagined I'd live to see this moment. I started at the age of 8, at a time when youth leagues didn't exist. So I had to play with athletes almost twice my age. Of course, I was lucky; my parents were crazy enough to let me do it, and my coach back then believed in me. But many girls weren't as fortunate.

That's why seeing this generation step onto the field with their own age group is so powerful. We're living a special moment in the sport, where kids everywhere are being invited to fall in love with the game from day one. And it's only the beginning.

It's the perfect introduction to sports. It builds confidence, body awareness, and discipline, all in a positive environment.

Nowadays, those same kids grow and can become national team players, college champions, or coaches. But they can also keep playing on weekend leagues or with friends after work. Some may compete at World Championships or make it to the Olympic Games.

The sport has come a long way. The changes we've seen in the past 10 years are almost unbelievable. What once was a casual backyard game is now part of structured leagues, sanctioned by federations, and even recognized by universities. Today, young athletes are receiving scholarships to play flag football, something that didn't even seem possible just a decade ago.

This game is evolving fast, and it's creating opportunities in every direction. Whether your goal is to compete at the highest level or just get moving and have fun, there's a version of flag football waiting for you. The community is welcoming, the games are exciting, and the energy is contagious.

If you've never played before, this is the perfect time to jump in. All it takes is one game to fall in love. Trust me, it may just change your life.

Tracking flag football's history

Flag football wasn't created in a boardroom. It came to life out of a real need, a need to keep athletes active, engaged, and safe. During World War II, soldiers on military bases craved a way to play football without the risk of injury that came with full contact. So, they stripped the game down to its core. No tackles. No pads. Just a ball, belts, and pure strategy. That was the beginning of what would eventually become flag football.

From those humble roots, the sport started to take hold. Soldiers brought it home. Communities started playing it in parks. Recreational leagues popped up. College intramurals adopted it. And as more people experienced its fast pace and inclusive nature, it began to grow, quietly at first, then exponentially.

Rules got cleaner. Plays got sharper. And players? They got faster, more skilled, more creative. Flag football wasn't just surviving; it was evolving. What started as a safer alternative had transformed into a competitive, strategic, and globally respected sport.

That's the official story of how flag football began. But the truth is, this game found its way into life in different countries in different ways. In Mexico, for example, it all started in the streets, literally. College students began organizing games out of pure love and passion for football. There were no flags yet; it was more like "touch football," a way to play without tackling. It wasn't formal, but it was full of heart.

Slowly, that raw version evolved. The rules took shape. Influence from the United States helped bring structure, and eventually, flag football became recognized as a formal sport. It moved from the pavement to parks, from casual games to school tournaments and federated leagues. And now, Mexico is one of the world leaders in the game, both in performance and passion.

Today, flag football is no longer just a version of football. It's its own game, one that's now played by millions around the world, with world championships, professional tournaments, and a spot on the Olympic stage.

That journey, from dusty military fields and college sidewalks to the world's biggest arenas, is still being written. And now you're part of it.

World Cups

Flag football's competitive history is more exciting than many imagine. The first IFAF Flag Football World Championship was held in 2002, marking the beginning of an international era for the sport. It wasn't flashy back then, just a small group of passionate nations coming together to compete, with the dream of something greater.

Through the 2010s, the game steadily gained momentum. Countries like the United States, Mexico, Canada, and Austria started to emerge as powerhouses. Their rivalry helped elevate the level of play and inspired other nations to step up and invest in the sport.

Then came the 2021 World Championship in Jerusalem. That tournament was a turning point. It brought together a record number of teams, with fierce battles on both the men's and women's sides. The energy was electric. New contenders emerged. The sport had truly gone global.

In 2024, the World Championship made another leap forward. The competition expanded, more countries reached the podium, and new nations like Japan (in the women's division) and Switzerland (in the men's) made history. You could feel the shift — flag football wasn't just growing, it was thriving. Nations were no longer just participating; they were contending.

Every World Cup has written a new chapter in this story. From the early days to the latest editions, each tournament has showcased how far the sport has come and how much further it can go. And now, as flag football continues to evolve, the World Cup remains one of its brightest stages — a place where dreams are tested, new stars are born, and the world comes together around the same ball.

I dive deeper into this journey in Chapters 17 and 18.

Perusing Various Levels of Play

One of the most beautiful things about flag football is that you can find a version of the game for every stage of life. It doesn't matter if you're five years old, picking up a ball for the first time, or a seasoned athlete dreaming of representing your country, there's a place for you on the field.

Kids often start in recreational leagues in their communities or school programs. These early experiences are built around fun, movement, and basic football skills. In many countries, programs like NFL FLAG provide a structured way for youth to play the sport in a safe, inclusive environment.

As players get older, the game follows them. In many states across the United States, flag football is now an official high school sport. That means real competition, regional championships, and even state titles. College campuses are buzzing with club teams, varsity programs, and elite athletes who train year-round to compete at a high level.

Then come the adult leagues, where former college stars, weekend warriors, and national team hopefuls all meet on the same turf. These leagues aren't just for fun (though fun is definitely part of it). They're fierce, strategic, and filled with talent. What's even more exciting is that in countries like Mexico, colleges have now adopted flag football as an official sport, and they're even offering scholarships to student-athletes. This is a game-changer, opening doors for young talent to compete, study, and dream bigger than ever before. At the top of that pyramid, elite athletes represent their countries in IFAF competitions, World Games, and now, the Olympic Games.

Wherever you are in your journey, flag football meets you there. And it's ready to take you further.

Flag football in the NFL

The NFL isn't just a supporter; it's a major driver of flag football's explosion. In fact, flag football has been closer to the NFL than most people think. For many professional players, flag football was part of their foundation. It helped them develop their agility, vision, and awareness of space long before they ever wore shoulder pads. Some of their earliest experiences in the game came through flag, and many of them have supported the sport through their own foundations and community outreach programs.

I talk more about some of these players in Chapter 21, and trust me, you may be surprised.

From funding youth leagues to hosting international flag tournaments, the NFL sees the future of the sport and is investing heavily in it.

Since 2023, the NFL Pro Bowl Games have replaced traditional tackle with 5-on-5 flag. That year marked a major milestone, not just for the NFL, but for flag football as a whole. The format made its debut in front of a massive audience, with over 6.2 million viewers watching across platforms. Digital highlights exploded online, and fans everywhere started seeing flag football through a new lens: not as an alternative, but as an exciting form of elite football.

But what made that moment even more special was the presence of two flag football athletes stepping into the spotlight in a groundbreaking way. I had the honor of making my debut as the offensive coordinator for the AFC, alongside Vanita Krouch, who took the reins for the NFC. Standing on the same sidelines as legends like Peyton Manning and Ray Lewis was more than just an unforgettable experience, it was a powerful statement.

To have the opportunity to lead these teams alongside legends was a big blessing, but also a clear signal of the moment we're living in. Female flag football athletes are leading worldwide, not just playing, but coaching, creating, and shaping the future of the sport. The Pro Bowl Games were the biggest stage flag football had ever seen, and to showcase the beauty and competitiveness of our game through the talent of NFL stars was simply unforgettable.

DIANA SAYS

I'll never forget looking up at the packed stadium, feeling the excitement from every corner, and watching fans get swept up in the energy of flag. That moment proved what many of us already knew: Flag football is ready for the world stage.

International competitions

International flag football is intense, but it's also incredibly inspiring. At the elite level, nations compete through IFAF's official structure: World Cups, Continental Championships, World Games, and now Olympic qualifiers. These tournaments are filled with energy, strategy, emotion, and national pride. I talk more in depth about each of these competitions in later chapters: Chapter 17 (IFAF International competitions), Chapter 18 (World Games), and Chapter 19 (the Olympic Games). But international flag football goes beyond official medals and titles.

All over the world, a growing number of tournaments are bringing the flag football community together, from youth athletes to adult competitors. These aren't just games; they're experiences. It's common now to see players packing their cleats and passports, traveling the world to compete in flag football.

You'll find tournaments in Mexico City that light up entire neighborhoods, elite championships in Panama where the crowd never stops cheering, competitive festivals in the United States that attract hundreds of teams, and international showdowns in places like Germany, France, and China. Athletes from every corner of the world are crossing borders, building friendships, and sharing a deep love for the game.

Some of these tournaments can host over 500 teams in a single weekend. Crazy, right? Imagine being part of a weekend full of flag football where, everywhere you walk, you see boys, girls, men, and women of all ages sharing the same passion, playing the same game. This kind of energy is happening in almost every continent, and it's a reminder of how universal this sport has become.

This global energy is one of the most exciting things about flag football. No matter where you go, someone is playing. And chances are, they'll welcome you with open arms, a fierce game, and maybe a plate of post-game tacos or pastries, depending on the country.

That's the spirit of flag. And it's only getting bigger.

The road to the Olympics (LA 2028)

Everything changed with the announcement that in 2028, flag football will make its Olympic debut in Los Angeles.

This isn't just a dream. It's real. And it's historic.

For the first time ever, football will be played at the Olympic Games in a way that welcomes the world. No helmets. No pads. Just speed, skill, and strategy. Flag football represents the spirit of accessibility and inclusion, and it's bringing a fresh energy to one of the oldest and most prestigious stages in sport.

The road to this moment has been long and filled with dedication. The sport's inclusion is the result of years of collaboration between the NFL, IFAF, athletes, and federations around the globe. It was built by grassroots players, passionate coaches, and a global community that refused to stop growing.

As someone who watched the Olympic Games as a little girl, dreaming of one day playing on that stage, this chapter of flag football history gives me chills. Knowing that thousands of flag football athletes around the world will now have the chance to chase Olympic gold makes all the effort, sacrifice, and heart poured into this sport more meaningful than ever.

And now . . . it's your turn to be part of it.

I share more about how this dream came true and what to expect from the sport's Olympic debut in Chapter 19.

**DIANA
SAYS**

Being part of the Olympic movement, representing athletes alongside the NFL and IFAF through the process of making flag football an Olympic sport was one of the biggest honors of my life. One thought echoed in my mind through it all: "This is bigger than us. This is for every little girl who ever dreamed of being on that stage." It wasn't just about flag football finally getting the spotlight. It was about representation, legacy, and a sport that's rewriting what's possible. It's more than just a game. Now it's a symbol of inclusion, progress, and possibility. And I'm beyond proud to have been part of the journey that helped make this a reality.

Chapter **2**

The Wear and Where of Flag Football

One amazing thing about flag football, beyond being an inclusive sport, is that it's one of the most versatile sports in the world. I've spent the last 20 years of my life on flag football fields across many countries, and I can tell you about the magic of this sport: The game knows no boundaries; it transforms any space into its arena. I've seen flag football played in massive stadiums, on dusty fields, in concrete courtyards, parks, on beaches, and even on streets. This sport truly has no barriers — it can be played by anyone, anywhere, plus very little is required in terms of equipment.

In this chapter, you find the basics of how to recognize marks on a flag football field, a few particulars of the game, and exactly what you need to play the game.

Where: The Field

The field of play is one of the most critical aspects of the game. Although flag football is a versatile sport that can be enjoyed on almost any type of terrain, from grassy parks to sandy beaches, competitive play demands specific standards to ensure fairness, safety, and an optimal playing experience.

This section outlines the essential requirements for a flag football field. I explore the necessary dimensions, surface conditions, and marking guidelines that create a regulated environment for competitive matches. Understanding these elements is key to understanding the game —whether you're a casual enthusiast or an aspiring competitor aiming to elevate your game.

Playing surface

I start with the surface because that is the field itself, and it's made of either natural grass or *turf* (artificial grass). Regardless of whether the surface is grass or turf, the playing field must be solid, level, and free of any obstacles. Nowadays, flag football is more commonly played at turf fields because they're easier to maintain compared to natural grass. Numerous games are typically played on the same field each weekend during a tournament or regular season, which makes it difficult to keep a natural field in optimal conditions.

If you ask me, both have their pros and cons. Artificial turf is much lighter to run on, but natural grass will always have a special mystique — there's nothing like a beautiful, soft, and green natural field. Plus, it doesn't hurt as much when you fall on grass. You inevitably get one or two skin burns when you fall on turf because it's not the friendliest surface when it comes to falls.

Turf is usually made of synthetic nylon fibers or woven fibers placed over cement, blacktop, or dirt. These materials make it a harder surface that also retains heat, creating a thermal sensation of 40 to 70 degrees higher than the surrounding temperature.

Field dimensions

The dimensions of the flag football field depend on the format: 5-on-5, on 7-on-7, or beach flag, all of which I describe further in Chapter 15. In this chapter, I focus on 5-on-5 because it's not only the most popular version of the game, but also the modality played at international competitions all over the world.

No matter the format, flag football field measurements look like this: 70 yards long × 25 yards wide. That includes a 50-yard *field to play* area (literally, the area where players are playing the game) and two 10-yard *end zones* (the area where players score).

The marks on the field

If you're watching or playing flag football for the first time, all the white lines and marks on the field may seem confusing. But don't worry; I've got you, and learning what they mean is actually pretty easy. Every line and mark has a meaning and serves a purpose, as shown in Figure 2-1.

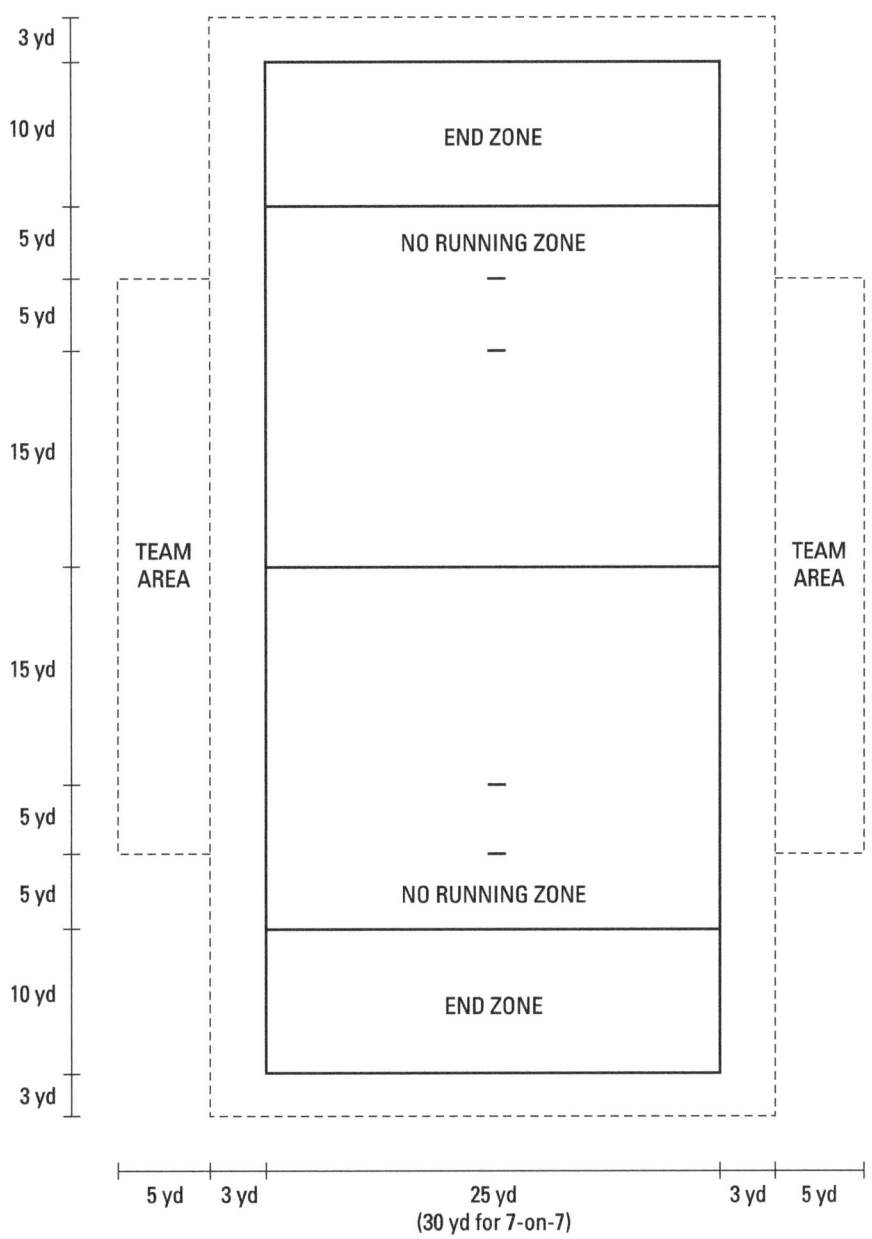

FIGURE 2-1: Knowing the line marks helps you understand how the game is played.

Among all, these are the most important line marks you should be aware of when playing or watching a game:

>> **End lines:** The boundary lines at the back of each end zone, *end lines* mark the end of the field.

>> **Sidelines:** These are the lines along the flag football field.

>> **Goal lines:** The *goal line* is the line that separates the end zone from the field to play and is marked 10 yards inside the end lines.

>> **Field to play:** This is the area in between the end lines and the sidelines — where all the action happens.

>> **Middle field line or first down line:** The flag football field is divided into two equal halves by a center line drawn at the 25-yard mark; this line is called the *first down line* (and is also referred to as the *mid line*). This is one of the most important marks on the field. When a player crosses this line the first time during their team's possession, the offense gets four more plays (a new set of downs) to advance the ball. This is called *winning a first down.*

>> **5-yard lines:** The first 5-yard lines marked after the end lines are where every offense starts their possession. The team faces the end zone where they aim to score, meaning they have to advance 45 yards to score. Unless there is an interception, every offense should start from their own 5-yard line.

>> **No-run zone:** The two areas between the goal lines and the first 5-yard lines (from each side of the field, marked with dashed lines) are called the *no-run zones.* When attempting to score a touchdown, an offense cannot use running plays when the ball is positioned anywhere in this area. No-run zones apply only for the offense in possession of the ball.

>> **End zones:** The *end zones* — or as I like to call them, the promised land — are the areas at each end of the field where teams score touchdowns. Each end zone covers an area of 10 yards between the end line and goal line and is delimited by the sidelines.

>> **Scrimmage line:** An imaginary line where the ball is placed before each play starts that separates the offense and defense and shows where the action begins.

Yard Lines

Yard lines are used to give the players and the fans a better idea of where the game ball is positioned and track how a team advances on the field. Although yard lines are technically marks on the field (see Figure 2-2), which I cover in the preceding section, yard lines play a significant role in tracking a team's progress — and that's why I cover them in their own section.

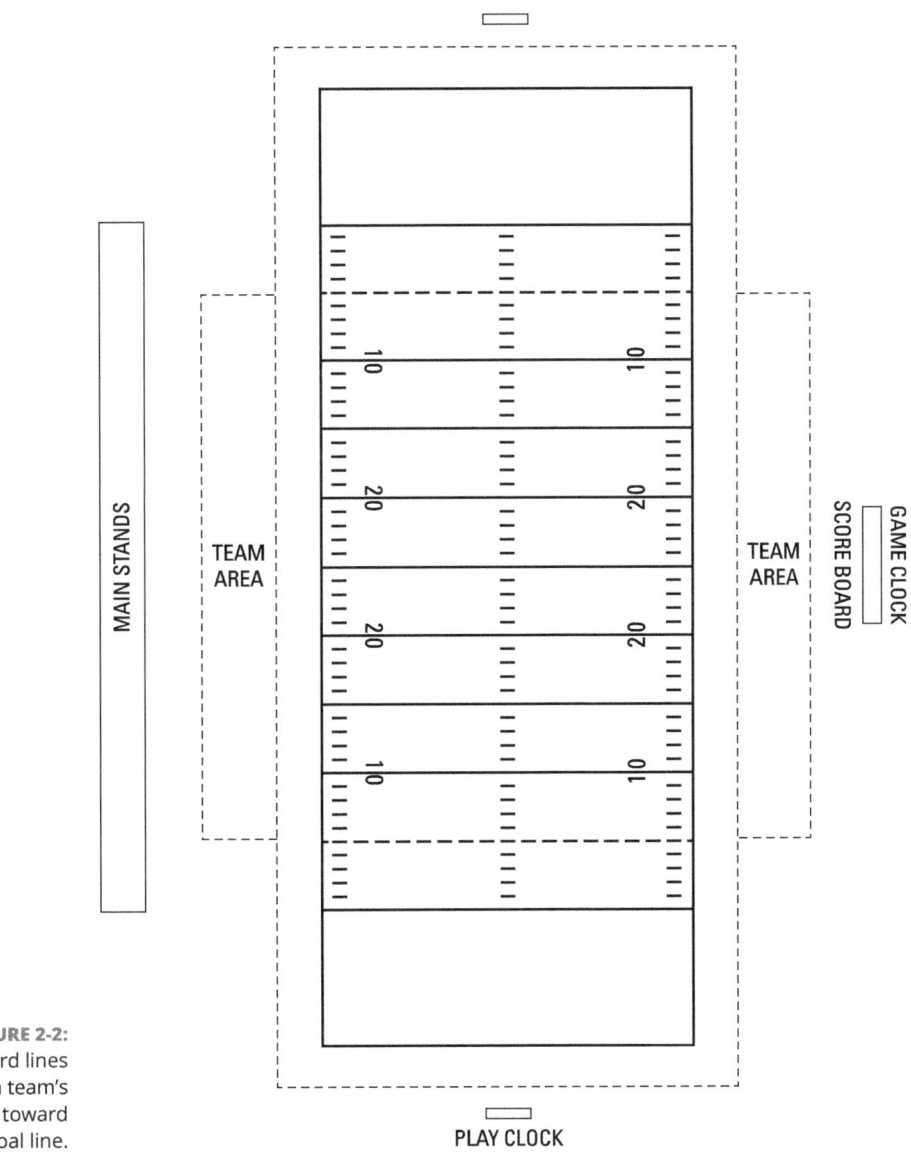

FIGURE 2-2:
The yard lines
show a team's
progress toward
the goal line.

On the field, marks along the sidelines 1 yard apart from each other start from the goal line. This means there should be 50 yard lines along the field marking the 25 yards from the goal to the middle of the field.

Every 5 yards is marked with a solid line stretching from one side to the other, except for the two most approximate to the goal lines, which are marked with dashed lines. Also note the numbers marking the 10- and 20-yard lines (these numbers are white on the field).

Out of bounds

The *field to play* area — literally, the part of the field where players play the game — is also called the *in-bounds* area. Everywhere else (including the sidelines and end lines themselves) is *out of bounds*. A player is out of bounds when they step out or over a sideline or end line, making this player automatically ineligible during a play. Also, a player is out of bounds when any part of their body touches anything out of bounds (like the marks or pylons) except another player or official. Whenever a player gets out of bounds while having possession of the ball — called a *dead ball* — the play automatically stops and the game clock stops running, too, until the next play is called.

To complete a pass or a touchdown, a player must have one foot inside the field to play or the end zone to be considered in bounds.

Other marks

In addition to the marks painted on the field, pylons or disk markers are used to make it easier to identify the *middle field line* and the *end zone area*. *Pylons* are placed at each corner of the end zone, while disks mark the intersection of the mid-field line with the sideline.

Down indicator

A *down* in flag football is a play or a chance that a team has to move forward on the field each time its offense has possession of the ball. When a team starts their possession, they have four downs (four plays) to cross the first down line (described in the section "The marks on the field"). If a team crosses the first down line, the team wins the first down, earning another set of four downs to try to score!

A *down indicator* in flag football is a visual marker used to show the current down (first, second, third, or fourth) during a series of plays. It is typically displayed on a pole or a digital device held by an official on the sideline, making it easy for players, coaches, and fans to track the progress of the offense as they attempt to gain the first down line or score a touchdown.

7-yard chain

A *7-yard chain* is literally that: a chain that connects two indicators. Similar to the down indicator, its only purpose is to indicate the starting point where the blitzer at the defense should be positioned before a play starts. This is where the term *rush line* comes from, because this is the imaginary line where the blitzer starts rushing to the QB. (A blitzer is a defense position, further explained in Chapter 14.) The chain is operated by one of the officials, starting from the down indicator and extending in the direction of the playing ball 2 yards outside of the sideline, making it easier for the defensive player to visualize.

Team areas

The *team areas,* which include player benches, are located 3 yards behind the sidelines and are 20 yards long (18.2 meters). This is the area where the players stand alongside the coaches and team staff watching their teammates play when they're not active on the field. See Chapter 3 to find out who's on staff for each team.

During international competitions, only the twelve active players from a roster and two coaches can stand in this area. See Part 5, which has chapters covering various levels of play.

Wear: Uniforms

When it comes to flag football, the uniform etiquette is simple and almost adapts to what every player finds more comfortable to play in. There are four key items you must have to play: a jersey, pants, flags, and a pair of cleats. I cover those four, plus the mouthpiece, and what isn't permitted.

The jersey

While passion, talent, and character are some of the most evident traits that distinguish each player, the jersey is often the first thing the world notices about them. A jersey instills in every athlete an unmatched sense of pride and belonging.

In my career, I definitely remember the first time I was given my first jersey for each of the clubs I played at. The national team jersey is the most special to me. After 10 years representing my country, the ritual of putting on the national jersey never gets old. The pride and emotion of wearing your country colors is indescribable, plus having your name at the back of your jersey is a privilege every player knows is earned, not given. That's why the act of exchanging jerseys between players is an act of profound respect and friendship.

Jerseys come in different styles and colors. Like other sports jerseys, they display the player's number, name, and club logo. A key difference between football and flag football jerseys — besides flag football jerseys being lighter and more fitted — is the numbering system. While football assigns specific numbers to different positions, flag football players can freely choose any number from 0 to 99, regardless of their position.

Make sure your jersey is either tight enough to fit over your hips or long enough to tuck in to avoid flag guarding penalties during a game.

Nothing should hide your flags or interfere with a defender's ability to pull them.

Pants

Whether you decide to wear shorts or compression pants (tight-fitting garments made of flexible fabrics such as spandex or nylon), there are two key aspects to consider: Make sure the shorts are not too loose to prevent defensive players from pulling them off (no one wants their pants pulled down during a game), and they must not have pockets! Avoiding pockets is super important as it helps prevent injuries caused by caught fingers.

Cleats

Wearing the right pair of cleats is super important for a player to have the right traction, support, and protection on the field. A good pair of cleats can make the player feel more confident and automatically translate to delivering a good performance during the game.

Types of cleats vary and come in three primary cuts: low-cut, mid-cut, and high-cut. Low-cut and mid-cut cleats are usually lighter, which can benefit skill positions since they enhance agility and speed. However, high-cut cleats are the best to offer support and stability and reduce the risk of injuries. In my opinion, these cleats are highly recommended for kids or players who are being introduced to the game.

TIP

Wear cotton socks and cleats half a size bigger than your usual size. This will prevent your toes from getting hurt inside the shoes during quick direction changes.

Flags

The flag (see Figure 2-3) is the key element for a flag football player since it is truly the essence of the sport. It is the main attribute of a noncontact game and what makes the game so versatile.

Flag

FIGURE 2-3:
The flag is the central piece of a flag football player's uniform.

This accessory consists of a belt with two identical flags attached to it, which hang down each of the player's hips. The flags are usually made of nylon, both in the same color and without sharp edges. They are 15 to 16 inches (38.1 to 40.6 centimeters) long and 1.8 to 2.0 inches (4.6 to 5.1 centimeters) wide.

When the flag detaches from the player's belt, it emits a popping noise, which makes it clear to everyone that the play has ended. Do not let the flags fool you; it is not as easy as it looks to pull a flag. A lot of coordination and reaction is needed for this task, plus adding the speed and agility factor from the players (making quick hip movements or changing the level of their hips) can make flag pulling a true challenge.

Because flags can come in different designs and colors that players can personalize for practice or some competitions, they're one of the most personal accessories in flag football, showcasing each player's unique style.

Mouthpiece

Even if it isn't mandatory, wearing a mouthpiece in flag football is highly recommended. It helps protect your teeth, mouth, and jaw from accidental impacts, ensuring you can play confidently and safely. While flag football is a noncontact sport, collisions can still happen, and a mouthpiece adds an extra layer of protection. Mouthguards are mandatory in youth flag football.

What is not permitted

While flag football's uniform rules are generally flexible, certain restrictions ensure fair play. Players must avoid wearing wide pants or attempting to hide their flags, as this would give them an unfair advantage. Other items that players should avoid include the following:

>> **Pants with stripes, patterns, or pockets as well as flags matching uniform colors:** These are not allowed because they make it harder for opponents to grab flags. The principle is simple: Everything must remain clearly visible.

>> **Detachable cleats or cleats longer than 0.5 inch (1.25 centimeters):** Additionally, cleats cannot be sharpened, pointed, or made of any metallic material. These are prohibited across all levels of play to prevent injuries to both the wearer and other players.

>> **Shoulder pads or helmets:** Headwear includes caps, hoods, bandannas, headbands, or the like, and is not allowed. Headwear may be legal, provided it does not endanger or offend other players.

Shoulder pads and helmets are generally not permitted because flag football is a noncontact sport, and any type of hard protection can harm other players if any incidental collision occurs.

The Ball

Flag football uses the same ball as American football. This is a one-of-a-kind ball. It's shaped like an oval with pointy ends, which helps it fly smoothly through the air and makes it perfect for throwing long, accurate passes or spinning like a pro.

Typically made from leather, often cowhide, the ball is durable and offers excellent grip, though synthetic materials are also common for recreational play. Its brown or tan color is accented with white laces and sometimes stripes, improving visibility during gameplay.

The ball comes in different sizes:

>> Regular balls measure approximately 11 inches in length with a 22-inch circumference.

>> Youth balls are slightly smaller at 10.5 inches long with a 19-inch circumference.

>> Junior balls are 10.25 inches long with an 18-inch circumference.

Women's categories typically use the youth-sized ball for better handling. All female participants ages 10+ use this same size ball (10+, middle school, high school, college, and IFAF).

A key feature is the raised laces running along one side, providing players with a firm grip and control for accurate throws and spins.

Chapter 3

The Who and How of the Game

lag football isn't just about the game itself; it's about the people who make it happen. Players, coaches, referees, and team managers (among others) all play a crucial part in making this sport as exciting and dynamic as it is. In this chapter, I break down who's involved in flag football and how the game is played.

Looking at Who's Involved in Flag Football

Flag football is a team sport of excellence. When the offense (discussed in Part 2) is on the field, any play can be ruined without the contribution of each one of the players — from the center to the quarterback and the receivers. It doesn't matter if not all of them touch the ball every time, but if one player doesn't do their job, the team's execution is affected.

Like a chain that is only as strong as its weakest link, the defense can only be as strong as the "weaker" player. The defensive team works as a block bridge, where each player represents a block, and when they're all in the right position, they create a strong, unbreakable structure. If one block is missing or out of place, the bridge becomes weak and is easier to break through. Thus, every member has an important role while trying to stop the other team from advancing on the field.

Players are the shining stars in the field; however, a team relies on more people than the players only. The sport isn't just about scoring touchdowns or making the perfect pass; it's about teamwork, mentorship, and community. Throughout the rest of this section, I talk about the key people who make flag football happen and the role each plays both on and off the field.

Coaches: The beating heart of a team

A coach is more than just someone who calls plays and yells from the sidelines. Coaches are leaders, mentors, and sometimes even like a second family to their players.

Coaches not only oversee the function of a team, but they also set the tone for the team, build strategy, develop skills, and, most importantly, shape the mindset and culture of the team, as I discuss in this section. But first, I answer the question, what makes a good coach a good coach?

If you only look at a coach's resume — the number of championships they've won or the years they've been coaching — you may think that's what defines their greatness. But in my experience, the best coaches aren't just the ones with the most wins; they're the ones who change lives and make impactful contributions to the game. They help players believe in themselves, push through challenges, and grow both on and off the field.

DIANA SAYS

In my career, I've been super lucky to be able to play for different teams, in different countries, which has given me the opportunity to learn from different coaches, cultures, and game systems. Each experience has taught me something valuable, and while every coach is different, the few who have made a big impact on me beyond the field had one thing in common: They knew how to build confidence, emotional strength, and a relentless mindset in me and other players.

To achieve this, a coach should develop several key skills and qualities to ensure the continuous evolution of their team both on and off the field. So, what does it take to be a truly great coach? I break it down in the following sections.

Leadership and mentorship

A great coach is more than a strategist; they are a leader and mentor. Leadership in coaching means setting high standards, leading by example, and cultivating a team-first mentality. The best coaches inspire players to believe in themselves, push through challenges, and work toward common goals.

Mentorship extends beyond the field. Coaches play a crucial role in shaping young athletes' lives by teaching values such as discipline, teamwork, and perseverance. Their impact often lasts far beyond their players' playing days.

Game strategy and preparation

Expertise and experience are key differentiators in coaching. Regardless of how many years a coach has been in the game, flag football never stops evolving. To stay ahead, a coach must continuously study the game, watch film, analyze opponents, and adapt strategies:

>> **Game analysis and study:** Reviewing game footage is essential for understanding strengths, weaknesses, and tendencies in both their team and the opposition.

>> **In-game adjustments:** Great coaches can read the game in real time and make necessary adjustments to maximize their team's chances of success.

>> **Player development:** Every athlete has unique strengths and weaknesses. A coach must recognize and tailor their guidance to help each player reach their full potential.

You can read more about game strategies in Parts 2 and 3 of the book, where I cover offensive and defensive positions, respectively. But it is very important to understand that, from a coaching perspective, not every game style or strategy fits every team. That depends on your athletes and their strengths and characteristics as individuals and as a group.

REMEMBER

In any sport, most of the coaches who have built a legacy are the ones who have made contributions to the game, some of them by sharing their unique way to view the game, and others by making contributions to the way it's played. Sport remains in continuous evolution, so if you're a coach, don't be afraid of innovating on your game style and strategy. Stay curious and be open-minded. Sometimes the answer you're looking for will come from your players.

Building team culture

This is something that often gets overlooked, but trust me, it matters. The culture of a team can make or break its success. A good coach creates an environment where players feel supported, motivated, and part of something bigger than themselves. Coaches need to teach the following values to their players (through words and by setting an example):

>> **Inclusivity:** Flag football is a sport for everyone. A great coach makes sure every player, regardless of experience, skill level, or background, feels valued and included.

>> **Discipline and accountability:** Fun is important, but so is structure. Coaches who set clear expectations and hold players accountable help build a team that operates like a well-oiled machine.

>> **Communication:** If a coach can't communicate their vision, strategy, or feedback effectively, they'll struggle to get their team on the same page.

Handling challenges and setbacks

Let me be real, coaching isn't always easy. There will be losses, conflicts, and tough moments. But the best coaches know how to navigate these challenges with patience, empathy, and resilience:

>> **Patience:** Not every player develops at the same pace. A great coach understands this and knows how to guide each player's growth without frustration.

>> **Empathy:** Sometimes, what a player needs most isn't more drills; it's someone who understands what they're going through and supports them.

>> **Resilience:** A great coach doesn't dwell on losses. They use setbacks as learning opportunities and teach their players to do the same.

Motivation and earning players' trust: the foundation of a great coach

In addition to the points in the preceding sections, one thing that separates a good coach from a great one is their ability to motivate and earn the trust of their players. Remember, the best coaches don't just teach X's and O's — they inspire, push, and build strong relationships that extend beyond the field. They know how to connect with their players on a deeper level — mentally, emotionally, and even personally.

So how do you do that? It all starts with trust.

Trust isn't given — it's earned. And it doesn't happen overnight. Players trust a coach who believes in them, challenges them, and leads with integrity. Here's how great coaches build trust:

>> **Be consistent:** A player needs to know that their coach is reliable. If you say you're going to do something, follow through. If you set standards for the team, stick to them. Inconsistency in leadership leads to doubt, and doubt breaks trust.

>> **Show you care (beyond the game):** The best coaches don't just care about winning — they care about their players as people. Take the time to check in on your players. Ask about school, work, family, or anything that matters to them. When a player feels valued off the field, they'll run through a wall for you on the field.

>> **Be honest and transparent:** Players respect coaches who tell them the truth, even when it's not what they want to hear. Sugarcoating things doesn't help anyone improve. However, honesty should always be in the form of constructive criticism and with the intent to motivate rather than tear a player down.

>> **Admit when you're wrong:** At the end of the day, we are all humans. In life, we all make mistakes; in sports, no coach is perfect. If you make a mistake, own it. A simple "That was on me" goes a long way in showing players that you lead with humility. It also teaches them that mistakes aren't failures — they're opportunities to grow.

>> **Lead by example:** Players don't always listen to what you say, but they always watch what you do. If you demand discipline, effort, and respect, make sure you embody those qualities yourself. Leadership starts with your own actions.

The power of motivation: Keeping the fire burning

Some days, players show up ready to compete. Other days, they're tired, frustrated, or doubting themselves. That's when a coach's ability to motivate makes all the difference. The right words, at the right moment, can have a big impact on a player's attitude toward the game and life.

This list highlights ways to ignite a player's passion and push them beyond their limits:

>> **Find what drives each player:** Not every player is motivated by the same thing. Some are driven by competition, others by personal goals, and some by team camaraderie. A great coach understands each player's "why" and uses that to fuel their fire.

REMEMBER

The only way you can determine your players' "why" is by observing and engaging with them through conversation. Among all your responsibilities on the field, make sure you still take time to connect with your athletes.

>> **Set the tone with energy:** Have you ever noticed how a coach's energy affects the entire team? A high-energy, passionate coach naturally creates a high-energy, passionate team. However, not every coach has to act in that way if it's not in keeping with their personality. Find your own style and make sure you channel that energy every time you're about to work with your team. Do not play a role that isn't the real you in front of them; players will always notice when someone is being authentic in their words and actions, and who is only acting.

REMEMBER

Stay authentic, bring the intensity in your own way, and your players will follow.

>> **Use positivity — but keep it real:** Motivation isn't just about hyping players up; it's about making them believe in themselves. Positive reinforcement goes a long way, but it needs to be genuine. Empty praise doesn't motivate — it just creates complacency. Instead, acknowledge progress, reward effort, and challenge them to keep improving.

>> **Build a culture of accountability:** Motivation shouldn't only come from the coach. I've experienced the power that comes from teammates who motivate each other, and let me tell you, a team that trusts, supports, and encourages each other is unstoppable. That doesn't take talent, and it goes beyond winning or losing games. Create a culture where players push one another, hold each other accountable, and celebrate each other's successes.

>> **Never let a player feel like they're alone:** The mental side of sports is just as important as the physical. Players will struggle. They will fail. They will have moments of doubt. A great coach makes sure that no player ever feels like they're fighting alone. Remind them of their strengths, reinforce their value to the team, and help them see past their setbacks.

Coaching beyond the game

At the end of the day, motivation and trust are what create lifelong impact. Players may forget a specific play or strategy, but they will never forget a coach who believed in them, inspired them, and helped shape them into better athletes and better people.

Flag football is more than just a game. It's an opportunity to teach discipline, resilience, teamwork, and confidence. A coach who understands this will not only win games but will change lives.

Managers: The team's backbone

If coaches are the heart of a team, managers are its backbone. They may not be on the field calling plays, but trust me — without them, the team would struggle to function smoothly.

A manager's responsibilities can vary depending on the level of play, but they usually include the following:

>> **Handling logistics:** Scheduling practices, coordinating travel, and ensuring everything runs on time

>> **Keeping track of equipment:** Making sure jerseys, flags, and footballs are ready before every game

>> **Communication bridge:** Keeping players and coaches informed about schedules, rule updates, and other team matters

Athletic trainers: Keeping players in top shape

Flag football is a high-speed, explosive sport. Injuries can happen, and that's where athletic trainers come in.

Athletic trainers serve the team in two important ways:

>> **Injury prevention:** Helping players avoid injuries with warm-ups, strength training, and proper stretching techniques.

>> **Rehabilitation programs:** Helping injured players recover and safely return to the field.

As I discuss in Chapter 12, athletic trainers aren't just for pros. Even in recreational leagues, having a trainer on staff makes a huge difference not only in athletes' skills but also in player safety and longevity.

Referees and officials: The guardians of fair play

Without referees, flag football would be absolute chaos. Imagine a game where everyone argues over what counts as a touchdown or whether a flag was pulled in time — yeah, not fun.

Referees and officials enforce the rules, ensure fairness, and keep the game moving smoothly by making split-second decisions under pressure. Whether they're blowing their whistles to signal a play or pulling out what I call "the dreaded yellow flag" to call a penalty, referees are a crucial part of the game. They may not always be the most popular people on the field (players and coaches tend to have *opinions* on calls), but their job is essential.

An official flag football game typically has at least three referees to make sure the game runs in the best possible way. The roles of the officials during the game are as follows:

>> **Head referee:** Typically positioned right at the back of the offensive team, this is the main official who oversees the entire game and makes final rulings on plays.

>> **Field judges:** Positioned on the sidelines, they watch for penalties, out-of-bounds calls, and scoring plays.

>> **Back judge:** Focusing on deep passes and defensive coverage, the back judge watches for holding, illegal contact, and defensive fouls.

>> **Game clock official:** Positioned on the sideline, this official ensures that time is managed correctly, especially in the final minutes of a game.

DRESSED FOR THE JOB: THE REFEREE'S ICONIC LOOK

You can always spot a referee before they even make a call, thanks to their distinctive black-and-white striped jersey. This uniform isn't just for show; it serves a purpose:

- **The black and white "zebra" look:** The stripes make referees easy to identify on the field, ensuring they stand out from players.

- **The hat:** Most referees wear a black or white cap, depending on their role. The head referee typically wears a white hat, while other officials wear black hats.

- **Black pants or shorts:** Depending on the level of play, referees wear either black athletic pants or black shorts (with a thin white stripe down the hip) for comfort and mobility.

- **The whistle:** Referees use a whistle to call the beginning and the end of a play. This means the clock usually starts running whenever the whistle is blown (I discuss this in more detail in Chapter 4) and ends when it is blown again after a flag has been pulled or a penalty has been called. It also indicates when a touchdown is confirmed and when there's an incomplete pass or dead ball situation.

- **Bright yellow flag:** Every official on the field carries a bright yellow flag, usually attached to their bottoms, ready to be pulled out whenever a penalty must be called. It also marks the exact spot where the penalty happened, helping officials determine the right enforcement.

- **Small bean bag:** Instead of signaling a foul, referees toss the bean bag on the ground to mark a spot. It could be where a fumble happened, where the ball was intercepted, or the exact spot where a player's flag was pulled, if it needs to be recorded. Think of it as the referee's "bookmark" for the play, helping them track important moments and keep the game fair and organized.

- **Running shoes or cleats:** Yes, referees run too! They need proper footwear to keep up with the fast pace of the game. Referee footwear needs to be black.

- **The down indicator:** This is a small elastic band they wrap around their fingers to track downs. You may not see this band, but a lot of the officials do carry one.

- **Stopwatch:** Usually only the referee in charge of the game clock carries a stopwatch to make sure time is tracked, including timeouts, two-minute warnings, and running clock situations.

Love them or hate them, referees play a vital role in keeping the game structured, competitive, and fair.

The players: The stars of the game

At the end of the day, the players are what make flag football so exciting. Their speed, creativity, vision, and heart are what bring the game to life. Every position on the field plays a unique role in shaping the outcome of a play, a drive, and ultimately, the game itself.

I dive deeper into each position, their characteristics, responsibilities, and skillsets in the chapters ahead (you can take a look at Parts 2, 3, and 4 for a full breakdown). But for now, this is your crash course on how players are classified, what they do, and why each one matters on the field, starting with the two main groups flag football players fall into: offensive players and defensive players.

Offensive players

Offensive players are the ones in charge of moving the ball down the field and scoring touchdowns. The offense is made up of five players that you'll quickly recognize because they're the team with ball possession every time they step onto the field. That doesn't mean every player is holding the ball all the time, but they're all part of the strategy that helps the offense reach the end zone.

Offensive players are creative, dynamic, and strategic athletes who bring the game to life. They're responsible for advancing the ball, executing plays, and ultimately scoring points. Whether it's reading the defense, running sharp routes, or making quick decisions under pressure, offensive players thrive on timing, teamwork, and precision.

In flag football, *ball possession* refers to the period when one team has its offensive players on the field and control of the ball. During this time, the team has the opportunity to run plays and try to advance the ball down the field to score. Possession continues until the team scores, turns the ball over, or uses up its allowed number of downs.

One thing I love about flag football is how it pushes players to be multi-dimensional. Depending on your strengths — speed, hands, vision, footwork — you can learn to play multiple positions and even switch between offense and defense from one series to the next.

In fact, one of the coolest things I've seen in this sport (and lived personally) is how players who started out in one position eventually discovered their talent for another — sometimes even their true role on the field. A receiver becomes a rusher. A defensive back learns to throw and becomes a quarterback. It's all part of the learning journey, and trust me, the game rewards those who explore every corner of it.

DIANA SAYS

When I started playing flag football at just eight years old, my first positions were center and rusher. I was learning the basics of snapping the ball and chasing quarterbacks, just having fun and soaking it all in. Not long after, I transitioned to quarterback, where I found a new passion and challenge. But I didn't stop there — over time, I kept building my skillset and expanding my roles. I played wide receiver, linebacker, center, rusher, and, of course, quarterback again at the highest level with Mexico's national team. Being able to perform in multiple positions didn't just help me become a better athlete; it made me a better teammate, a better leader, and a deeper student of the game. That versatility shaped my entire journey.

TIP

From a team standpoint, this versatility is gold. It gives coaches more options when building game plans and lineups. And from the player's perspective, it keeps things fun, challenging, and constantly evolving. You grow not just physically, but also mentally. You start seeing the game from different angles, understanding your teammates' roles better, and becoming a more complete athlete.

I explore each offensive position in detail in Part 2, but for now, just know this: Offense is about creativity, making plays, and getting into the end zone. It takes everyone working together to make it happen.

Defensive players

While the offense is trying to move the ball forward, the five players on defense are doing everything in their power to stop them. Their mission? Pull flags, shut down passes, apply pressure, and force turnovers. They may not get as much glory on the highlight reels, but ask any serious flag football player and they'll tell you: Defense is an important part of winning games.

Defensive players are aggressive, quick thinkers with great field awareness. They anticipate plays, communicate constantly, and adjust in real time depending on what the offense is trying to do.

Just like on offense, many defensive players switch roles based on the situation and defensive strategy. The best defenses are built on discipline, versatility, and communication.

And here's the thing: Many flag football players play on both sides of the ball. It's not uncommon at all to see a player catching a touchdown on one drive, then making a game-saving flag pull on the next. That's part of what makes flag football so special; you get to be a complete athlete.

Part 3 has the details of each defensive position, but just know this for now: Defense isn't just about stopping, it's about disrupting, adapting, and making game-changing plays.

The spirit of the flag football player

Whether you're lining up on offense or defense, what makes a flag football player stand out isn't just speed or athleticism: It's awareness, creativity, versatility, and grit.

This sport demands that you read the field, think fast, and react even faster. It challenges you physically and mentally. And most of all, it pushes you to work as part of a team. There's no such thing as a one-person show in flag football; every role matters, every play counts, and every player has a chance to shine.

As you read this book and start exploring each position in depth, remember: This chapter is just your first step into the huddle. In flag football, a *huddle* is when the players on a team gather in a small circle before a play to quickly discuss the strategy or play they're about to run. It's usually led by the quarterback and helps make sure everyone is on the same page.

Your position isn't just where you line up, it's how you contribute, how you lead, and how you grow.

The Big Picture: How the Game Is Played

In this section, I give a crash course on how the game is played, including the fundamentals, key skills, and basic game flow. Although different leagues have their own rule variations, the core fundamentals stay the same. Chapter 4 covers the international rules, the most popular format; Part 5 covers other game styles.

A game of flag football consists of two teams, usually with 5 to 7 players (depending on the format) on the field for each team. The goal? Get the ball into the end zone and score more points than the other team.

Unlike in tackle football, where strength and size can dominate, flag football is a game of agility and smart playmaking. The most successful players and teams know how to use their speed, creativity, and quick decision-making to outmaneuver their opponents.

In Chapter 20, I explore various skills needed to get started playing flag football, but here are the three most important skills every player needs to master:

>> **Passing:** Most offensive plays revolve around passing. A quarterback needs accuracy, arm strength, and great decision-making to get the ball where it needs to go. See Chapter 5 for more details about the quarterback position and Chapter 6 for more about passing.

>> **Catching:** Wide receivers and other offensive players must have good hand-eye coordination and route-running skills. Catching cleanly and securing the ball before making a move is crucial.

>> **Pulling flags:** Since there's no tackling in flag football, the key to stopping an opponent is pulling their flag. This requires quick reflexes, proper positioning, and solid technique.

IN THIS CHAPTER

» **Seeing how the game clock works and how timing can influence strategy**

» **Understanding how the coin toss impacts the start of the game**

» **Breaking down the downs and yards systems**

» **Exploring how teams score**

» **Clarifying the responsibilities of the officials**

Chapter **4**

Regarding the Rules

Flag football comes in different formats. The most popular ones are 5-on-5 and 7-on-7. In this chapter, the focus is on 5-on-5 rules. It's the format most widely played around the world and the official version used at World Cups, The World Games (you can check out the difference in Chapter 18), and other major international competitions like continental championships.

Flag football is an easy sport to grasp and play. It's fast, fun, and feels natural once you're on the field. But even though it's intuitive, the game runs on specific rules that keep it dynamic and fair.

Remembering the Golden Rule of Flag Football

Before diving into the details of the rule book, I want to remind you of what I like to call the golden rule:

Flag football is noncontact.

Blocking, tackling, and kicking are not allowed. Any kind of contact, holding, or shielding leads to a foul — and that foul brings a penalty. Here's what these words mean in flag football:

>> **Penalty:** A consequence applied to a team that commits a foul. This can mean loss of yardage, loss of down, automatic first down for the opponent, or even disqualification. If the penalty includes a loss of down, it still counts as one of the four downs in the series (see the later section, "Getting the Gist of Downs and Yards" for more info on downs).

>> **Foul:** A foul is a rule infraction for which a penalty is prescribed by rule.

>> **Contact:** Making physical impact with an opponent. Simply brushing against someone without impact is not a foul.

>> **Holding:** Grabbing an opponent or their gear and not letting go right away, especially if it affects their movement.

>> **Shielding:** Getting in someone's way — without touching them — but blocking their path on purpose. If a player doesn't have the right of way and disrupts a pass route, chases down the runner, or interferes with a legal blitzer, that's shielding.

Noting the Ins and Outs of the Game Clock

Just like in any sport, time management in flag football can make or break a game. Knowing how the game clock works helps you stay in control — whether you're trying to score before time runs out or protect a lead.

A 5-on-5 flag football game is played in two halves, each lasting 20 minutes, with a 2-minute intermission between halves. The clock runs continuously during most of the half, which means it doesn't stop between plays like in tackle football. So once the clock starts, it keeps ticking . . . unless something specific happens.

The game clock starts once the ball is legally snapped to begin a play. This applies at the start of each half, after a time-out, or following a change of possession — basically, as soon as the referee signals the ball is ready for play.

During most of the game, the clock operates on what's called a *running clock.* This means it continues to run even when a play ends — unless there's a time-out, injury, or a referee signal to stop it. The running clock keeps the game moving at a fast pace and adds a layer of strategy, especially when time is winding down. In the last two minutes of each half, the clock stops in more situations — like what you'd see in traditional football. During this time, the clock will stop for the following:

>> Incomplete passes

>> Players stepping out of bounds

>> Penalties

>> Scores

>> First downs

>> Time-outs

>> Change of possession

>> Referee decisions or injuries

If your team is trailing and needs time, those final two minutes are your golden window.

REMEMBER

Each team gets two time-outs per half, and each one lasts 30 seconds. Use them wisely — sometimes stopping the clock is just as valuable as gaining yards.

Once the ball is set and the referee signals ready, the offense has 25 seconds to snap the ball. If they take too long, it's a delay-of-game penalty. That play clock keeps things moving and adds pressure in crunch time.

Now, what happens if the game is tied at the end of regulation time? Don't worry — it's not over yet; the game goes to *overtime.* In my experience, I haven't been in many overtime situations, but I've still developed a bit of a love/hate relationship with them. Sure, they're the moments that make a game unforgettable, the ones you talk about for years. But if I'm being honest, I try to avoid getting into those situations as much as I can.

When a game heads to overtime, both teams get a fair shot. Each team has the chance to score from a set distance — usually starting from the opponent's 5-yard line. The goal is simple: Score and stop the other team from scoring. It's intense, it's nerve-wracking, and it brings out the clutch plays when they matter most.

Checking Out the Coin Toss

Every game starts with a coin toss, but don't let the simplicity fool you. That little flip of the coin sets the tone for how you'll begin the game.

Before the game starts, the referee gathers both team captains at midfield. The captain from the visiting team calls heads or tails while the coin is in the air. The team that wins the toss gets to choose to put the ball in play first by a snap at its own 5-yard line in either the first half or the second. The other team will choose which side of the field they want to start their offense on.

In the second half, the choices flip: Whichever team didn't get first choice in the first half gets it now. So both teams get a turn at making the first call — it's fair and balanced.

Most teams prefer to start on defense as part of their game plan. The idea is to stop the opponent early and then start the second half with the ball, hopefully with a lead to build on.

DIANA SAYS

Personally, I like to start on offense. My mindset is to score first and set the tone — a strong, early touchdown can really shake up the other team's energy. It creates a mental edge that shifts the whole vibe of the game.

At the end of the day, there's no right or wrong choice. It all comes down to your team's style, strengths, and a bit of gut feeling.

Getting the Gist of Downs and Yards

This is where game strategy really starts to unfold.

The field is 50 yards long, but each drive only uses 25 yards — from the 5-yard line to midfield, then midfield to the end zone. This creates two key "zones to gain":

>> **From the 5-yard line to midfield:** You're playing for a first down.

>> **From midfield to the end zone:** You're going for the touchdown.

In 5-on-5 flag football, each team begins its possession at its own 5-yard line. From there, the offense has four downs — basically, four chances — to advance the ball at least 20 yards. If they reach or cross midfield, they earn a new set of four downs to try to score.

DIANA SAYS

Getting to midfield is slightly easier than scoring a touchdown. You only need 20 yards to earn a new set of downs, but reaching the end zone from midfield takes the full 25. Keep that in mind when building your playbook — some plays work better depending on where you are on the field.

If the offense fails to reach the next zone in four downs, they lose possession. The opposing team takes over with a fresh set of downs, starting from their own 5-yard line.

That's why every down matters. In tight games, one smart decision — or one mistake — can swing momentum fast.

The referee is responsible for spotting the ball and deciding whether the offense has reached the next zone. In some leagues or high-level tournaments, this call can be challenged, but that depends on the rules of the competition.

Also, keep in mind the no-run zone: the last 5 yards before the end zone. If the ball is in this area, running plays are not allowed — the offense must pass. It's a detail that often gets overlooked, especially when pressure is high and emotions are running hot. While running plays are not allowed, handoffs and laterals still sometimes occur to trick or confuse the defense; it isn't a run play until the ball carrier crosses the line of scrimmage (LOS).

REMEMBER

From experience, I've found that knowing your team's strengths and having strong field awareness and time management skills make a huge difference. I go deeper into strategy in Part 2, but for now, just keep this in mind: Every down is a chance to shift momentum. Master this part of the game, and you're already a step ahead.

Scoring Points

Flag football may be noncontact, but when it comes to scoring, the action is anything but soft. Every point counts, and momentum can swing fast. Whether it's a bold extra point call or a game-saving sack, understanding how scoring works can help you make smarter plays.

Touchdowns

Just like in tackle football, a *touchdown* is worth six points. To score, the ball must break the plane of the opponent's goal line while in possession of the runner or receiver. You don't need to dive or run through anyone — just control the ball and cross that line.

Extra points: One or two points

After scoring a touchdown, the offense has a chance to earn *extra points.* They'll line up for one additional play and choose from two options:

>> 1-point attempt from the 5-yard line

>> 2-point attempt from the 10-yard line

The team must pass or run the ball into the end zone — remember, there's no kicking in flag football. Most teams stick to the 1-point try for consistency, but if you're feeling the pressure or playing catch-up, the 2-pointer can be a bold move.

When you go for a 1-point conversion, you're in the no-run zone and must pass only to convert.

Safeties

A *safety* occurs when the offensive team is downed in their own end zone. This could be due to a sack, a bad snap, or a flag pull while the ball is still behind the goal line. When this happens, the defensive team is awarded two points — and they also get possession of the ball.

A *sack* happens when the quarterback's flag is pulled behind the line of scrimmage before the ball is thrown. Sacks don't score points, but they're momentum killers. A couple of big sacks can push the offense backward, force risky plays, or even put them close to their own end zone, which can lead to a safety.

I personally think safeties are underrated most of the time because they only add two points to the board. They rarely occur during a game, but they can be a true momentum shifter.

Stay sharp, because knowing how and when these scoring moments happen can be the difference between a win and a "What just happened?"

Recognizing the Roles of the Officials

Flag football moves fast — and with no contact allowed, making the right call at the right time is key to keeping the game safe and fair. That's where the officials come in.

In 5-on-5 flag football, two primary officials are on the field: the referee (R) and the field judge (FJ). These two are essential; a game isn't considered official unless both are present.

Some games are played with three officials: a referee (R), a field judge (FJ), and a down judge (DJ). Others use four officials, adding a side judge (SJ). The number of officials depends on the importance of the game. For example, at the World Cups, most games are played with three officials. But for the championship game, you'll always see four. That final game demands precision on every single call.

Here's a breakdown of their main roles.

The referee

The *referee* is the lead official, positioned in the offensive backfield. Their responsibilities include

>> General oversight and control of the game

>> Final authority for the score and rule decisions

>> Inspecting the field before the game and reporting any irregularities

>> Jurisdiction over player equipment

>> Managing the game clock and play clock

>> Positioning the ball after each play

>> Indicating when the ball is ready for play

>> Awarding a new series of downs

>> Administering penalties and notifying both teams of any disqualifications

>> Ruling on plays behind the line of scrimmage after the snap

>> Coverage of the quarterback

>> Signaling all fouls and enforcing penalties

>> Calling the ready-for-play and whistle signals

>> Monitoring the quarterback's actions, including passes and pitches

>> Observing illegal contact, illegal pitches, and forward pass infractions

Basically, the referee sees it all — from timing to rule enforcement — and makes sure the game runs safely and fairly.

The field judge

The *field judge* lines up on the defensive side, often near the line to gain (line that needs to be crossed to earn the down or score). Their duties include:

>> Watching the line of scrimmage and monitoring the 7-second pass clock (QBs generally have just seven seconds to hand off or pass once receiving the ball from the center)

>> Signaling when the ball crosses midfield or the goal line

>> Observing defensive and offensive fouls (like flag guarding or pass interference)

>> Keeping count of players on the field and tracking substitutions

>> Ruling on the play and forward progress once the ball crosses the line of scrimmage, focusing on their side of the field

The down and side judges

Now, when the game requires more precise officiating, the down judge and side judge step in:

>> **Down judge (DJ):** Positioned at the line of scrimmage on the sideline, holding the down indicator. They're responsible for tracking downs and the line of scrimmage.

>> **Side judge (SJ):** Positioned 7 or more yards deep on the sideline, also with a down indicator. They help with timing the game or supervising the game clock, and focus on receivers on deep routes, the status of the ball, and forward progress in their area.

Other official responsibilities

Together, the officials constantly communicate and coordinate to ensure accuracy, fairness, and flow.

Beyond what's visible during a play, officials also:

>> Conduct the coin toss

>> Confirm player equipment and field conditions before kickoff

>> Manage sideline behavior and sportsmanship

>> Pause the game for injuries or unexpected situations like bad weather (rain or thunderstorms)

In my experience, the most competitive and respectful games happen when players understand and trust the role of the officials. You may not always agree with every call (I've definitely had my moments), but they're there to protect the integrity of the game.

Familiarizing yourself with the referees' signals

Let's be honest — sometimes watching the officials can feel like you're seeing a choreographed dance. They throw their flags, wave their arms, and flash hand signs you may not understand, especially if you're watching from the stands and can't hear what's being said on the field.

That's why I've put together this quick guide to help you decode the most common referee signals in flag football. Whether you're playing or watching, these signs will help you follow the action like a pro.

Check out the image shown in Figure 4-1 that features all the key signals. I walk you through what each one means.

To make it easier for you, I've divided the most popular signs into three categories: game management, scoring and possession signals, and penalty signals.

Game management signals

These signals keep the game moving or alert everyone when the play ends, or a half or game is finished:

>> **S1 — Ready for play:** The referee points one arm downward to indicate the ball is ready to be snapped.

>> **S2 — Start the clock:** Circular arm motion signals the game clock should begin.

>> **S3 — Stop the clock:** Both arms are extended horizontally to the sides; the clock stops due to an incomplete pass, out of bounds, or other stoppage.

>> **S14 — End of period:** One arm raised with the hand forming a fist signals the end of a half or game.

FIGURE 4-1:
Each of the referees' signals has a unique meaning.

Scoring and possession signals

These signals keep track of each team's offensive series and indicate when a team adds points to their score:

>> **S5 — Touchdown:** Both arms raised straight above the head. Six points on the board!

>> **S6 — Safety:** Hands together, forming a triangle above the head. Two points to the defense.

>> **S8 — First down:** Arm extended forward horizontally. A new set of downs for the offense.

>> **S9 — Loss of down:** Hands placed behind the head. Offense loses a down, usually due to a penalty.

>> **S10 — Incomplete pass:** Both arms waved horizontally across the body. Pass did not connect.

Penalty signals

These 12 signals are the most feared in a game, but they ensure fair play is maintained. They indicate when a foul has been made and lead to a team penalty.

>> **S18 — Offside/Illegal blitz:** Hands on hips — used when a player crosses the line of scrimmage early.

>> **S19 — False start/Illegal procedure:** Arms crossed at the wrists in front of the chest.

>> **S21 — Delay of game/Delay of pass:** Arms folded across the chest. Offense took too long to snap, or the quarterback exceeded the 7-second rule.

>> **S22 — Illegal participation/Illegal substitution:** One arm extended diagonally across the body, touching the opposite shoulder.

>> **S27 — Unsportsmanlike conduct:** Arms extended sideways at shoulder height — can apply to players or coaches.

>> **S33 — Pass interference:** Hands in a grabbing motion in front of the chest — called when a defender or receiver interferes with a pass.

>> **S35 — Illegal forward or backward pass:** Arm crossed diagonally across the back.

>> **S38 — Illegal contact:** One hand extended outward with the other arm crossed over.

>> **S43 — Shielding:** Arms crossed in front of the body below the chest — used when a player illegally obstructs another's path without contact.

>> **S47 — Disqualification:** Thumb extended over the shoulder, like a "get out" gesture.

>> **S51 — Jumping/Diving:** Arms move in a downward motion. Flag football doesn't allow diving to advance the ball.

>> **S52 — Flag guarding/Illegal flag pull:** Hand sweeps downward across the front of the body — used when a player uses their hands or arms to block flag access.

Penalties and other violations

Penalties in flag football are meant to keep the game fair, safe, and flowing smoothly. Each penalty comes with a consequence — most commonly, loss of yardage. In some cases, it can also mean a loss of a down, an automatic first down, or even disqualification.

WARNING

A loss of yardage means the team that is playing offense will have to continue their drive from behind the point where the foul was made. How far back they have to go depends on the violation and the resulting penalty.

To make things easier, in this section, I provide a breakdown of the most popular penalties based on yardage, using the official IFAF Rulebook (`americanfootball.sport/wp-content/uploads/2023/05/FlagRules2023.pdf`) as a guide.

5-yard penalties

These are typically procedural or minor infractions. They don't usually change the course of a drive, but they can add up quickly. This list describes the 5-yard penalties:

>> **Delay of game:** Offense takes too long to snap the ball (more than 25 seconds). The ball must be snapped within 25 seconds from the ready to play whistle after the ball has been spotted.

>> **False start:** Offensive player moves illegally before the snap. An example of this is when a player flinches and makes a movement while on the line of scrimmage prior to the snap.

>> **Offsides:** Defensive player crosses the line of scrimmage before the snap.

>> **Illegal blitz:** Blitzer crosses the line before the 1-yard buffer or without proper declaration.

- **Illegal snap:** Snap not performed correctly or cleanly, meaning the center picks up or rolls the ball before snapping it.

- **Illegal formation:** Not enough players on the line of scrimmage.

- **Illegal motion:** More than one player moving at the time of the snap.

- **Encroachment:** A movement by the defender to intentionally draw a player offsides.

10-yard penalties

These are considered more serious because they impact player safety or provide an unfair advantage. Here's a quick look at the 10-yard penalties:

- **Flag guarding:** Any body part or football being used to impede the progress of a defender to pull the ball carrier's flag. In IFAF, if a player's jersey is untucked and covers the flag when a defender attempts to pull it, the referee can call a flag guarding penalty.

- **Illegal contact:** Making contact with an opponent in a restricted way.

- **Pass interference (offensive or defensive):** Impeding a player's ability to catch the ball.

- **Illegal participation/substitution:** Entering the field illegally or with too many players.

- **Illegal forward pass:** A second forward pass, or one thrown beyond the line of scrimmage.

- **Illegal pitch:** A lateral or backward pass that doesn't meet the rule, like a pitch downfield or beyond the line of scrimmage.

- **Shielding:** Impeding a player's path without making contact.

- **Jumping or diving:** Leaving your feet to avoid a flag pull or advance the ball.

- **Unsportsmanlike conduct:** Includes taunting, inappropriate language, or excessive celebration.

Automatic first down/loss of down/ disqualification

Some penalties come with additional consequences beyond yardage, such as these:

- **Automatic first down:** Typically awarded after certain defensive penalties, such as defensive pass interference.

>> **Loss of down:** Some offensive penalties (like flag guarding or an illegal forward pass) may include loss of down.

>> **Disqualification:** Repeated unsportsmanlike conduct, flagrant fouls, or dangerous behavior can result in ejection from the game.

TIP

Understanding these penalties not only helps you avoid them, but also allows you to play smarter, take calculated risks, and better recognize how penalties can shift momentum during the game.

Offense

Get into the mindset of a quarterback.

Break down route trees, compound routes, and the fundamentals of catching, movement, and flag evasion.

Explore key formations and core skills to enhance your team's running game.

IN THIS CHAPTER

» Strategizing to put points on the board: the offense

» Discovering the unique demands of playing quarterback

» Exploring the mindset, leadership, and core skills that define a great QB

» Understanding the fundamentals that shape a QB's performance

» Breaking down coverages and reading defenses like a pro

Chapter **5**

The Quarterback

When you think about the quarterback, think about the heartbeat of the offense. The quarterback is the player who sets the tone, leads the team, and keeps everything moving forward. Every play starts with the ball in the quarterback's hands, and what happens next in the game depends a lot on their decisions, skills, and instincts. This chapter focuses on the role of the quarterback, but first, I provide an overview of the offense in general.

Understanding the Role of the Offense

The offense is the squad in charge of putting points on the board and helping a team win the game. In flag football, the offense usually lines up with five players on the field: the quarterback (QB), the center (C), and three wide receivers (WRs). Depending on a team's game style, these positions can shift; some teams swap a wide receiver for a running back (RB) or use different formations based on their strengths and strategies.

DIANA SAYS

I've played both sides of the ball throughout my career, but I've always been drawn to the offense. In many ways, the offense has the power to control the flow of a game, not just by scoring touchdowns, but by setting the rhythm of the action. That rhythm comes from a mix of factors: the team's playing style, players' individual skills, clock management, and the team's overall philosophy (whether it's more conservative or aggressive in decision making).

At its heart, offense is all about developing a strategy that maximizes your players' strengths and adapts to every opponent. It's about creating a competitive edge, either by building a playbook that highlights your team's best abilities, perfecting your execution to stay consistent under pressure, or finding ways to attack your opponent's weaknesses.

Building a strong offensive system is never a one-and-done job. It's a constant process that demands study, creativity, and communication, especially between the quarterback and the offensive coordinator, who form the brain and heartbeat of any offense.

I like to compare an offense to a clock's inner workings: every piece must perform its individual job perfectly, but also stay tightly connected to the others, especially to the quarterback, to keep the whole system running smoothly and on time.

Many things contribute to a successful offense, but here are five key factors I believe every coach and offensive player should focus on:

>> **Execution:** Every player must run their routes and assignments with precision, hitting the right spot at the right time. Perfect execution gives the quarterback cleaner reads and helps the offense build consistency and confidence.

>> **Timing:** In flag football, timing is everything. Receivers must arrive at their route windows just as the quarterback finishes their read and releases. Great timing creates unstoppable plays.

>> **Team connection:** Communication and synergy fuel an offense, both on and off the field. A strong connection helps teams adapt quickly, handle adversity, and stay sharp in every situation.

>> **Focus:** No matter the scoreboard, the best offenses stay calm, intense, and locked in. Staying focused on execution and the game plan, no matter what, is a factor that separates good teams from great ones.

>> **Clock management:** Managing the clock wisely allows an offense to control not just the flow of the game, but the game's outcome. Every second matters when you're trying to win.

Now that you know what makes an offense tick, it's time to meet the player who keeps everything running: the quarterback.

The Quarterback: More Than Just a Strong Throwing Arm

The job of the quarterback goes way beyond just throwing the ball. A quarterback must be a strategist, a leader, and a decision-maker all at once. They must read the defense before and after the snap, stay calm under pressure, and trust their teammates while inspiring them to give their best on every play.

One of the most powerful things about the quarterback position is that it demands a unique combination of mental strength and physical skill. Great quarterbacks don't just have strong arms — they have sharp minds, quick thinking, and the ability to adapt to anything the defense throws at them. They're like the eyes and brain of the offense, processing information in real time and acting with confidence.

At the same time, quarterbacks carry a huge responsibility. Wins and losses often get tied to how well the quarterback performs. It's a position that requires heart, courage, and a constant drive to keep improving.

I started playing quarterback around the age of 10, and I instantly fell in love with the position. It challenged me in so many ways, and even today, every new challenge teaches me something different. What captured my heart the most was the connection it created with my teammates. Playing quarterback has taught me more than just how to read defenses; it taught me how to observe and understand people. Sometimes, people say more with their body language than they do with words.

DIANA SAYS

One of the greatest lessons I've learned as a quarterback is that true leadership isn't just about constantly cheering and hyping up your team. It's about leading by example, staying accountable even during the hardest moments, and transmitting positivity, confidence, and calm through your attitude and actions. Leadership is also about helping others bring out the best in themselves, both on and off the field.

Throughout the rest of this chapter, you discover what makes a quarterback truly great. Even though every quarterback has their own style and unique gifts, I share some of the key traits that, in my experience, make a real difference. I also dive into the fundamentals of good throwing mechanics, how to read defenses, and how to lead a team when the game is on the line.

DOES SIZE MATTER FOR A QB?

DIANA SAYS

This is a question I've heard throughout my entire journey, and my answer is clear: no, size doesn't matter. What matters is your mindset, your leadership, your willingness to study the game, and how well you maximize your own abilities.

This issue is deeply personal to me because growing up, I often heard people, including coaches, say that I wouldn't make it as a quarterback at the highest level because of my size. Back then, there was a misconception that the quarterback's job was simply to stand tall and throw over defenders, nothing more. No movement, no creativity, no evasion, just catch, throw, and keep the ball above the rush. If you weren't tall enough, people assumed you wouldn't be able to see the field clearly or get the ball over the blitzer. But that view is outdated. The game has evolved, and so has the role of the quarterback.

I never let those opinions define me. Instead, I focused on building every part of my game: my speed, my awareness, my decision making, and my ability to evade pressure. And that mindset changed everything. Not only did it help me lead my team to compete and win at the highest level, including a gold medal at the 2022 World Games, but it also contributed to redefining what a quarterback can be in today's flag football game.

The game is constantly evolving, and so should you. No matter your size, your biggest strength will always be the size of your commitment, your passion, and your work ethic. That's what truly sets great quarterbacks apart.

Qualities of a Successful Quarterback: From Mentality to Precision

Every quarterback brings their own unique strengths to the position, but a few key qualities set the truly great ones apart. Being a quarterback isn't just about having a strong arm, as I explain in the previous section; it's about mastering the mental game, leading with heart, and executing with precision under pressure.

In this section, I break down some of the core qualities every quarterback should strive to develop. These qualities work together to shape a quarterback who can not only deliver results on the field but also inspire trust and belief from their entire team. And it all starts with developing the right mentality and mindset.

Arm strength and release

Having a strong arm helps a quarterback throw deep passes and fit the ball into tight windows. But arm strength alone isn't enough. Quick and clean release mechanics are just as important. A fast release gives defenses less time to react and makes the quarterback's throws more effective and harder to defend, especially in flag football where a QB has 7 seconds to get rid of the ball (that's a rule). Yes, seven seconds! I know it may sound like a considerable time for decision making, but it is not, especially if you don't have an offensive line (as in tackle football) ready to protect you and buy you some extra time. That's why a quick release is a game changer for every QB on the field. You have to make sure you have the power to execute fast and clean at any moment.

REMEMBER

In flag football, according to the IFAF rulebook (see `americanfootball.sport/wp-content/uploads/2023/05/FlagRules2023.pdf`), a QB has seven seconds to get rid of the ball before incurring a penalty.

Accuracy (and timing)

On such a small field, accuracy is extremely important — and it separates good quarterbacks from great ones. It's not just about throwing to the right player; it's about hitting them in stride, making it easier for them to catch and gain yards. Accurate passes build trust between the quarterback and their receivers and keep the offense moving forward.

Nevertheless, accuracy doesn't come alone. For an offense to be elite, QB accuracy needs to be developed alongside good timing between the QB and the receivers to make sure both — the ball and the WR — hit the same spot at the same time.

Positive leadership

Leadership is the backbone of a successful quarterback. It's not just about giving pep talks; it's about showing up for your team in every moment, especially the tough ones. A great quarterback leads by example: staying composed when things get rough, being accountable for mistakes, and radiating confidence and calm that others can lean on. True leadership helps elevate everyone around you, making the whole team stronger and more connected.

Competitiveness

To be a great quarterback, you must have a competitive fire that pushes you to be better every single day. Competitiveness means wanting the ball in your hands when the game is on the line. It means striving for excellence in every practice, every throw, every decision. A competitive quarterback fuels the team's drive to fight for every yard and every point.

Intelligence

Football is a thinking game, and quarterbacks are the ultimate thinkers. Great quarterbacks are like on-field coaches, leading the offense and making adjustments as necessary on the go. A good quarterback executes the plays by throwing the ball to the WR, reading defenses, adjusting plays, and making quick decisions under pressure — that's all part of the QB's job. Intelligence isn't just about memorizing the playbook; it's about understanding the flow of the game, recognizing patterns, and always staying two steps ahead of the defense.

Strategy

As I mention in the preceding section, a quarterback must always think a few steps ahead. Strategy is about understanding not only your team's strengths but also your opponent's weaknesses. Strategy involves setting up plays, disguising intentions, and making decisions that give your team the best chance to succeed. Strategic quarterbacks can outsmart even the toughest defenses.

Emotional intelligence

Staying calm under pressure, reading the energy of your teammates, and managing emotions during high-stress moments are all part of emotional intelligence. A quarterback with high emotional intelligence can sense when the team needs a boost, when a teammate needs support, and when it's time to stay composed and steady, no matter the situation.

Agility

In today's flag football game, agility is a game changer. A quarterback who can extend plays and even gain yards with their legs becomes a nightmare for defenses. Flag football relies heavily on speed and agility — agility isn't just a resource for extreme situations; it can shape the entire style of an offense. An agile quarterback can buy extra time for their players when a play breaks down, but even more, they can add versatility and an extra danger factor to the offense, making it harder for defenses to predict and stop the game plan.

Vision

A great quarterback sees the whole field, not just the primary target, but also the defensive coverage, the secondary options, and the open spaces that develop during a play. Good vision allows a quarterback to make better decisions faster and take advantage of opportunities that others may miss.

Mastering the Fundamentals

Even with all the right traits (see the preceding section), a quarterback can't succeed without mastering the basics. Fundamentals are what hold everything together, from the stance at the start of the play to the throwing motion that sends the ball flying. These small details make a big difference when it comes to precision, timing, and overall execution.

Whether you're new to the position or looking to fine-tune your skills, getting the fundamentals right is where it all begins. Fundamentals may seem simple, but they're the building blocks of every great quarterback. When you lock them in, everything else becomes easier and a whole lot more fun.

Stance: Balance starts here

The quarterback's stance is the foundation of every play. A good stance helps you stay balanced, explosive, and ready for anything. Keep your feet shoulder-width apart, knees slightly bent, and your weight evenly distributed. Your hands should be ready to receive the snap, and your eyes should already be scanning the defense. A solid stance sets you up for a smooth drop back (see the later section on dropbacks) or any other move you need to make to get away from the blitzer so you can quickly make a clean transition into your throwing motion.

DIANA SAYS

What has worked for me when it comes to my stance is keeping my weight slightly forward, focused on the balls of my feet rather than across the entire foot. This small adjustment helps me react quicker, whether it's to avoid a blitzer, drop back smoothly, or sprint out for a rollout when needed.

Eventually, every quarterback figures out the stance that works best for them. Some prefer to keep their feet even and shoulder-width apart, while others, like me, bring one foot slightly forward to stay balanced. This kind of preference comes with time and repetition, so don't be afraid to experiment and adjust until you find what feels natural and helps you move efficiently.

Quick feet

Footwork can make or break a quarterback. Quick feet allow you to move confidently, adjust your position, evade the blitzer, and set up your throws with accuracy. Drills that focus on lateral movement, shuffles, and directional changes are key to developing this skill. The faster and more controlled your footwork is, the more time you buy yourself to read the defense and make the right decision.

Dropping back

A *dropback* is when a quarterback takes some steps backward after receiving the snapped ball; they do this to see what's happening on the field before making a pass. In flag, the three-step drop back is the most used due to the speed of the plays, and it's also used to set the tempo for the entire play and gives your receivers time to get open. The dropback is all about rhythm and timing. The key here is to keep your eyes downfield while maintaining proper foot spacing and posture, moving smoothly and efficiently, always ready to plant and throw.

Whether you drop back is determined by the nature of the play, the pre-snap read from the QB, and how far the QB is positioned from the line of scrimmage (this is usually 7 yards, but some QBs can call the snap from even 12 yards away!). When the routes are longer than 5 yards, usually a snap is needed to give the receiver enough time to finish the route, especially when it comes to throwing a deep route. This helps a lot with timing. In the next chapter, which is about passing, I break down all routes so you can have a better idea of what I'm talking about here.

From the QB perspective, this is one of those fundamentals that demands repetition until it becomes second nature: smooth, consistent, and automatic every single time.

Getting a good grip

Ball control starts with the *grip* (basically, how the quarterback holds onto the ball), but here's the thing: Every quarterback has a slightly different one. That's because something as simple as hand size can totally change how you hold the ball.

While many coaches will show you a "correct" way to grip it, what I've learned is that there's no "one-size-fits-all." There are key elements that help, including spreading your fingers across the laces, keeping your fingertips (not your palm) in contact with the ball, and leaving a small space between your hand and the ball to help generate a clean spin.

In the end, it's about what feels natural and gives you control. Comfort and confidence in your grip are what truly matter, especially in those high-pressure moments where muscle memory takes over.

Power comes from the hips

Many people think arm strength is all about the shoulder, but real power comes from the ground up. Your hips generate the torque needed for a powerful and controlled throw. As you step into the throw, your hips should rotate naturally while your upper body follows through. Proper hip movement improves both distance and accuracy.

In Chapter 11, I show you some drills and exercises you can add to your training to improve hip mobility. This will help you maximize power and efficiency in your throws by creating smoother, stronger motion from the ground up.

Three keys to a great throw: Timing, accuracy, ball positioning

A great throw isn't just about getting the ball to the right place; it's about when and how you get it there. Timing and accuracy go hand in hand. They aren't exclusive of each other; they complement each other. You can throw an accurate pass, but if it's late, the opportunity may be gone. And you can throw right on time, but if the placement is off, it may lead to an incomplete pass — or worse, a *turnover* (when a member of the other team catches it). A well-timed, well-placed throw is the magic combination that keeps drives alive and makes an offense dangerous.

During my time working with two of the best quarterback coaches in the United States, Jordan Palmer and Mike White, I discovered a new way to look at accuracy. These coaches have worked with some of today's top NFL quarterbacks, and the way they break down the mechanics of throwing completely changed my perspective. They made accuracy easier to understand and, more importantly, easier to apply.

Of course, with practice, these ideas become second nature. But if you're just getting started, or even if you've been playing for years like me, it's always worth going back to the fundamentals. I wish I had understood this when I was younger; it would've saved me a lot of trial and error, so I want to share it with you.

According to their approach, accuracy can be broken down into three main pillars:

» **Ball positioning:** This refers to where the ball is placed in relation to your receiver's body and their route trajectory. A well-placed ball is one that only your teammate can catch, and that usually means understanding leverage, timing, and defensive coverage.

» **Ball speed:** This is how fast the ball gets to your receiver. Speed matters because it gives defenders less time to react and helps the play stay on rhythm.

» **Ball trajectory:** This is the path the ball takes, or how high or flat you throw it. Changing the angle of your throw helps you fit the ball into tight spaces or float it over defenders when needed.

REMEMBER

These three layers of accuracy — positioning, speed, and trajectory — are what take your passing game to the next level. Mastering them can transform how you approach every throw, no matter what kind of defense you're facing.

Reading the Defense

Once the fundamentals are in place, it's time to tackle one of the quarterback's most important responsibilities: reading the defense. A great quarterback isn't just reacting; they're anticipating. Being able to understand and recognize what the defense is doing (or is going to do) gives you a major edge and allows you to make faster, smarter decisions.

The process of reading the defense starts with watching film, studying your opponents, and identifying their tendencies. This gives you a solid foundation for understanding what the defense in front of you may do, but it doesn't stop there. Defensive coordinators are doing the same thing on their end, analyzing your offense and preparing their counters. That's where the real challenge begins: anticipating their adjustments and adapting to whatever the game throws at you. That back and forth is part of what makes the quarterback position so mentally demanding and so much fun.

The pre-snap read

Your job as a quarterback starts before the ball is even snapped. The moment you line up, you should be scanning the field. Are the defenders in man or zone coverage? Is the defense showing blitz? Where is the safety lined up? Where is the linebacker positioned? It's not just about where defenders are on the field; their stance can speak too. The way a defender is standing can give you clues about their intentions. Are they leaning forward and ready to explode? That may signal an aggressive move. Are they more relaxed, playing off the line? That usually means they're playing it safe, giving your receivers room to develop their routes.

Over time, you'll start noticing even more subtle details, like where their eyes are focused, or how their weight is distributed. These little indicators can tell you a lot about what's coming and help you decide whether to stick with the original play or adjust on the fly. The more you pay attention, the more you'll realize that defenses often reveal their plans before the ball is even in your hands.

Reading the defense pre-snap is all about observation and pattern recognition. The more you study film, the more you start to notice tendencies. And the better your pre-snap read, the less time you'll need to figure things out once the play is live.

REMEMBER

But don't get too confident in your pre-snap read! Many defenses, especially the more experienced ones, use clever tactics to disguise their coverage. They may rotate, shift, or change responsibilities the moment the ball is snapped. That's why it's crucial to stay alert and be ready to make a second read once the play is live. The defense you saw before the snap may not be the one you're actually facing, so trust your instincts, react quickly, and adjust on the fly.

7-second rule

After the snap, things move fast, really fast. At IFAF international competitions like the World Cups, as soon as the quarterback gets the ball in their hands, a clock starts ticking: The QB has 7 seconds to read the defense, make a decision, and execute the play. This isn't just a mental benchmark; it's an actual rule. If the quarterback doesn't release the ball within those 7 seconds, the play is considered dead, and a loss of down is applied. But it doesn't stop there. In reality, a quarterback often has much less time to throw the ball due to pressure from a blitzer.

On average, in flag football, you typically have about 3 seconds, sometimes even less, before the blitzer reaches you and makes a sack. That makes every moment on the field high stakes. In that tight window, you must scan the coverage, find your target, make a quick decision, and deliver the ball with precision. It's a mental sprint that demands both speed and control.

REMEMBER

A sack (introduced in Chapter 4) happens when the blitzer pulls the quarterback's flag before they can throw the ball. Just like any other flag pull, it causes the offense to lose yards and counts as a down. If the sack takes place while the quarterback is standing inside their own end zone, it results in a safety — which gives 2 points to the other team. It's a big momentum play for the defense and a tough hit for the offense.

Note: At the highest level, a blitzer can reach the quarterback in just 2.4 seconds on average. That's incredibly fast, and it's why quarterbacks need to process information quickly, stay composed, and get the ball out efficiently. Every second counts.

That's why practice and preparation are so important. The more you've seen in film and in reps, the faster you'll be able to react in real time. You're not just reading defenders, you're reading leverage, spacing, and movement. You're reacting to what unfolds while staying calm.

Coverages

There are several basic coverages that defenses run, and every quarterback should know how to recognize them. I walk you through them one by one so you can recognize them and know how to take advantage of them.

Cover 1

This is a man-to-man coverage where each defender will have a personal coverage on each one of the offensive players, meaning they are going to follow their matchup no matter what.

Cover 1 allows defenses to bring extra pressure to the offense, which means the quarterback needs to make quick reads and take advantage of one-on-one matchups. It's aggressive and risky; if the offense can beat their man, there's usually not a lot of help in the backfield.

You can spot a Cover 1 from the pre-snap read by looking at where the defenders are positioned and how they're standing. Defenders usually line up about 3 to 5 yards in front of their assigned receiver, squaring their shoulders and locking their focus directly on their matchup. Unlike zone coverage, where defenders tend to read the quarterback's eyes, in man coverage, their attention is fully on the receiver, not the ball. Their body language often feels more aggressive, with a reactive stance that shows they're ready to mirror every move. Recognizing that energy and alignment help you confirm what kind of coverage you're facing before the play even begins.

TIP

A one-on-one matchup means identifying which of your players has an advantage over the defender in front of them. That edge can come from athletic skills like speed or sharp route-running, or from the way the defense is lined up; sometimes their stance or positioning leaves a clear window your receiver can exploit. Spotting that mismatch and acting fast can lead to big plays.

Figure 5-1 depicts how the players are lined up in one-on-one coverage. Note the offensive players in the bottom row: Wide receivers (denoted by WR) and the center (denoted by C). The QB (not shown) lines up behind the center. Defensive players appear in the top row: Cornerback (CB), free safety (FS), and linebacker (LB).

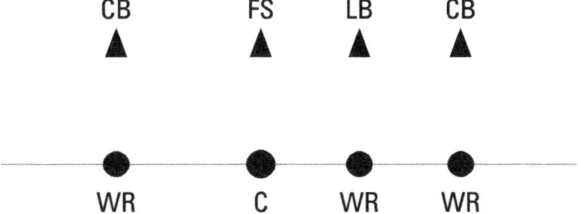

Here are some tips on how to attack this coverage:

>> Identify your key matchups.

>> Look for crossing routes and slants to create separation.

>> Use motion to identify man coverage and force defenders to adjust.

>> Quick throws are key. Get the ball out before pressure gets in.

REMEMBER

In the figures in this chapter, the blitzer is missing in the diagrams to make it easier for you to spot the FS and CBs, but the blitzer will always be positioned 7 yards away from the line of scrimmage in front of the center. I talk more about this position in Chapter 9.

Cover 2

Cover 2 is a zone coverage often used as a preventive defense (see Figure 5-2). That means defenders aren't overly aggressive on the ball or the offensive players. Instead, they focus on covering specific zones of the field and preventing big plays. In this formation, the two safeties split the deep part of the field in half. Each one is responsible for protecting one side over the top, typically lining up 10–12 yards off the line of scrimmage. Meanwhile, the remaining defenders drop into short and intermediate zones, each one holding down their area.

Imagine dividing the field into four quadrants, two deep zones and two short ones, with defenders positioned strategically to protect their space. This creates a balanced, layered defense that forces the offense to earn every yard through precise execution and smart decisions.

FS CB

CB LB

WR C WR WR

In 5-on-5 flag football, this coverage is probably the most basic one because of the balance it provides when it comes to the defense, where they can equally protect the short and the deep zones. This defense helps protect against deep passes and keeps everything in front of the defense. It can be particularly effective against offenses that rely on vertical routes, but it also creates opportunities underneath for the quarterback to exploit.

TIP

You can recognize Cover 2 from the pre-snap read by watching the safeties. If both are aligned deep and evenly spaced apart, it's a strong indicator that the defense is splitting the field. One corner, and the LB will commonly play short in this case.

Here are tips for attacking this coverage:

>> The middle of the field and the sidelines are common weak spots in this coverage. Defenders are spread out to cover their zones, which can create soft areas between the safeties and the short defenders, especially along the deep middle and near the boundaries.

>> Use deep middle routes like post or seam routes to attack the gap between the safeties.

>> Flood one side of the field with layered routes (short, medium, deep) to overload the zone.

>> Check down underneath — curl and hitch routes often find soft spots behind the linebacker and cornerback responsible for the short zones. These routes are especially effective when timed correctly, as they take advantage of the natural gaps that form in the middle and flat areas of Cover 2.

TIP

Cover 2 can be challenging if you hesitate. If you spot the safeties splitting early, be decisive and attack the soft spots before the defense can close in. Precision and timing work hand in hand. Aim to deliver the ball just before your receiver reaches the open zone. This gives them a better chance to make the catch in stride and take advantage of the space before defenders react.

Sometimes defenses try to reduce the disadvantages of Cover 2, especially the vulnerable areas in the middle of the field and near the sidelines, by slightly staggering their positioning. Instead of being aligned in a "box" formation, defenders adjust their depth and angles to minimize open windows and close down space more quickly. This subtle variation (shown in Figure 5-3) adds complexity for the quarterback, who now has to identify shifting zones on the fly.

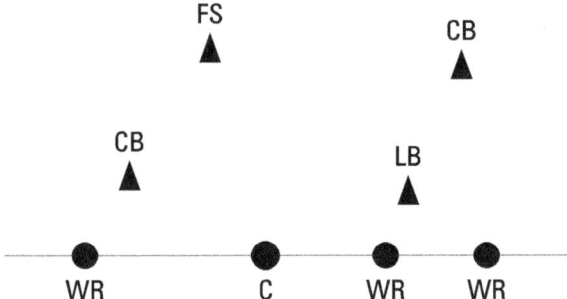

TIP

No matter the variation, your first job as a quarterback is to identify the coverage as quickly as possible. The sooner you recognize the structure, the sooner you'll understand the responsibilities of each defender, and that knowledge gives you the power to attack with confidence. Use it to your advantage. No matter how complex the look may be, the defensive principles remain the same, and the fundamentals will always guide you through.

Cover 3

Cover 3 is a zone defense designed to stop deep passes by placing three defenders in the backfield. These are usually the two cornerbacks and the free safety (see Figure 5-4), each responsible for covering a third of the deep field. Their main job is to prevent any explosive plays downfield.

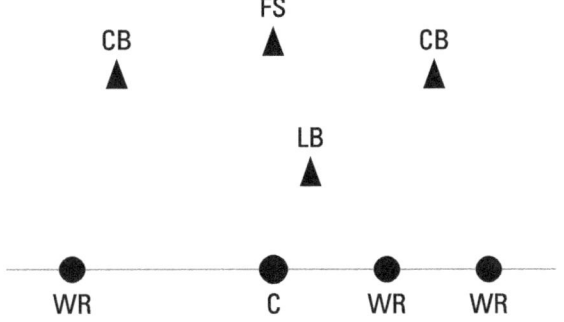

In 5-on-5 flag football, this means the defense prioritizes depth, sometimes giving more cushion to routes developing underneath. The remaining defender, usually the linebacker, is responsible for the short zone, typically positioned near the middle of the field. This player often shades slightly toward the strong side of the offense (where there are more receivers).

Here are my tips for attacking this coverage:

>> **Take advantage of the short space:** Drag routes, curls, and quick outs underneath the deep coverage often work well.

>> **Flood one side of the field:** Stack two or three receivers at different depths to challenge the zone responsibility.

>> **Look for holes between zones:** Seams between the corner and safety can open up if timed well.

TIP

Patience is key. Cover 3 invites you to take the underneath routes. Don't be afraid to move the chains bit by bit until the deep zone opens. Recognizing the deep triangle early will help you decide where to strike.

Cover 4

From a quarterback's perspective, Cover 4, also known as *quarters coverage* and shown in Figure 5-5, can be deceptive. All four defenders are responsible for their own quarter of the field, covering both short and deep zones. In 5-on-5 flag football, this coverage is not only used to stop deep passes but also to lock down crucial areas like the red zone or the midfield line. It's a balanced defense that allows players to sit back and read the play as it unfolds, rather than aggressively attacking the ball.

FIGURE 5-5:
All four defenders, two cornerbacks, a safety, and a linebacker, aligned at the line to gain, each covering one-fourth of the field.

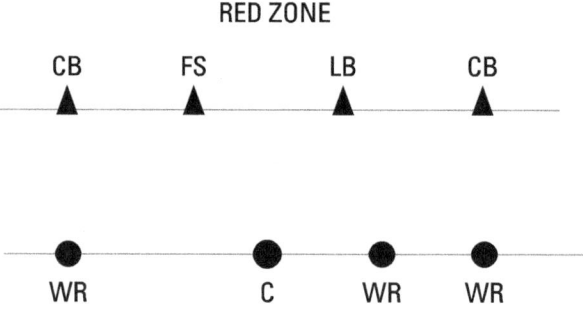

DIANA SAYS

As a quarterback, what makes Cover 4 tricky is that defenders are watching you the entire time. With all eyes on your movement, you must be precise and intentional with your fakes, eyes, and throwing motion. It's important to understand that while the defense appears passive, they're simply waiting for you to commit.

You'll often recognize Cover 4 when defenders are evenly spaced and aligned 10–12 yards off the line of scrimmage, especially when the defense expects the offense to cover a long field. Their priority in this case is to protect the deep zone. On the other hand, if the goal is to defend a first down or the end zone, defenders will be positioned right at the line to gain or the goal line. Their depth and balance make it harder to find immediate open receivers unless you force them to commit with route combinations.

Tips for attacking this coverage include the following:

>> Mix in route combinations that put pressure on one defender's zone (smash or flood concepts) to force a decision.

>> Be intentional with your fakes!

>> Exploit the flat areas. In Cover 4, these zones are often left open if the defenders drop too early.

>> If the defense is aligned deep, use short routes like hitches, outs, and quick slants to take advantage of the cushion defenders give.

TIP

Cover 4 may seem focused on stopping deep passes, but it actually leaves a lot of space open underneath. As a quarterback, stay calm and take what the defense gives you; throw short, safe passes to move the ball. Once defenders start stepping up to stop those, that's your chance to go deep and hit a big play.

I go deeper on offensive plays and concepts in Chapter 13, but for now, here is a quick definition for the smash and flood concepts:

>> **Smash concept:** This strategy is often used to create stress for a specific defender in a zone coverage, forcing them to choose between a short or a deep route and creating an open window for the quarterback.

>> **Flood concept:** The flood concept is a route combination that overloads one side of the field by sending three receivers at different depths: short, intermediate, and deep into the same zone.

Cover 3-1

This cover can be one of the trickiest to identify. That's because it mixes the structure of Cover 3 with deceptive pre-snap looks, making it harder to read until the ball is snapped. In this formation, shown in Figure 5-6, one safety drops back into a deep zone while the two cornerbacks and the linebacker stay underneath, covering the short middle.

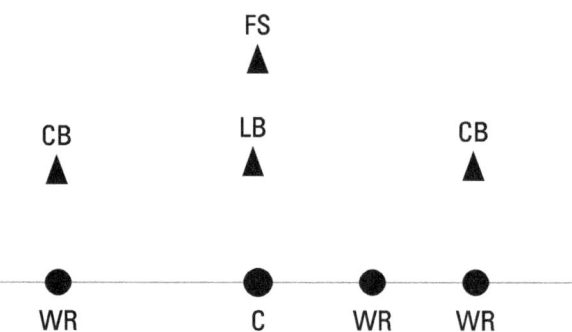

FIGURE 5-6:
The free safety drops into a deep zone while both cornerbacks and the linebacker stay underneath, covering short zones across the field.

What makes Cover 3-1 unique is that defenders may initially show a different look, like Cover 2 or man coverage, and then rotate into their actual assignments right after the snap. This post-snap shift is designed to confuse the quarterback and bait a mistake.

You can sometimes spot Cover 3-1 by watching how one safety stays slightly deeper and more central while others hold neutral stances that allow for a quick drop. But the real key is staying disciplined and reacting once the picture becomes clearer after the snap.

Here are my tips for attacking this coverage:

>> Be patient and trust your post-snap reads. Don't lock into a receiver too early.

>> Hit short or intermediate routes quickly before the defense settles into position.

>> Use motion to force early shifts and expose the rotation before the snap.

TIP

Hybrid coverages challenge your ability to adapt on the fly. The more confident you are in your fundamentals and film study, the better you'll be at recognizing the disguise and taking advantage of the windows they leave open.

Reading in the red zone

Things tighten up when you're close to the end zone. The defense doesn't have to cover as much space vertically, so everything gets faster. Timing, anticipation, and precision become even more critical. Defenders tend to sit on routes more aggressively, so you must be sharp with your reads and trust your receivers to get separation.

Use these tips to help you attack this coverage:

>> **Know your timing windows:** With less space to work with, the timing of your routes and throws has to be nearly perfect.

>> **Make quick decisions:** Defenders are closer and can close gaps fast. Hesitation kills drives inside the 20.

>> **Use motion and formation:** Shift your receivers to reveal coverages and isolate mismatches.

>> **Throw with intent:** Every throw needs to have a purpose. Put the ball where only your receiver can get it — high, low, or away from coverage.

>> **Trust your instincts:** The red zone rewards decisive play. Read the leverage, understand your matchup, and commit.

REMEMBER

Film study, reps, and in-game experience are what really sharpen this skill. The more you face these situations, the better you'll get at spotting the clues and delivering under pressure.

Reading defenses is a skill that never stops developing. The more time you invest in learning how defenses work, the more confident you'll be when it matters most and the easier it becomes to take full command of the game.

Chapter **6**

The Passing Game

Flag football thrives on speed, creativity, and precision, and nothing shows that better than the passing game. Whether you're watching a deep bomb fly into the end zone or a quick slant that turns into a big gain, passing is the heartbeat of most offensive strategies. It brings energy to the game and gives players the chance to show off their athleticism and connection as a team.

Unlike in tackle football, where running the ball can often dominate, flag leans heavily into passing. With smaller rosters and no blocking, the quarterback must rely on quick throws, well-timed routes, and players who know how to make space and turn short gains into long ones. Wide receivers bring the magic to flag football. They're the playmakers, the route artists, and the highlight reel creators. With quick feet, sharp minds, and fearless hearts, they make this sport one of the most fun and exciting to watch and even better to play.

This chapter takes you into that world, from understanding the role of receivers to breaking down route running, catching techniques, and how to read man-to-man coverage.

The Anatomy of a Playmaker: Wide Receiver Essentials

Not every receiver is the same, but the best ones all bring a mix of speed, sure hands, field awareness, and a fearless mindset. Some are tall and rangy, perfect for jump balls in the end zone. Others are quick and shifty, able to break ankles with sharp cuts and take short throws the distance. And then there's the reliable target who always finds a way to get open and make the catch.

A *playmaker* is a player who makes things happen on the field — whether that's throwing key passes, completing effective runs, or making defensive stops. When it comes to the position of wide receiver, a true playmaker doesn't just run routes; they read the defense, adjust on the fly, and keep building chemistry with their quarterback. A lot of the passing game is about rhythm and trust. It's not just about being fast but being in the right place at the right time.

In this section, I break down the traits that make a great receiver, whether it's a wideout (another term for wide receiver) stretching the field or a center sneaking out for a first down.

Speed and endurance

Speed gets you open. Endurance keeps you dangerous throughout the whole game. Flag football demands both. Receivers run multiple routes in a row, often at top speed, and they need to recover quickly to line up for the next play.

Hands

Soft hands make all the difference. (*Soft hands* refer to when receivers relax their hands to let the ball enter their grasp.) Great receivers don't just catch the easy passes; they haul in throws under pressure, in tight coverage, or just out of reach. Strong fingers, hand-eye coordination, and confidence are key.

Field awareness

Knowing where you are on the field helps you work the sidelines (running toward and along the sidelines to find an open path), find *soft spots* in a zone (an area of the field where there aren't any or many defenders), and avoid the *rush zone* (the area behind the line of scrimmage where defensive players are allowed to rush the quarterback). Great receivers have a sixth sense for space, and they know how to use it.

Competitiveness

The best receivers have that "give me the ball" mentality. They want the pressure. They fight for extra yards, go all-in to win 50/50 balls (when a ball is loose and up for grabs by either side), and come back to the huddle ready for more.

Consistency

Flashy plays are fun, but being reliable is everything. You must keep consistent, making sure you catch the hard balls and the easy ones every single time to build the trust of your quarterback, so the coach and the QB know they can rely on you no matter the situation.

Timing

In flag football, timing is everything. With a short rush count and no blockers, the window to get the ball out is tight. Receivers must hit their breaks on cue and be ready the second the quarterback releases the ball.

TIP

To earn the trust of your QB, catch every single ball thrown your way and be consistent in your execution. On top of that, communicate clearly with your QB, share what you see on the field, suggest adjustments, and help make their reads easier. That connection can make or break a play.

Wide Receivers

Being a great wide receiver starts before the ball is even snapped. From how you line up to how you explode off the line, every detail matters. These fundamentals build the foundation for sharp routes, clean releases, and big plays down the field.

Lining up

Lining up correctly helps the offense stay organized and avoid penalties. As a receiver, you must line up at least one yard behind the line of scrimmage to avoid an illegal formation. Know your alignment in each formation, always be alert and ready for motions or shifts before the snap, and make sure your spacing is right — too close and you'll clog up routes, too wide and you'll throw off timing. I talk more about these formations in Chapter 13.

Stance

Start in a balanced, athletic position. Feet should be shoulder-width apart with a slight bend in the knees. Lean slightly forward with your weight on the balls of your feet, ready to explode. Keep your hands relaxed and don't tip the route you're about to run.

Release

The *release* is how you get off the line and into your route. Quick feet and sudden movement are key. Against man coverage, the first few steps decide everything. Stay low, stay fast, and don't waste time dancing; get vertical. Think of it like a sprinter exploding out of the blocks — those first steps can be the difference between getting open or being locked down. I walk you through each one of these skills in Chapter 11.

Motions

Pre-snap motion adds confusion for the defense and helps receivers get a better matchup. Whether it's a simple shift or a full-speed motion, stay in control and time it perfectly with the snap. Motion can also help you identify man versus zone coverage.

WARNING

You are not allowed to motion toward the line of scrimmage, ever. If a player crosses the line of scrimmage before the snap, that's known as being *offside* or a *false start* and carries a 5-yard penalty.

Center

The center doesn't just snap the ball and get out of the way. In flag football, the center can be a major passing threat, especially in short yardage or red zone situations (the *red zone* is the area between the 20-yard line and the goal line). Because of their position on the field (as the name says itself, the center is right in the center of the field), they can sneak out on quick routes and catch the defense off guard since they have a wider range of possibilities for the routes.

Stance and snap

Start in a stable stance, just like any offensive lineman would, but be ready to move quickly. Set your feet shoulder-width apart with a slight bend in the knees.

Drop into a three-point stance and grip the ball firmly, holding it in front of your head but making sure it doesn't cross the line of scrimmage. This position gives you a strong base and allows you to snap the ball cleanly and explode into your route. The snap needs to be fast and accurate, either directly into the quarterback's hands or via a short toss. The cleaner the snap, the faster the play develops.

Quick release

After snapping the ball, the center should be ready to release it into a route right away. Most of the time, this means a quick out, slant, or hook. Timing is critical here: Delay too long and you'll miss your window; move too early and it can throw off the snap.

Field vision and awareness

A smart center knows how to find space. Look for open pockets in the defense, especially if they're playing zone. In man coverage, beat your assignment with a clean break and quick footwork. You're not just a snapper, you're a weapon.

WARNING

Make sure to avoid the rushers' path to the QB; obstructing their path generates a penalty.

Route Tree

The *route tree* is like the playbook's alphabet; it's how receivers communicate which path they'll take on each play. Each route is numbered and named, giving players a common language to work with. Mastering the route tree helps you understand spacing, timing, and how to attack different coverages.

You may notice that different teams use slightly different route trees, depending on the offensive strategy or coaching preferences. The routes themselves don't change much, but the numbers assigned to them sometimes do. The version I show you here (see Figure 6-1) is one of the most popular and widely used across flag football.

>> **0 – Stop:** A quick route where the receiver takes a few steps forward, usually 5 yards, then abruptly stops and turns back to face the quarterback. It's used for timing throws and to catch defenders off guard with sudden movement.

>> **1 – Go:** Also known as the fly or streak route. The receiver sprints straight down the field, aiming to outrun the defender and stretch the defense vertically. Speed and timing are crucial.

>> **2 – Slant In:** A sharp, diagonal route toward the center of the field. The receiver takes a few steps forward and cuts inside at about a 45-degree angle. Great for quick completions and beating tight coverage. (Plant foot is the outside foot.)

>> **3 – Slant Out:** Similar to the slant in, but the receiver breaks to the outside instead. It's effective against defenders playing inside leverage and offers a quick, sideline option. (Plant foot is the inside foot.)

>> **4 – In (also known as the dig):** A mid-to-deep route where the receiver runs upfield and then breaks sharply toward the middle of the field, usually at a 90-degree angle. Perfect for attacking weak windows in zone coverage.

>> **5 – Out:** Like the dig, but the break goes to the sideline. Run at a precise depth (usually 5, 10, or 12 yards), it's ideal for sideline throws.

>> **6 – Curl:** The receiver runs straight upfield and then quickly turns back toward the quarterback, curling into a stop. This route is designed to create separation from a backpedaling defender.

>> **7 – Comeback:** Starts like a go route, but then the receiver plants and cuts back at a 45-degree angle toward the sideline. Requires sharp footwork and precise timing with the quarterback.

>> **8 – Post:** The receiver runs straight, then cuts toward the middle of the field, aiming for the goalpost. It's a deeper route designed to split safeties and exploit gaps in zone coverage.

>> **9 – Corner:** A deep route that breaks at a 45-degree angle toward the corner of the end zone. Great for one-on-one matchups and big plays, especially near the red zone.

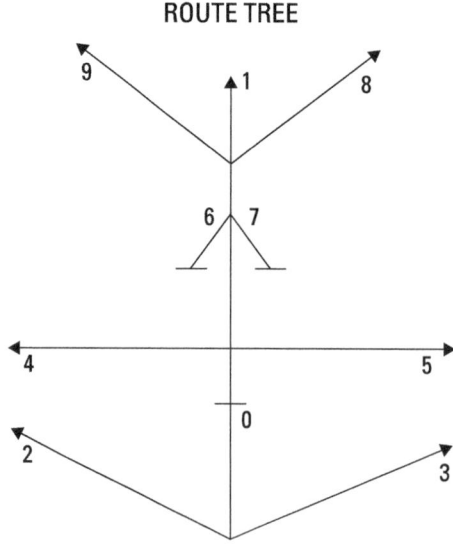

ROUTE TREE

FIGURE 6-1: A popular and widely used route tree diagram.

REMEMBER

Your *plant foot* is the foot you plant firmly on the ground for power and stability when throwing the ball or pivoting. When you're doing routes toward the sideline, your plant foot is your inside foot. When you're working toward the middle of the field, your plant foot is your outside foot.

Compound Routes

A *compound route* is a combination of two or more basic routes strung together in one fluid movement. These routes, also called *double moves,* are especially effective in flag football, where quick changes of direction and agility are key. They're designed to create separation, bait defenders into reacting to the first move, and then beat them with the second. When executed well, they're deadly, especially against man-to-man coverage.

Here are a few of the most basic and effective compound routes you'll see on the field (see Figure 6-2), but keep in mind, there are more varieties of these routes:

>> **Stop-and-Go:** A second example using a short stop before launching deep. It's a classic double move that's all about timing.

>> **Out-and-Go:** Looks like a sideline out route, but the receiver quickly turns upfield. Designed to freeze corners and go over the top.

>> **Slant-and-Go:** A sharp inside slant followed by a vertical burst. A great option to burn tight man coverage.

>> **Back-and-Go:** Begins with a stop or hitch, then the receiver restarts and goes deep. Perfect for baiting aggressive defenders.

>> **89 Post-Corner:** Starts on a post route, then sharply breaks to the outside toward the corner. This move catches defenders leaning inside.

>> **84 Post-In:** Fakes the deep post, then breaks into an in/dig route. Great for pulling deep defenders out of position.

As you can see in the preceding list, some of the routes are referenced with the numbers of the individual routes involved. For example, a post-corner is called "89": 8 for post, 9 for corner.

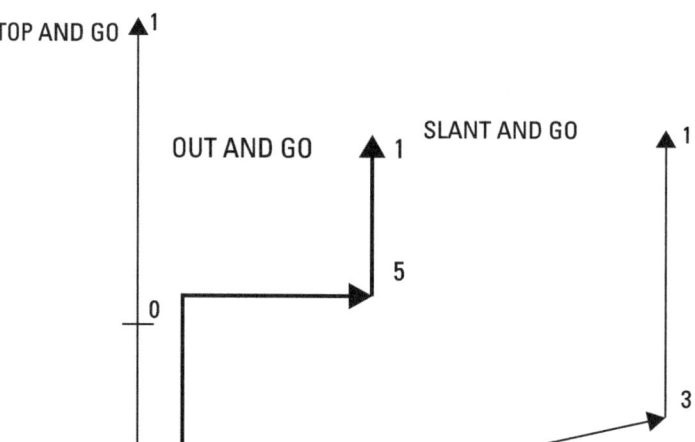

STOP AND GO

OUT AND GO

SLANT AND GO

FIGURE 6-2:
Examples of a
few compound
(or double
moves) routes.

Personally, these are my favorite routes to throw. I love the creativity they allow and the trust they require. As a quarterback, seeing the defender bite on the first move and then watching the receiver burst free on the second part of the route is one of the most rewarding plays in the game. But these routes only work if the timing is perfect and the chemistry between QB and receiver is rock solid. You must anticipate the break, throw with confidence, and trust your receiver will be exactly where they need to be. When that connection is there, these routes become killers, especially against man-to-man coverage, where every step counts and the smallest hesitation by a defender can cost a lot.

DIANA
SAYS

I encourage you to be creative when it comes to practicing new compound routes! They not only can be killer during a game but also will help you expand your range of possibilities while running a route on the field and be more dynamic.

Catching the Ball

Making the catch is one of the most important jobs of a receiver and also one of the hardest. A great catch doesn't happen by accident. It comes from focus, technique, and relentless repetition. In this section, I break down how to become the kind of receiver your quarterback can always count on.

Eyes on the ball

Always keep your eyes locked on the ball from the moment it leaves the quarterback's hand until it's secured. That means tracking its speed, spiral, and trajectory. The more you train your eyes to focus under pressure, the more natural it becomes to adjust mid-route or make last-second grabs.

Hands ready

Extend your arms and create a triangle or diamond shape with your thumbs and index fingers (as shown on the left in Figure 6-3) when the ball is coming straight at you (at chest height). If the pass is lower than chest height or off to the side, adjust your hand placement (keeping your pinkies together) — but always keep your fingers relaxed yet strong.

Thumbs together   Pinkies together

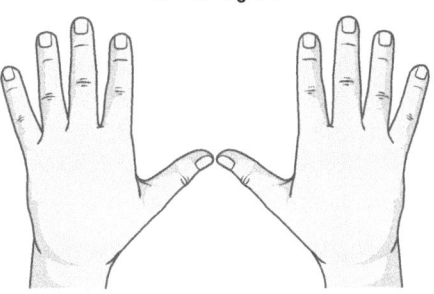 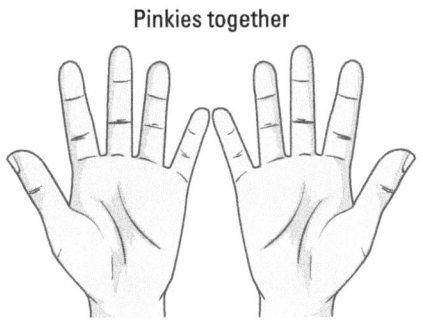

FIGURE 6-3: Always use your fingertips to catch the ball and keep your fingers relaxed yet strong.

WARNING

Avoid catching with your body! That reduces control and increases the chance of a drop.

Catch softly, which means absorbing the ball instead of letting it bounce off of you. Use your fingertips, not your palms, to secure the ball; then immediately tuck it away. A clean catch isn't finished until the ball is secured against your body and protected from defenders.

Body positioning

Position your body between the ball and the defender whenever possible. This makes it harder for defenders to reach in and increases your chances of a clean catch. Whether it's a curl, slant, or deep ball, controlling your space is key.

Finishing the play

After the catch, immediately turn upfield and get into a runner's mindset. Don't celebrate too early, because some of the best plays happen after the catch. Be ready to shake off a flag pull attempt, use a quick hip move, and keep moving the ball.

REMEMBER

Great receivers don't just make catches, they make plays! Making plays starts with focus, footwork, and fundamentals, and keeps the player always moving forward.

Beating man-to-man coverage

In flag football, defenders aren't allowed to make physical contact like they are in tackle football. That means winning the matchup comes down to skill, not size or strength. If you're the better athlete with sharper technique, you'll win most battles.

To beat man-to-man coverage, the key is separation. That comes from three main ingredients: speed, clean footwork, and precise route execution:

>> **Speed** allows you to create natural distance from your defender.

>> **Footwork** helps you stay sharp through breaks and use quick changes of direction to your advantage.

>> **Route execution** ensures you're where the quarterback expects you to be on time and in rhythm.

Add to that a solid understanding of field positioning and perfect timing with your quarterback, and you've got a recipe for success.

TIP

Take advantage of the space on the field. Use motion to identify coverage and gain leverage. Use fakes, head movement, and sudden breaks to keep defenders guessing. And above all, trust the connection with your QB. A perfectly timed throw beats even the best defender when the route is clean and the timing is tight.

Gaining yards after catch

In flag football, the play doesn't end with catching the ball; your ability to gain extra yards can make or break a drive (known as YAC, or yards after catch). Without contact or blocking, it all comes down to quick decisions, sharp cuts, and body control. *It's all about speed, agility, and body control.*

Evading a flag pull in flag football is all about mastering the fundamentals of movement. In Chapter 11, I go deeper into how to develop these skills through practical training that can level up your ability to extend plays after the catch and become a true threat with the ball in your hands. But here's where we break down why they matter so much. These are the tools that let you turn a simple catch into a big gain, and maybe even a touchdown.

Quick feet

This is, in my opinion, one of the most important abilities to develop in a flag football player. Since the field is not too big and the games tend to go so fast, having the ability to move your feet fast —making tight jukes and cuts to make sure no one snags your flag — on the field is key. Long strides may look fast, but quick feet win in tight spaces.

Hips and dips

Your hips are your biggest weapon after the catch. A quick dip or hip fake (known as *changing your level*) can throw off a defender's timing just enough to slip by untouched. Stay low, stay sharp, and stay unpredictable. This is where body control becomes your best ally. You need enough mobility and flexibility to shift direction and the ability to move your hips fluidly while maintaining top speed. It's not just about making a move; it's about making the right move at the right time while staying fast, balanced, and in control.

REMEMBER

The more hip movements you make, the more the flags on your hips move, and the harder it is for the defender to pull them.

Field awareness

Scan the field as soon as you secure the ball. Anticipate where defenders are coming from and look for open space. Plan your cut or turn before the defender gets close. In this case, mixing speeds is just as effective as changing direction. A sudden slowdown followed by an explosive burst can leave your defender flat-footed.

No contact or blocking

Because physical contact isn't allowed, the advantage goes to the player with stronger agility, footwork, and decision making. Work on reacting quickly and using your body language to keep defenders guessing.

REMEMBER

The goal is not just to catch the ball but to keep moving the ball! Aim to avoid the flag pull and maybe even break free for a touchdown. True playmakers are the players who always remain hungry for more.

Thinking Smart: Mastering Game Situations

What separates a good wide receiver from a great one isn't just athletic ability; it's *game IQ*, which is knowing how to read the game and adjusting decisions based on the situation. Because flag football is such a fast-paced sport, players must process information quickly. That includes the down, distance to the first down, time on the clock, and overall offensive strategy. The best wide receivers have a high game IQ.

DIANA SAYS

Every player on offense should know exactly what the situation is. When everyone's on the same page, the offense flows smoother, decision making is faster, and execution gets sharper. Small details can have a huge impact on the outcome of a drive.

I walk you through an example so you can picture this better:

> Imagine your team gets a great first down and moves the ball to the 10-yard line. That means you're exactly 10 yards away from another first down. On second down, the wide receiver catches the ball and does a great job evading a flag pull, gaining 12 yards across midfield, and finally getting captured at the 22-yard line.

At first glance, this looks like a solid play; 12 yards is a great gain, right? Not quite. By crossing the first down marker on second down, the offense resets the count and now only has 4 plays left to score instead of 6. That's two fewer chances to reach the end zone.

It's a subtle situation, but it shows how knowing the game can change the play. In this case, if the receiver had gone out of bounds at 9 yards or taken the flag pull just before the first down, the offense would've had 2 more plays before reaching the red zone, and then after making the first down, another set of 4 plays to punch it in.

Every choice on the field has an impact. Sometimes the smart move is knowing when *not* to get the extra yard. The secret is to balance athletic instincts with strategic thinking. Know your situation. Play your cards right. Be smart.

IN THIS CHAPTER

» **Understanding how a running play complements the passing game**

» **Identifying who can run the ball**

» **Exploring key formations (and variations) that expand the playbook**

» **Breaking down the core skills every runner needs**

» **Recognizing the no-run zone rule**

» **Seeing how smart runners evade flag pulls with hips, dips, and creativity**

Chapter **7**

The Running Game

Speed is at the heart of flag football, and the running game is one of the best ways to put it on display. Depending on the format, running plays are used differently. In 5-on-5, they're sometimes underestimated. With a short and narrow field, many coaches would rather take the quick five-yard pass than bet on a run that could be shut down early.

But don't be fooled. A strong running game, especially when it features a true running back or a hybrid player in the backfield, someone who can both run and throw, can be a total game-changer. I've seen it time and time again: Even the best defenses struggle when more than one player behind the line of scrimmage is a threat to take off running. There simply isn't enough coverage to account for every possibility.

And when that threat is real, the playbook comes alive. Creativity takes over. Suddenly, there's a whole new world of trick plays, motion, and misdirection. One of the teams that does this to perfection at the highest level is Team Japan. Their speed, mixed with how smart and unexpected their plays are, makes their offense nearly impossible to predict and even harder to stop.

Something I absolutely love about my team, Team Mexico, is how we bring that same creativity to life. It's one of the things that defines us. Whether it's one, two, or even three players behind the line of scrimmage, we find ways to make the game more entertaining, exciting, and unpredictable. Those moments where the defense doesn't know who's going to run, pass, or trick them? That's where the magic happens. And I can tell you, it's as much fun to execute as it is to watch.

When Is a Running Play Used?

Running plays are usually called when the offense wants to take advantage of open space or keep the defense on its toes. In formats like 5-on-5, where passing is often the go-to strategy, running can be the perfect curveball. It's especially useful when defenders start dropping too deep in coverage or when you spot a mismatch in speed or positioning.

Running can also help control the pace of the game. Short runs that move the chains force the defense to play closer to the line of scrimmage, which in turn opens up the passing game. It's all about balance. And in close yardage situations, like 3rd and short, a well-timed run can break through for just enough yards.

However, you have to be smart to know when you can or cannot run. According to the IFAF 5-on-5 Flag Football rulebook, the no-run zone is a 5-yard area located only before the opponent's end zone (see Figure 7-1). Inside this area, the offense is not allowed to run the ball and must attempt a forward pass that crosses the line of scrimmage. This rule is designed to promote more challenging and skill-based plays near the scoring zone.

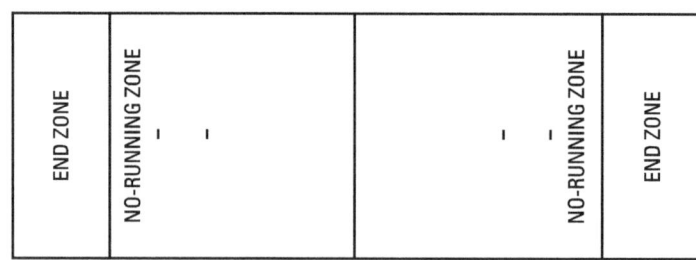

FIGURE 7-1:
The 5 yards before each end zone is the no-run zone.

WARNING

If a team runs the ball in the no-run zone, it results in a 5-yard penalty and a loss of down. Awareness of field position is key, especially in red zone situations, so the offense doesn't waste a crucial opportunity with a penalty.

REMEMBER

If you're in the no-run zone, you can still hand the ball off or lateral it *backwards.* Some teams use these types of plays as trickery. A play is not considered a run until the ball carrier breaks the line of scrimmage.

The key is to be unpredictable. If the defense knows you're only going to pass, they'll adjust quickly. But if they have to respect the run? That's when you start winning the mind game.

Who Can Run the Ball?

Flag football is full of surprises, and the running game is no exception. While the term *running back* (RB) is still used, it doesn't always mean a traditional, exclusive role. In most cases, RBs are some of the fastest wide receivers on the team. They play as *hybrid players,* meaning they may run the ball or run downfield to catch a pass. This makes it harder for the defense to know when a run is coming versus a pass.

That unpredictability is part of what makes flag football so dynamic. The only player who can't run the ball immediately is the quarterback. Everyone else? Yes! They can — as long as the play includes a legal hand-off, reverse, or any kind of ball exchange behind the line of scrimmage. Once that happens, any player who receives the ball becomes a runner, even if they're usually a receiver.

Here's a twist: If the ball is legally exchanged to another player behind the line of scrimmage and then returned to the quarterback, the QB becomes eligible to run. That type of play opens up even more creative opportunities and makes the offense even harder to defend.

A forward pass can also result in a running opportunity once it's caught. When it comes to designed runs, though, those sneaky behind-the-line exchanges are where the magic happens. Mixing up who gets the ball and how keeps the defense guessing, and that's exactly what you want.

DIANA SAYS

Do not be afraid to try different combinations and play options. There's no one good or right thing to do when it comes to being creative on the field and creating strategic advantages for your offense. Here's an example of how dynamic the game can be when you add different running options to the game. Imagine this setup:

> The QB takes the snap and immediately hands off the ball to a receiver coming in motion. That receiver then flips it back to the QB behind the line of scrimmage. Now the QB has the green light to run. The defense is forced to react quickly — is it a pass, a double reverse, or a QB run? By the time they figure it out, the QB is already sprinting downfield.

This kind of creative play isn't just exciting; it's strategic. It stretches the defense and gives your offense the upper hand. I dive deeper into these types of plays in Chapter 13, so stay tuned for more tricks and setups you can add to your playbook!

Lining Up: Hand-offs and Reverses

When it comes to lining up for a running play, it varies depending on the team's strategy. Some plays will show a running back (RB) lined up next to the quarterback, ready to take a hand-off or fake it. Other times, the run will come from a wide receiver (WR) who starts at the line of scrimmage and then comes around in motion to execute a reverse.

A *hand-off* happens when the ball is exchanged hand-to-hand between the QB and another player behind the line of scrimmage; see Figure 7-2.

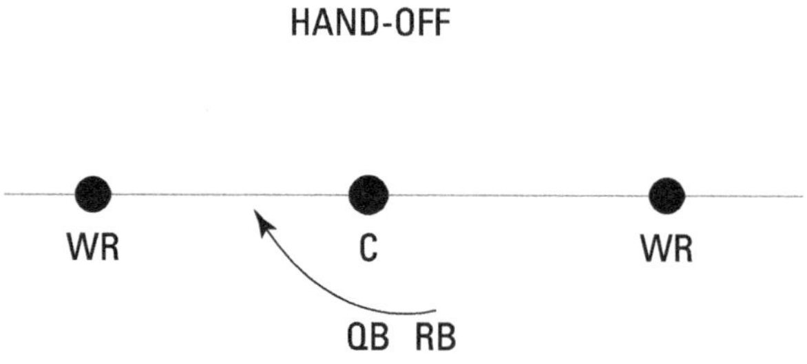

HAND-OFF

FIGURE 7-2:
Executing a hand-off behind the line of scrimmage.

WR   C   WR

QB   RB

⚠️

WARNING

However, understanding a key rule is important here: Once a player receives the ball through a hand-off, they can no longer throw a forward pass. If they do, it's considered an illegal forward pass under the IFAF rulebook. The penalty for this is a loss of down and a 5-yard penalty from the original line of scrimmage. To remain eligible to throw, the ball must be returned to the QB or passed laterally before any forward pass is attempted.

A *reverse* typically involves a WR coming from the outside and looping behind the QB to receive the ball, as shown in Figure 7-3. Since this exchange also happens behind the line of scrimmage, the receiver has the same options: run or pass. These subtle differences can completely change how the defense reacts to a play and how much space your offense can create.

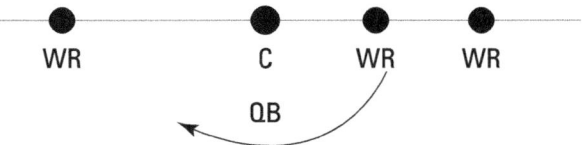

REVERSE

FIGURE 7-3:
Executing a
reverse behind
the line of
scrimmage.

Variations on Running Formations

The previous section covers the basic setups for hand-offs and reverses. Now I want to go a bit deeper into formations that open up new possibilities for running the ball. I walk you through examples of how you can position players to kick off a run, but I don't break down the full play or route development. That part is up to your creativity; think of these as building blocks to get your imagination going.

Formation 1, shown in Figure 7-4, is one of the most basic and balanced formations for a running play. By placing the RB directly behind the quarterback, the offense keeps the direction of the hand-off unpredictable, making it harder for the blitzer to commit to a path right at the snap. This setup is especially useful for short-yardage situations where quick execution is key and there's no time for the defense to adjust.

FORMATION 1

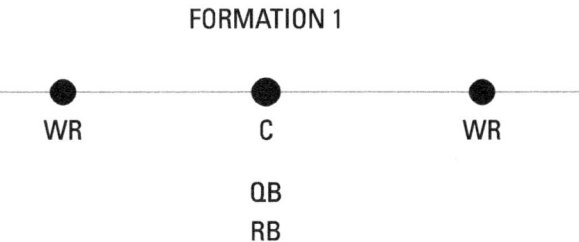

FIGURE 7-4:
Basic running
formation with
the RB lined up
behind the QB.

Because the defense doesn't get an early read on the direction of the play, the first few seconds become critical. The runner has to explode into space immediately and rely on pure speed to get ahead before defenders collapse in. If timed well, this simple formation can catch the defense flat-footed and set up consistent yard gains.

In the formation variation shown in Figure 7-5, the RB lines up to the side of the quarterback instead of directly behind the QB. This formation allows the offense to play with angles and timing. It opens up possibilities for quick hand-offs, inside or outside runs, or even motion plays where the RB shifts right before the snap to create confusion.

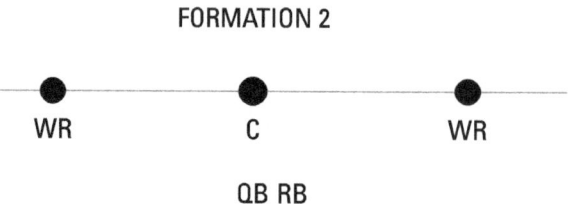

Having the RB on the side can also help with fakes and decoys. A well-executed fake hand-off in this setup can freeze defenders for just long enough to give another player the space they need. The hand-off path becomes clearer for the QB, and depending on how the defense shifts, the runner can quickly decide to cut inside or bounce out wide.

TIP

It's a flexible and commonly used formation that supports a fast-paced style of offense and keeps the defense guessing.

The setup shown in Figure 7-6 gives the offense more flexibility and movement options. With one RB lined up directly behind the QB and the other to the side, the formation creates multiple opportunities for hand-offs and fakes. The real magic of this formation lies in its ability to keep the defense uncertain and force them to hesitate. It allows the QB to read the defense as the play unfolds and decide which runner is in the best position to gain yards.

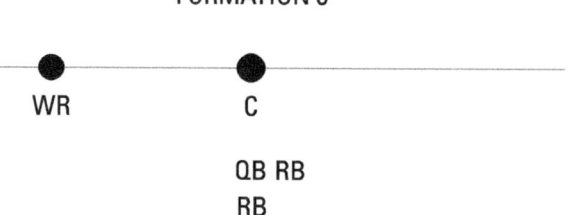

This kind of formation is great for running fake hand-offs and keeping the defense guessing. The QB may fake to the back behind them and instead hand it off to the side RB or vice versa. Because of the split backfield, defenders must stay alert and disciplined, or they'll end up chasing shadows. It's a great way to stretch the defense horizontally and open up space.

DIANA SAYS

I personally enjoy this type of formation because it not only helps open up space for wide receivers to run a variety of routes, but it also creates one-on-one opportunities when the defense drops down to cover the running backs. This makes the offense more dynamic, unpredictable, and honestly, way more fun to watch and play.

Figure 7-7 shows a formation that puts the quarterback directly under the center, with one RB lined up a few yards behind and a WR positioned close to the center in a tight formation. This design is perfect for quick plays that develop right after the snap. The tight alignment can confuse the defense and force them to play closer to the line, opening up possibilities for short but explosive runs.

FIGURE 7-7: This basic running formation puts the QB directly under the center, with one RB lined up a few yards behind and a WR positioned close to the center.

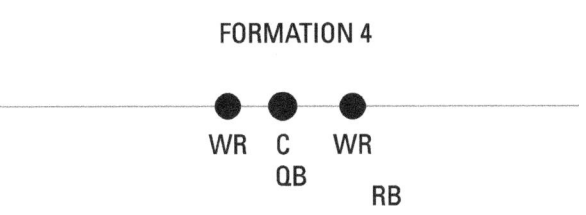

FORMATION 4

The formation in Figure 7-7 is especially effective when combined with motion or a fake hand-off, giving the QB multiple options right from the snap. With so much action concentrated in a tight space, defenders often hesitate or overcommit. In this setup, the QB can fake a reverse with the WR, hand the ball off to the RB, or toss a lateral that puts the ball back in the RB's hands, now giving them the freedom to either take off running or throw to a crossing route. These layers of options make the offense much harder to read and defend.

The Basic Skills for Running the Ball

In flag football, there's no contact or shielding, so the only way to avoid getting your flag pulled is through body control, quick feet, and sharp movements. Once the ball is in your hands, it's go time. But great runs don't happen by chance. They're built on a few core skills that every runner needs to sharpen for flag football, specifically, where no blocking or contact is allowed.

Whether you're a QB, RB, or WR, understanding how to run effectively can help you become a more complete and unpredictable player. And let's be real: Watching or executing a play where a runner escapes defenders with smooth hips, quick jukes, and clean flag evasion is one of the most entertaining things in the game. These skills aren't just effective; they're flashy, fun, and a showcase of true athleticism.

Receiving the hand-off

In flag football, the hand-off must be quick and clean; there's no room for error. Because defenders don't need to tackle you but just grab your flag, any hesitation at the exchange can cost yards. A solid hand-off starts with good body positioning, as shown in Figure 7-8. The runner forms a pocket with their arms just outside the stomach, which is sometimes referred to as the "bread basket."

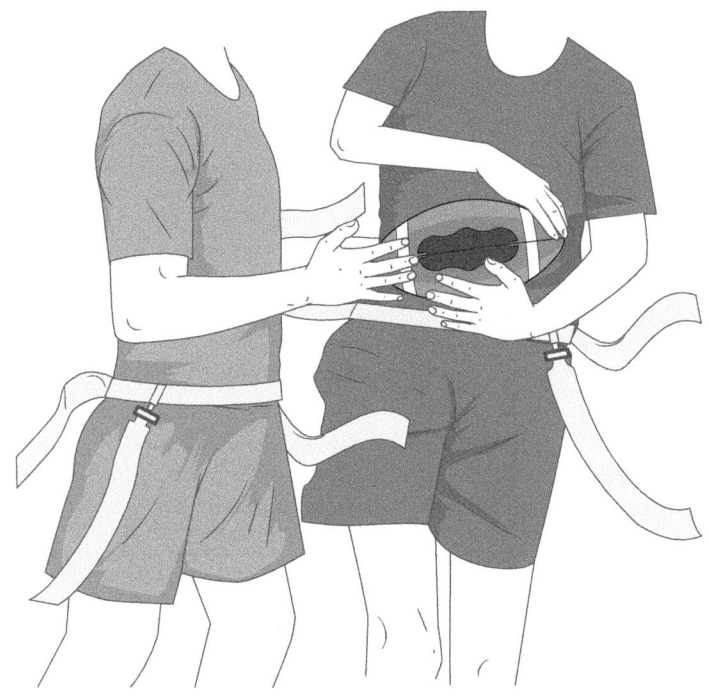

FIGURE 7-8: Hand and body position are important to receiving the hand-off quickly and cleanly.

It's important that the arm receiving the ball — the one closest to the quarterback — stays low, while the opposite arm comes down over the top to secure the ball. For example, if the hand-off is coming from the QB's right side, the runner should receive the ball with their left arm underneath and use their right hand to secure the top.

If you're faking a hand-off, go through all the same motions as if you were really handing off the ball to make your fake look real.

TIP

Running at top speed

Acceleration is everything in flag football. The quicker you can go from zero to full speed, the harder it is for a defender to catch up and grab your flag. Great runners know how to explode forward from their plant foot, usually the opposite foot of the direction they're cutting toward, and reach their top speed within a couple of strides. Body mechanics matter here: a slight forward lean, strong arm drive, and square shoulders help create maximum momentum without losing control.

And here's the good news: Speed and explosiveness can be trained. In Chapter 11, I share some of my favorite drills to help you improve these abilities and become more dangerous every time you touch the ball.

Seeing the field

Field awareness is one of the biggest separators between average and elite runners. In flag football, you're constantly reading defenders, looking for gaps, and reacting in real time. The best players have strong peripheral vision, allowing them to see not just what's directly ahead but where help defense may come from. This can be improved through specific vision and focus drills, like tracking multiple objects at once or using colored cone drills to force quick recognition under movement.

TIP

Check out Chapter 11, where I share some helpful exercises to strengthen this part of your game. Knowing when to slow down, speed up, or change direction based on the defenders' movements can turn a short gain into a highlight run.

Being agile

Elite running backs train for lateral agility, balance, and hip mobility. Hips play a massive role here, especially when using moves like the *dip,* a move where the runner lowers their hips mid-sprint (similar to a lunge) to dodge a defender's hands while continuing to move forward. Combined with fast cuts and smooth transitions, these tools help a runner stay elusive and unpredictable.

Evading the clean flag pull

Training yourself not to instinctively protect your flags with your hands is a must. This may feel natural at first, almost like a reflex, but doing so results in a penalty called *flag guarding,* causing a 5-yard loss. According to the official rules, flag guarding includes swiping, stiff-arming, or even lowering your arms or hands near the flag area to prevent a defender from making a clean pull. In other words, if your hands are used in any way to block access to the flag, intentionally or not, it's a penalty. Developing body awareness and clean running form is key to avoiding this costly mistake.

Here are a few effective ways you can use to evade a flag pull:

>> Moving your hips away from the defender while running full speed

>> Making some jukes to escape from the defenders

>> Doing a 360 spin on the go to make the flags fly (and harder to pull)

See Chapter 11 for drills to help you work on these moves.

3
Defense

Discover the linebacker's role, where the LB lines up, and main skills that make a great LB.

Recognize the blitzer as the heart of the defense.

Understand the key roles of cornerback and free safety.

IN THIS CHAPTER

» **Understanding the linebacker's role as a hybrid defender**

» **Identifying where and how a linebacker lines up**

» **Exploring the key traits that define great linebackers**

» **Breaking down the LB's physical stance and mental focus**

» **Mastering how to read offensive formations, motion, and quarterback cues to stay one step ahead of the play**

Chapter **8**

The Linebacker

In flag football, the linebacker is, in my opinion, one of the most challenging and fun positions on defense. That's because this player's responsibilities are broad and their decisions can shape the entire flow of a drive. A linebacker can bring clarity and calm to a defense when the job is done right or create total chaos when it's not. Whether they're covering the backfield, locking into a one-on-one matchup, or simply reading the quarterback, linebackers can't afford to take a single play off. Even when they're not directly involved in the action, their choices influence how the offense reacts, and that alone can change the course of a drive.

This is also one of the positions I've had the chance to play on defense, and it's one of my personal favorites. Throughout my journey in flag football from the early days all the way to the highest level, I've played both offense and defense, and in 2016, I competed at the World Championship playing both linebacker and blitzer at defense and wide receiver (WR) at offense, but that's a story for another time.

DIANA SAYS

Being a hybrid player has given me a much deeper understanding of the game. Playing both sides of the ball teaches you not only about strategy, but also about the mental game that unfolds between defenders and offensive players. That mental chess match is especially intense at the linebacker position since, as I explore further in this chapter, linebackers are often the first to react to what's developing. They read, they adjust, and their choices open or close windows for the rest of the defense to do their job more effectively.

Looking at What the Linebacker Does

The linebacker (often referred to as the "LB") is the player responsible for patrolling the middle of the field, which means they're constantly reading the quarterback, tracking receivers, and reacting to what unfolds in real time. Their job requires a mix of anticipation, quick thinking, and athleticism.

What makes the linebacker truly special is the ability to see the whole field. They must be communicating shifts, calling out motions, and reacting to pre-snap cues. Their movement often dictates how the rest of the defense lines up and reacts. They're the players who close gaps, make split-second decisions, and most importantly, help cover the "gray area" of the field, the space between short and deep coverage where offenses often attack.

When done well, playing linebacker feels like playing chess at full speed. It's about reading eyes, predicting intentions, and being one step ahead without losing your fundamentals.

Filling a hybrid role

Unlike a blitzer who goes straight for the quarterback or a defensive back who usually focuses on deep coverage, the linebacker must balance both worlds. Sometimes they drop into zone coverage to guard short or intermediate routes. Other times, they match up man-to-man against a receiver. In some situations, they may be asked to "spy" the quarterback or crash into the backfield to disrupt a handoff or reverse.

You can recognize an LB on the field because they're the ones constantly calling out offensive motions and communicating with the rest of the defense. You'll often see them pointing and shouting adjustments, especially to the blitzer or cornerback when identifying potential crossing routes or when multiple receivers are flooding a zone.

Playing downfield and backfield

One of the linebacker's most important responsibilities is to operate both downfield and in the backfield, and knowing when to move between these two spaces is key.

The linebacker often supports the blitzer, especially in plays involving a hand-off, reverse, or *double quarterback*, meaning two quarterbacks (QBs) have lined up. When the offense introduces more than one player behind the line of scrimmage (either two QBs or a QB and a running back [RB] as shown in Figure 8-1), it's crucial that the linebacker reacts quickly. This extra support creates pressure, kills the timing between the second quarterback and the receivers, and gives the defense a huge advantage.

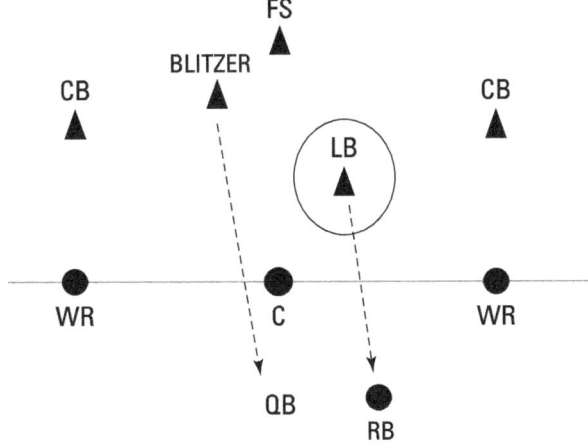

FIGURE 8-1: The linebacker supports the blitzer in plays involving a hand-off, reverse, or double quarterback.

Here's an example of how a play like this can develop: Imagine a hand-off or reverse happening behind the line of scrimmage; in this case, the linebacker must stay alert and wait for the ball to be exchanged before applying pressure. According to the rules, the LB is only allowed to cross the line and go after the runner once the ball has left the quarterback's hands.

TIP

Time is key! The longer a quarterback has to throw without pressure, the harder it becomes to cover receivers, and the game turns into a series of one-on-one matchups. That's why communication between the blitzer and the linebacker is so important, especially when the offense is running creative plays with multiple throwers.

On the flip side, the linebacker must also be ready to drop into coverage and protect against short slant routes, as shown in Figure 8-2. These quick plays may look harmless due to the few yards they initially gain, but with a speedy receiver, they can turn into massive gains after the catch. Because these plays often attack the sideline, generally fewer defenders are in position to pull the flag, which makes early coverage even more important.

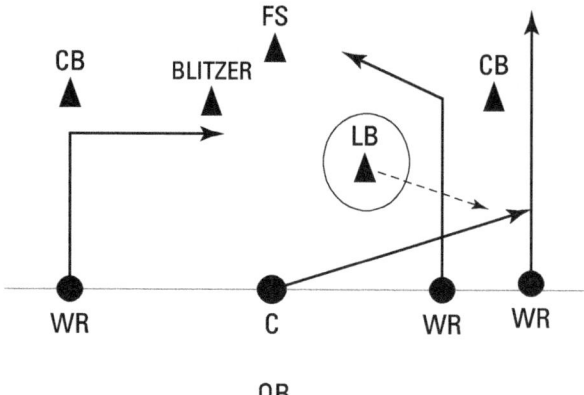

FIGURE 8-2:
The LB is responsible for covering a short route (in this case, a slant) to prevent the offense from gaining yards.

Linebackers also have the hard job of reading the quarterback's eyes and intentions, especially when the short area of the field is flooded with multiple potential routes (see Figure 8-3). This is where instincts, discipline, and athleticism come into play.

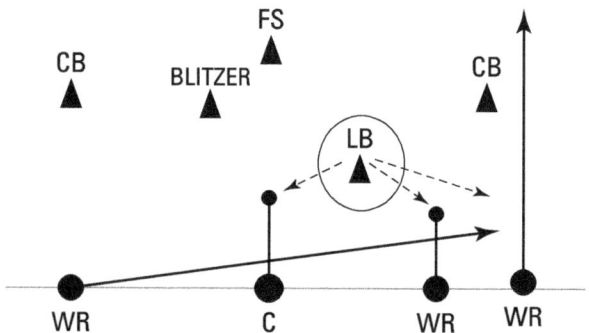

FIGURE 8-3:
The LB must be ready to cover any of multiple short routes.

The best linebackers don't just react to what's happening on the field; they provoke mistakes. They know how to bait the quarterback into making a bad read or force a throw that turns into an incompletion or, even better, an interception. And when that pick comes from a linebacker, it often results in big yardage or even a touchdown, because there usually aren't many players left on the field to pull their flag.

TIP

Offenses often flood the short game to bait defenders into creeping forward. Don't fall for it! As soon as multiple defenders bite and leave their assignments, the offense will look to strike deep, using a trick play to attack the windows in the backfield. Stay patient and trust your coverage.

Seeing Where the Linebacker Is Positioned

You can usually identify the linebacker by their position. They're typically lined up right in the middle of the defense (see Figure 8-4), about 3 to 5 yards in front of the center. This central position gives them the best chance to react to a wide range of short routes, including stops, slants, ins, outs, and hitches, all of which fall under the linebacker's zone responsibilities.

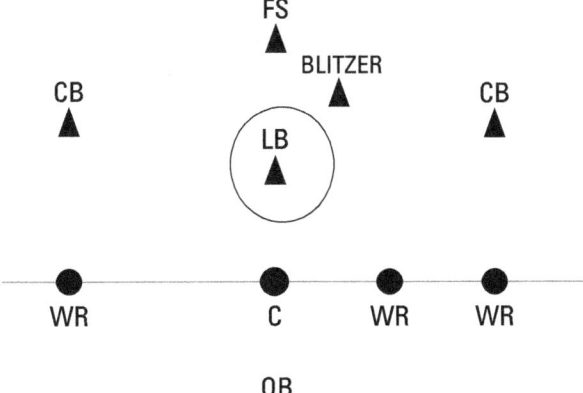

FIGURE 8-4: A linebacker usually lines up at the middle of the field, 3 to 5 yards in front of the center.

As you can imagine, this also means the linebacker can't cover everything all at once. Even the fastest player can't shut down every route across the middle. That's why alignment is everything. Pre-snap positioning can give the linebacker the upper hand or leave the defense exposed.

To avoid tough mismatches, linebackers often shift slightly toward the strong side of the offense (the side with more receivers). By doing this (see Figure 8-5), they place themselves in a better position to help defend where the action is most likely to go. But this strategic decision comes with trade-offs. While it allows the linebacker to reinforce the strong side, it often leaves the weak-side cornerback more vulnerable. That defender now has to handle one-on-one coverage or cover more ground, which can wear them down over time.

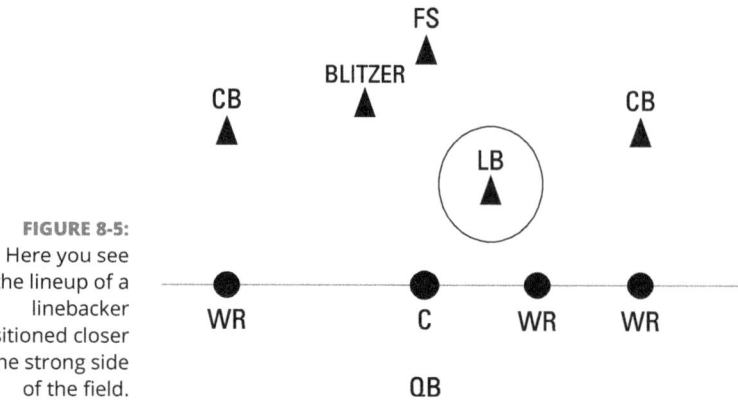

FIGURE 8-5: Here you see the lineup of a linebacker positioned closer to the strong side of the field.

This is where communication becomes key. A linebacker who slides toward the strong side should immediately signal the adjustment to the blitzer and defensive backs, especially the weak-side corner. That teamwork ensures everyone shifts together, maintaining balance across the field.

Considering the Core Traits of a Dominant Linebacker

To be a great linebacker in flag football, talent isn't enough. As shown in the previous examples, it takes awareness, communication, and a deep understanding of the game. This position demands versatility. One moment you're reading the quarterback's eyes and dropping into coverage; the next, you're crashing down to help stop a reverse. To handle all that, a linebacker needs a specific set of traits, which I detail in this section.

Quickness

Speed is important, but quickness and the ability to change direction fast and react instantly are what separate good linebackers from great ones. Alongside the blitzer, linebackers are often the quickest players on the field. Their reaction time has to be lightning-fast, especially since they're usually responsible for more than one player at a time. A single false step or a late reaction can open up space for the offense to strike. Your first move can be the difference between an incomplete pass, a pulled flag, or giving up a big play.

Mental quickness is just as important. Making a read and deciding how to react in a split second is part of the job. The best linebackers process what's happening around them almost instantly, and their ability to do that consistently can dictate how well a defense holds up.

Vision

The best linebackers see more than just the ball. They scan the offense like they're looking at a chessboard, analyzing formations, tracking pre-snap motion, and reading the quarterback's eyes. Since linebackers are primarily responsible for defending the short zone, they have to monitor both what's happening in the backfield and what's developing underneath. Whether it's a hand-off, a reverse, or a crossing route sneaking in behind the rush, they must be ready to react.

REMEMBER

Vision is not only about what you see but also how early you see it. It's an ability that comes with reps, film study, and in-game experience. Great linebackers trust what they see and move with purpose. They don't wait to confirm; they anticipate and strike.

Instinct

Instincts are that extra edge that sets elite players apart. Yes, they come with experience, but some players have a sixth sense for the game. It's that feeling that tells you to jump a slant or sit tight in a zone a second longer to bait the QB. The best linebackers are constantly studying the game and their opponents. They look for patterns in offensive play-calling and telltale signs in a quarterback's behavior. They don't just play the position; they try to get into the quarterback's head and disrupt the play before it even starts. That's what instincts at linebacker are all about: timing, intuition, and calculated disruption.

Communication

A dominant linebacker doesn't just do their job; they help the entire defense stay connected. Communication is part of their role. They call out motion, signal adjustments, and warn teammates of crossing routes. Especially in flag football, where there's less time and space to recover (because the field is short and quick decisions are necessary), as a defender, you don't have enough time to adjust on the go. That's why great communication can shut down an entire offensive series.

Stance

A linebacker's stance is all about balance and readiness. Since they don't know if the play will require them to drop into coverage, crash the backfield, or move laterally to cut off a route, their body needs to be in a neutral and reactive position. The stance must allow for quick acceleration in any direction.

Start with feet shoulder-width apart and knees slightly bent. This keeps your center of gravity low, which is key for balance. The linebacker's weight should be distributed evenly, staying on the balls of the feet, never the heels. This athletic stance keeps the body loose and spring-loaded, ready to move forward, sideways, or backward at any moment.

Hands should be relaxed but active, ready to react, redirect, or signal a teammate. Eyes are up, scanning the field, especially the quarterback's body language and the movement of offensive players. The posture must communicate one thing: I'm ready.

TIP

A linebacker's stance is never static. Great linebackers make tiny, constant adjustments before the snap: shifting slightly with motion, leaning forward if anticipating a run, or adjusting foot position based on formation. These micro-movements allow them to be fully tuned into the play and explode into action the moment the ball is snapped.

Reading the offense

Reading the offense is one of the most valuable skills a linebacker can develop and one of the hardest to master. Unlike other positions that often react after the snap, the linebacker has to start processing information before the ball is even hiked.

It begins with watching the quarterback: body language, eye movement, and pre-snap behavior all give clues. A quick glance to one side may hint at the primary target. A delayed cadence or hand gesture can signal a trick play or motion.

Then comes the alignment of the offensive players. Is the formation balanced? Are there stacked receivers on one side? Are they running a bunch set or spreading the field wide? These details shape what the linebacker should expect and how they should adjust.

Reading motion is also crucial. When a receiver moves across the formation, it may indicate a reverse, a pick play, or just a decoy. Great linebackers don't just follow the motion; they analyze the why behind it.

During the play, the job becomes even more intense. The linebacker must keep track of developing routes, monitor the quarterback's posture, and scan the back-field for hand-offs, double passes, or any unusual action. All of this must happen in real time, with zero hesitation.

TIP

Don't stare at the ball. Train your eyes to read the offense as a whole: the alignment, the spacing, and the rhythm. Often, the ball ends up where your instincts told you it would, even before it got there.

Reading the offense well means playing smart, not just fast. When done right, it turns the linebacker into a player who leads not only by voice, but also by vision and awareness.

Chapter **9**

The Blitzer

The *blitzer* (also known as the rusher) is the heartbeat of a fast, disruptive defense. Their job? Simple to describe, but tough to master: Get to the quarterback before the play unfolds. From the moment the ball is snapped, the blitzer's mission is to close the gap with explosive speed and force the quarterback to act fast, often too fast. Their pressure can break timing between the QB and the receivers, force poor throws, or even lead to turnovers. And the best part? They start doing all this even before they lay a finger on the quarterback's flags.

In this chapter, I explain the role of the blitzer and describe the core traits needed to be an effective blitzer. The blitzer's role goes far beyond just sprinting at the quarterback. Between hand-offs, reverses, and flooded backfields, there are dozens of possible situations a defense can face in a game, so I end the chapter by sharing a few common blitzer maneuvers.

Reviewing a Blitzer's Role and Responsibilities

Despite how crucial this role is, blitzers don't always get the recognition they deserve. To the untrained eye, it may look like all they're doing is sprinting straight at the QB. But don't let appearances fool you; being an elite blitzer takes way more than just raw speed. I describe blitzer traits in the next section, but this position demands explosiveness, laser-sharp focus, split-second reaction time, and an unbelievable amount of mental and physical endurance.

I've seen how this position can be underestimated on the field. I've even heard people say, "All they do is run!" But here's what most people don't realize: A blitzer can sprint *15 yards over 60 times* in one game, and not just casually — elite blitzers can do this consistently in around 3 seconds each. These are all-out bursts, with the pressure of being the one player counted on to disrupt every play. That kind of effort takes not only top-tier athleticism but also an intense ability to stay locked in, even when the legs are burning and the score is tight.

Here's the thing: Even at the highest level, a great blitzer may only have one or two truly impactful plays per game: a sack, a tipped pass, or blowing up a hand-off. That's what makes this position so demanding. You're sprinting every down, making reads, adjusting to fakes, and pouring in everything you have, knowing your chances to shine are slim. But when that one chance comes . . . it's everything. It can shift the entire momentum of the game. A perfectly timed blitz can be the spark that lifts a defense, energizes the sideline, and completely changes the outcome. It's a play that resonates far beyond the stat sheet — it's a statement.

Here's a fun fact: A blitzer may cover more total sprint distance in a single game than a wide receiver, but they don't get the glory of touchdowns or high-light catches.

The blitzer is a position that requires confidence, game awareness, and a bit of controlled chaos. You have to know when to go full throttle, when to hold, and how to throw off the offense's rhythm without ever crossing into illegal contact. Blitzing isn't just about being fast. It's about being smart.

As soon as the ball is snapped, the blitzer must explode off the line with maximum acceleration. This moment requires top-tier reaction time; every fraction of a second counts. The faster the blitzer reacts to the snap, the faster they close the gap between themselves and the quarterback. That reaction between the sound of the snap and the first step is one of the most crucial pieces of the position. However, the blitzer must be careful not to start the sprint before the ball is snapped.

WARNING

According to the IFAF Flag Football Rules (Rule 9, Article 4), blitzing early results in an illegal rush, penalized with a 5-yard penalty and an automatic first down for the offense. One early movement can cost the team momentum and field position, so timing is everything. However, it is not an illegal rush until the rusher crosses the line of scrimmage. If they leave early and don't break the line, there is no penalty.

The blitzer must commit to a straight-line sprint toward the quarterback, at least until crossing the line of scrimmage. This is important because by rule, the blitzer must have a clear, unobstructed path to the quarterback prior to crossing the line. Breaking this rule results in a penalty, so maintaining a legal angle and alignment is key.

Once across the line of scrimmage, things get more dynamic. Some blitzers raise their arms mid-sprint to try to block the quarterback's vision or deflect a pass. Doing this while running at full speed takes coordination, timing, and body control. These little disruptions can affect the QB's comfort and force off-target throws. But the blitzer must be careful not to come into contact with the QB while attempting to block a pass!

The most important moment comes as the blitzer gets close enough to make a play. This is where the real challenge kicks in: pulling the quarterback's flag, making a sack. It sounds simple, but in real-time action, it's one of the hardest things to do. The quarterback is moving, pivoting, sometimes even spinning to escape. The blitzer must match their speed, mirror their moves, and time the flag pull perfectly. One slight hesitation or misstep, and the QB is gone. This is why hand-eye coordination, balance, and body control are essential. A successful flag pull at this moment can be a game-changing play.

In flag football, a *sack* is defined as the action of pulling the quarterback's flag behind the line of scrimmage before a pass is thrown. A sack always requires team effort. Even if the blitzer is the one who finishes the play, it's often the result of great coverage by the rest of the defense. Tight man-to-man or smart zone defense can force the quarterback to hesitate or hold the ball just a little longer, giving the blitzer that extra second needed to make the play.

REMEMBER

It is absolutely crucial to avoid any kind of contact with the quarterback. Whether it's bumping into them, touching the throwing arm during release, or using excessive force during a flag pull, these actions can result in penalties.

WARNING

According to the IFAF Flag Football Rules (Rule 9, Article 1), any physical contact with the quarterback, including touching the throwing arm during release or running into the player, is considered roughing the passer. The penalty for this infraction is an automatic first down and a 10-yard gain for the offense. If deemed flagrant, it can also result in player disqualification. Always aim to pull the flag cleanly and avoid any contact to keep your defense out of trouble.

To avoid these penalties, elite blitzers master acceleration *and* deceleration. Being able to stop or adjust direction quickly while in full sprint helps keep control and reduces the risk of contact. In Chapter 11, I go over specific drills you can use to improve your body control and game awareness so you can blitz faster, smarter, and safer.

Understanding the Core Traits of a Dominant Blitzer

So, what does it take to go from a good blitzer to a great one? It's not just about raw speed or physical ability, although those help. The best blitzers are a mix of elite athleticism and mental sharpness, combining reaction, control, and grit every single play. In this section, I break down the core traits that define a dominant blitzer.

Speed

Blitzing starts with acceleration. The moment the ball is snapped, the blitzer has to close ground as quickly as possible. Speed isn't just about running fast; it's about exploding from a still position, accelerating through every stride, and sustaining that pace all the way to the quarterback.

Reaction

Elite blitzers don't just move fast; they move first. Reaction time is the split-second difference between missing a flag, pulling it late, or making a big play. The quicker a blitzer responds to the snap, the better the chances of causing disruption before the quarterback can make a move.

But the need for fast reaction doesn't end there. A great blitzer must also react instantly when the quarterback rolls out, makes a sudden juke, or a fake hand-off is executed. These moments demand full-body reactivity, not just foot speed. Being able to shift direction mid-sprint and stay locked on the target can make all the difference between making a play or being left in the dust.

And then after the QB releases the ball, the blitzer turns around and sprints downfield chasing the play to support the defense. Reaction time is everything!

Body control

Flag football doesn't allow contact, so blitzing is all about control. You've got to be able to change direction quickly, slow down near the QB, and maintain perfect balance while reaching for the flag. Without body control, a fast blitzer becomes a penalty risk.

The following traits are especially important in helping a blitzer to avoid penalties:

>> **Hand-eye coordination:** Pulling flags on a mobile quarterback takes timing, sharp eyes, and great hand placement. A blitzer must keep their vision locked on the hips and hands while moving at top speed. One wrong swipe can mean a missed opportunity.

>> **Focus:** Blitzers don't get to take plays off. Every down requires the same intensity and commitment. It's easy to get frustrated when you're inches from the quarterback but can't quite finish the play. A great blitzer stays locked in, play after play, regardless of the outcome.

>> **Perseverance:** This position is a grind. Blitzers will often sprint 15+ yards dozens of times a game, only to have the ball released just before they arrive. But the great ones never stop coming. They bring the same energy on the last drive of the game as they did on the first.

>> **Mental game (reading the QB):** Top blitzers don't just chase; they analyze. Having the ability to read the quarterback's eyes, body language, and movement can give you an edge. Sometimes, a blitzer can anticipate a rollout or a delay simply by studying the QB's stance or cadence. Getting into their head and staying unpredictable is a powerful weapon.

TIP

If you feel tired, the QB is probably hoping you'll slow down. Don't give them that relief. Keep pushing.

Lining up

The blitzer lines up exactly 7 yards behind the line of scrimmage (see Figure 9-1). This distance is set by rule and must be respected before rushing forward. Most often, the blitzer will align directly in front of the center, but they must subtly shift slightly to one side, either left or right. Why? Because once the ball is snapped, they need a clear path to the quarterback. If they run directly through a receiver or center and initiate contact, the defense will be penalized.

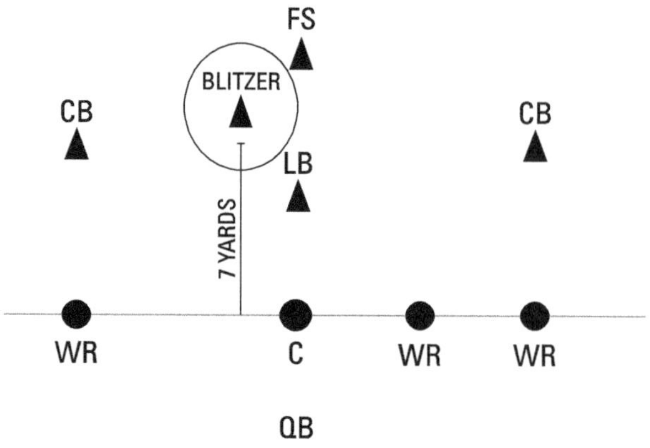

FIGURE 9-1: The blitzer lines up 7 yards away from the line of scrimmage, usually in front of the center, subtly shifting slightly to one side, either left or right.

Once the blitzer picks a side, they're committed. They can't change direction mid-rush and run into an offensive player. This means choosing your lane with intention, based on the offensive formation and the QB's dominant hand or tendencies, because according to the IFAF rulebook, "The blitzer must be at least 7 yards from the line of scrimmage at the time of the snap and must have a clear path to the quarterback. Contacting any offensive player while attempting to establish that path results in an illegal rush penalty."

However, the rule protects the blitzer, too. If the offense intentionally or unintentionally blocks the blitzer's legal path, or if any offensive player crashes into the blitzer while they are on their designated route, the offense will be penalized for obstruction. According to the IFAF Flag Football Rules (Rule 9, Article 3), this results in a 10-yard penalty and loss of down. The rule ensures fairness by recognizing the blitzer's right to pursue the quarterback safely within the boundaries of the game.

That 7-yard cushion may sound generous, but with the quarterback releasing the ball in three seconds or less, timing becomes everything. A single step too far inside or too wide can give the QB just enough time and space to escape.

Stance

Before the ball is even snapped, a blitzer is already setting the tone with their stance. This isn't just about looking ready; it's about *being* ready (see the nearby sidebar, "Crouched and ready," to see more of what I mean). Whether the blitzer is in a low three-point stance or an upright two-point stance like a wide receiver, the key is explosiveness, balance, and clarity.

According to the IFAF Flag Football Rulebook, the blitzer must raise one hand above their head before the snap to clearly identify themselves as the blitzer. This signal alerts the officials and the offense and ensures that the player is recognized as having the right to a free path to the quarterback.

To help with this alignment, a referee typically positions themselves on the sideline at the 7-yard mark, acting as a visual guide for the blitzer. This is critical. One step too far back, and the blitzer may arrive late, missing the sack opportunity. One step too close, and the blitzer risks drawing a penalty for rushing from the wrong depth. According to IFAF rules (Rule 9, Article 2), a blitzer who is not aligned at least 7 yards deep at the snap and initiates a rush is penalized with an *illegal blitz*, resulting in a 5-yard penalty and automatic first down for the offense.

A blitzer generally chooses between two stances before the snap:

>> The **three-point stance,** with one hand on the ground and a low, loaded position, is often the most explosive and commonly used among experienced blitzers.

>> The **two-point stance** mimics a wide receiver's upright start and allows for better vision of the quarterback and offensive formation; this stance works well for players who rely more on reaction than raw acceleration.

Regardless of the stance, the blitzer must remain still and focused. Any movement before the snap can result in a false start penalty or tip off the offense. The stance should feel like a coiled spring, waiting to fire.

DIANA SAYS

Use the stance that maximizes your personal strength. If you have great first-step explosiveness, go low. If your strength is vision and quick reads, stay tall and ready to adapt.

CROUCHED AND READY

You can easily spot the blitzer in any defensive formation — not just by their alignment, but by their body language. While other defenders may be communicating, shifting, or disguising their coverages, the blitzer usually stands still. There's a focus and intensity to their stance that gives away their purpose. It's like watching a cheetah crouched before the chase — silent, still, and ready to explode.

Studying Blitzer Maneuvers

Blitzing is often seen as a one-on-one duel between the blitzer and the quarterback, but in many plays, things get a lot more complex. When the offense places more than one player behind the line of scrimmage — such as a running back in position for a hand-off, a receiver coming in motion for a reverse, or a second passer lined up near the QB — the blitzer's job goes beyond a straight-line rush.

In these situations, the blitzer must rely not only on speed, but on intuition and elite reaction time to quickly diagnose who has the ball. A well-executed fake or misdirection play can easily throw off a defender charging in blindly. That's why blitzers must develop the ability to read exchanges in real time and respond with control.

This is also where teamwork becomes crucial. The linebacker is often the blitzer's best support in these moments. While the blitzer commits to attacking the ball carrier, the linebacker adjusts based on the play development, covering the second threat or collapsing the play from a different angle. The more coordinated these two positions are, the harder it is for offenses to execute trick plays or reverses.

These collaborative plays and reactions are called *maneuvers.* They aren't isolated actions, but shared defensive strategies that rely on pre-snap communication, player chemistry, and a deep understanding of the team's overall defensive system.

In many cases, the way a blitzer and a linebacker execute their maneuvers depends on the coverage or defensive scheme being run. For example, in man-to-man defense, the blitzer may stay locked on the QB while the linebacker follows a trailing receiver. In zone defense, roles shift fluidly depending on which zone is being attacked.

REMEMBER

Don't assume every play will be a clean sprint to the QB. Train your eye to recognize reverses, second passes, or lateral movement behind the line. Your awareness is just as important as your speed.

Reading hand-offs

One of the most common scenarios where blitzers must go beyond straight-line pressure is when the offense runs a hand-off. When a running back lines up behind or next to the quarterback, the possibility of a hand-off or a fake is on the table. Here's where the blitzer's instincts and reaction speed truly get tested.

As the play begins, the blitzer must identify whether the quarterback actually hands the ball off or fakes it; see Figure 9-2. This happens in a split second. A great blitzer doesn't hesitate; they track the ball carrier immediately and aim to close in fast, trying to minimize any gain on the play or force the player into a rushed decision.

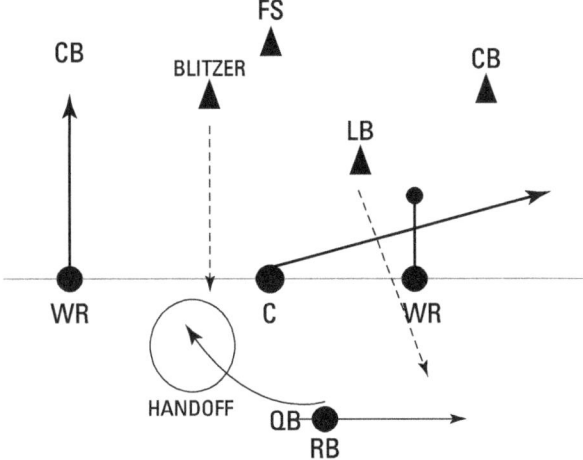

FIGURE 9-2: During a hand-off play, the blitzer must identify the player who keeps the ball.

Meanwhile, the linebacker becomes a critical piece of the defense. In this situation, the linebacker shifts into man coverage on the player who *doesn't* receive the ball. That way, both potential threats are accounted for: The blitzer attacks the ball, and the linebacker eliminates the option for a secondary pass or run.

In flag football, only the blitzer is allowed to cross the line of scrimmage at the snap. Here are a couple of exceptions:

>> If another player is aligned 7 yards away from the line of scrimmage

>> If the ball is handed off or passed behind the line of scrimmage and a defensive player willing to rush is aligned less than 7 yards away

Otherwise, if another defender crosses early without a legal exchange of the ball occurring, it's a penalty.

REMEMBER

According to the IFAF Rulebook Reference (Rule 9, Article 2), if a defender who is not the designated blitzer aligned less than 7 yards away, crosses the line of scrimmage before a hand-off or backward pass occurs, it results in an *illegal rush*. The penalty is a 5-yard gain for the offense and an automatic first down.

This rule protects offensive plays while keeping defensive pressure fair and structured. That's why communication between the blitzer and linebacker is key. Both players must understand who is tracking the ball and who is taking away the second threat, all while keeping their alignment legal.

DIANA SAYS

Always keep your eyes on the hips of the quarterback and running back. Fakes are designed to fool the eyes, but the hips never lie. Just as important, learn to be smart about when to go full speed and when to slow down to read the play. Blitzing is not just about intensity; it's about rhythm. Varying your pace can help you stay one step ahead of fakes and misdirection.

Defending a crowded backfield

Another common but more complex scenario is when the offense floods the backfield with two or more players. These formations usually involve a mix of hand-offs, fake hand-offs, and reverses, creating multiple potential ball carriers and passers behind the line of scrimmage. When executed well, this kind of offensive setup can confuse defenders and open up opportunities for big plays.

This is where coordinated defensive maneuvers come into play. Blitzers, linebackers, and even cornerbacks must work as a unit, as shown in Figure 9-3:

>> The blitzer, usually the fastest and most explosive defender, is often tasked with tracking the player who ends up with the ball, especially if that player has the ability to pass. The goal is to pressure the ball carrier quickly and limit the time they have to make a decision. By staying with the ball and closing the space, the blitzer neutralizes one of the offense's biggest threats.

>> The linebacker shifts focus to the second-closest offensive player, usually someone in position to receive a lateral pass or hand-off. The linebacker must be ready to cover, chase, or crash, depending on what unfolds.

>> If there's a third offensive player behind the line or floating near the sideline, a cornerback may have to step in. The corner becomes responsible for either covering that receiver if they release into a route or stepping up if they become a ball carrier.

This three-layered response is a common defensive maneuver used to stop deceptive backfield plays. It works best when players know their roles clearly and communicate early.

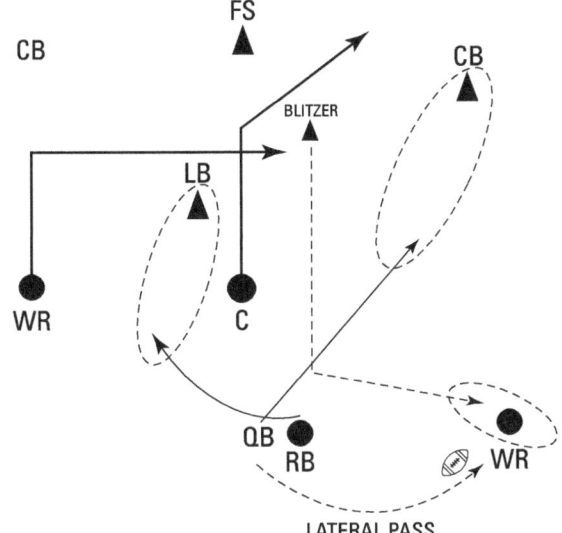

FIGURE 9-3: Defensive response to a crowded backfield, where multiple offensive players remain behind the line of scrimmage.

TIP

When facing a crowded backfield, don't focus just on the ball; scan the backfield pre-snap and count how many players are lined up to receive or move. This quick count helps you anticipate your role in the play.

When the blitzer has to cover

There are moments when the blitzer doesn't just rush toward the quarterback; they have to pivot and drop back into coverage. This typically occurs in special situations, depending on the game situation.

Another case is when, during a maneuver, the player they are matched up against takes off into a route. In this scenario, the blitzer must shift from attacker to defender in a split second.

Because of this, blitzers must not only focus on developing speed, reaction, and explosiveness but also spend time working on pass coverage skills. Covering a route demands awareness, footwork, and the ability to read the receiver, so the blitzer must dedicate time to drills and techniques that prepare them to defend passes effectively when called upon. That's why it's essential to stay ready, adaptable, and always prepared to step up whenever the defense needs it.

IN THIS CHAPTER

» Recognizing the secondary as the last line of defense

» Understanding situational football to use field position and time management to an advantage

» Reviewing the responsibilities of a cornerback

» Defining the free safety role

» Using clean and smart technique to avoid costly penalties

Chapter **10**

The Secondary

As I describe in this chapter, being part of the secondary takes much more than just physical ability. It's not just about speed or reaction — although those things are important — it's about communication, understanding game situations, and making smart decisions in real time. Cornerbacks and free safeties (collectively referred to as *defensive backs*) need to work in sync, adapt constantly, and use every detail they observe to their advantage. This position demands precision, discipline, and football IQ to turn small windows into big defensive plays.

In Chapter 11, I walk you through specific drills to help you improve your technique and instincts so you can sharpen these skills on the field.

Reviewing Core Traits of the Secondary Players

The secondary is the defense's last line of protection against the *deep ball* (a pass that's thrown way downfield, where a receiver has run into the opponent's territory). When this group does its job right, they create what coaches call a *no-fly zone,* an area of the field where quarterbacks hesitate to throw and receivers rarely make easy catches. This unit is made up of cornerbacks and the free safety, and they share one clear mission: Make sure nothing big gets past them.

To build a true no-fly zone, you need a mix of athleticism, awareness, and discipline. These are some core skills every defensive back must develop.

REMEMBER

Having all these attributes is essential to being a great defensive back. But these skills won't help without the ability to communicate and work together.

Speed and quickness

Whether you're sticking to a receiver in man coverage or closing in to help with a flag pull, speed matters. The best defensive backs don't just run fast, they accelerate quickly, recover when beaten, and close space in the blink of an eye. Quickness is that short-area burst that helps you change direction and react in tight coverage.

Vision

Seeing the whole play is what separates good defensive backs (DBs) from great ones. It's not just about watching the receiver, it's about reading the quarterback's drop, scanning the field, and recognizing patterns. A smart DB reads routes before they fully develop.

REMEMBER

Defensive backs include cornerbacks and free safeties. I explain each of these positions in more depth later in the chapter.

Hands

Catching may not be a DB's primary role, but when the chance for an interception shows up, it must be taken. Even a simple deflection can swing momentum. Good hands are also essential for clean flag pulls when receivers catch the ball.

Body control (noncontact) and reaction

In flag football, you're not allowed to tackle or bump your opponent. That means DBs need elite balance, awareness, and poise. Sticking close to a receiver without making contact takes control and discipline. Reaction refers to the ability to respond instantly to different stimuli, like a sudden cut or a pass in the air, and quickly change direction without losing balance.

WARNING

Because flag football is a noncontact sport, one of the most important things to remember about body control is to avoid contact. Any type of interference with a receiver during their route or at the moment of a catch can result in serious penalties. Defensive players must avoid pushing, grabbing, or obstructing the receiver, even if unintentional.

Two of the most critical infractions are:

>> **Illegal contact:** Called when a defender initiates physical contact with an offensive player during their route. Even small bumps or obstructions that disrupt the receiver's movement are penalized. Results in a 10-yard penalty from the previous spot and an automatic first down.

>> **Pass interference:** Happens when a defender interferes with a receiver's ability to catch the ball while it's in the air. This includes contact such as grabbing arms, playing the body instead of the ball, or cutting across the receiver's path. Also results in a 10-yard penalty and an automatic first down.

Other penalties to watch out for:

>> **Holding:** Grabbing or slowing a receiver down in any way during their route. This is penalized with 5 yards and an automatic first down if it occurs before the pass is thrown.

>> **Illegal flag pull:** Trying to pull the flag from a player who does not have possession of the ball. Results in a 5-yard penalty from the spot of the foul, with no automatic first down unless it significantly affects the play.

Flag pulling

If the catch is made, the play isn't over. Defensive backs are often the last hope to stop a touchdown. Clean flag pulling is about timing, reaction, and technique. Aim for the hips and finish the play.

TIP

Train your eyes as much as your body. The hips don't lie. Follow them instead of the shoulders when tracking a receiver or reading a fake.

Understanding the Game Situation

Playing in the secondary is like being in a chess match. Physical tools help, but smart decisions in the right moments change games. Great defensive backs (DBs) understand that the situation often dictates how to react, sometimes even when to take a calculated risk. Not every situation calls for a high-pressure, fast-paced defensive strategy. Playing aggressively all the time can work against the defense if it becomes too predictable or leaves open space behind. Sometimes, it's smarter to ease up the rhythm, disguise the coverage, or change the style of pressure to keep the offense guessing. That unpredictability creates hesitation and forces mistakes.

In this section, I provide some examples of situational awareness in action.

Knowing the down and distance

One of the most underrated skills is understanding when it's actually smarter to let the offense move the chains (move the ball far enough to earn a new set of downs, meaning move the down indicator and its chains). Sounds strange, right? But imagine this: It's second down and short, and you know they only need a few yards for a first. If you go all in to stop the short play and miss, they still get a new set of downs and may gain a chunk of yardage.

Now they're closer to scoring with more opportunities, not to mention that going all in to cover the first down line could be risky because the offense could come with a trap and go for a big play. But if you instead let them take those yards and get a first down while keeping the play in front of you, they restart their count of downs and now only have 4 plays to reach the end zone instead of 5 or 6. That means more chances for your defense to make a big play.

Here's another example. It's 2nd and 2 on the offense's 15-yard line. The offense completes a short pass, and your cornerback (CB) lets the wide receiver (WR) get 5 yards without going for a risky jump. It's now 1st and 25 on the middle field yard line. The clock keeps ticking. Now your defense tightens up, forces a flag pull behind the line, an incompletion, and finally a sack. Drive over. No points.

Forcing them to stay in bounds

When the clock becomes a factor, especially in the last two minutes, you can win games by just keeping the opponent from getting out of bounds. DBs should be ready to give up short completions in the middle of the field if it means forcing the offense to waste precious seconds.

On the other hand, quick sideline routes to stop the clock can give the offense control of the tempo. Smart DBs know how to close those options, forcing receivers to stay in bounds. Sometimes a well-timed flag pull just inside the sideline is more valuable than a deflection.

Adjusting according to the situation

Whether it's third and long, red zone defense (the red zone is within 20 yards of the opponent's end zone), the secondary must change its style accordingly. Playing zone or man-to-man coverage — each game situation calls for a different strategy.

A good example is understanding that it's not the same to play man-to-man on a 2nd down before midfield as it is on a 4th and long situation. In the second scenario, going full man coverage can be extremely risky, because all it takes is one fast receiver to win their matchup, go deep, and flip the game with a big gain or even a touchdown. When it's 4th and long, zone concepts or coverage that keeps the play in front is often the smarter call.

Formations, pressure strategies, and defensive alignments all depend on these game situations. The best secondaries aren't just fast or athletic, they're smart and they're masters at adapting in real time.

Cornerbacks

Cornerbacks (CBs; sometimes called simply corners) are usually the last line of defense alongside the free safety against the deep passing game. They're tasked with guarding wide receivers and shutting down outside routes. Depending on the coverage call, a cornerback may play man-to-man, zone, or a hybrid technique that combines both. While cornerbacks often contribute to deep zone coverage alongside the free safety, they must also be highly skilled in short zone defense and man-to-man coverage. Regardless of the scheme, the mission stays the same: Don't let your receiver get open.

What the cornerback does

Cornerbacks have a clear role: prevent completed passes, protect the deep sideline and often the mid or short outside zones, and quickly go for the flag after a reception. In man coverage, they mirror the wide receiver's every move. In zone, they're responsible for an area of the field, often the deep third or outside flat, depending on the formation.

DIANA SAYS

One of the most valuable tools a CB has is the ability to disguise intentions. They can control their body language to confuse the quarterback, maybe acting passive just before jumping a route or appearing ready for man coverage, only to drop into a soft zone.

Reading the QB's eyes and shoulders is crucial for a cornerback's success. Recognizing where the throw is going gives them a split-second advantage that can turn into a deflection, a flag pull, or even an interception. And when possible, a smart CB can even break off their own coverage to help a teammate's zone and make a play on the ball.

Communication is key for cornerbacks, especially with the free safety, when it comes to covering deep crossing routes that can stretch the defense. The connection with the linebacker is also essential on plays where multiple receivers run short routes or attack different depth levels; the CB and LB must coordinate to cover those layers effectively.

Cornerbacks are constantly adjusting based on the formation, motion, or split of the receiver. Reading body language pre-snap is a key part of the CB's job because receivers often give away subtle clues. A slight lean forward, the position of their feet, or how tense they seem can hint at whether they're about to run a deep or short route, or if the ball is likely coming their way. Recognizing these signals early can give the DB a valuable head start and make the difference between a deflection and a completed pass.

Another important concept for cornerbacks is to always keep a wide field vision. Don't just focus on what's happening right in front of you. Look for players aligned on the opposite side who may run across your zone. A deep crossing route behind your back can easily catch you off guard if you narrow your attention too much.

REMEMBER

Offensive players will often do everything they can to bait you into stepping forward to cover a short route. The moment you commit, they'll send someone behind you on a mid or deep cross. Stay patient. Keep your field of vision wide, track your main assignment, and don't get caught chasing the bait. Visualize the whole field and anticipate, not just react.

Positioning and alignment

The positioning of a cornerback depends largely on the defensive coverage being called. Cornerbacks (CBs) are usually placed on the outer edges of the formation, almost as if they're sealing the offense inside the field. The goal behind this setup is to keep offensive players running their routes toward the middle of the field, where more defenders are available to assist in pulling a flag in case of a reception. By steering receivers inward, CBs increase the chances of stopping the play quickly with a flag pull.

In zone coverages, as shown in Figure 10-1 (an example of a cover 3 defensive formation), corners must use smart leverage, meaning they position themselves based on where they expect help. If they have a safety inside, they may play outside leverage to force the wide receiver (WR) in. If alone, they have to balance speed and angle, usually aligning directly in front of their assigned receiver.

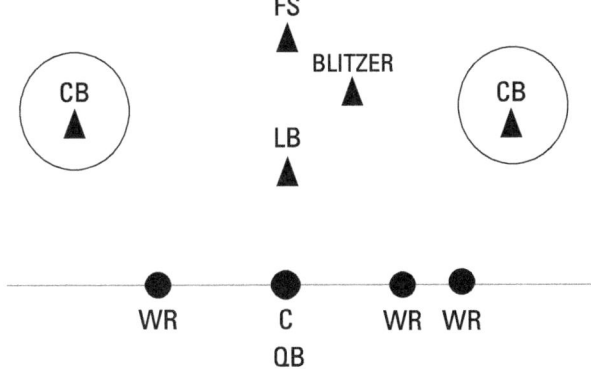

FIGURE 10-1: The CB in zone coverage is usually aligned on the outer edges of the formation, almost as if they're sealing the offense inside the field.

In man coverage, CBs must also play smart based on the alignment of the wide receiver. For example, if the WR is lined up close to the sideline, the CB should ideally align slightly inside. This forces the receiver to go outside, where space is limited, or to challenge the CB if they attempt to cut inside. Playing from inside leverage gives the CB an advantage if the WR runs a slant or drag, while also squeezing them toward the sideline on out-breaking routes.

On the right side of Figure 10-2, one CB is aligned 3 yards in front of the wide receiver, directly facing them to react quickly to any immediate move. On the opposite side, the other CB is positioned slightly inside the receiver, using the sideline as an extra defender and limiting the space available for out-breaking routes.

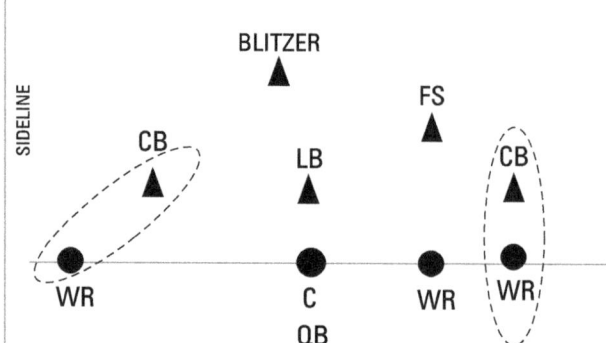

FIGURE 10-2:
Both cornerbacks
are lined up in
man coverage.

Most corners line up between 1–3 yards off the receiver in man coverage. This gives them the flexibility to stay patient and react, but at the same time keeps the distance short enough to close in quickly. In zone coverage, CBs tend to line up deeper and wider to keep the play in front. The extra cushion gives them more time to read and react to route developments.

**DIANA
SAYS**

Use every variable you can to your advantage! It's true that defenders often play from a reactive position, but if you understand how to use spacing, angles, and positioning to disrupt the receiver's route, you can create precious seconds to close in, deflect the pass, or even intercept the ball. Defensive intelligence can beat offensive speed if you know how to use it.

Free Safety

The *free safety* (FS; sometimes called simply the safety) has the widest view of the field and is responsible for identifying threats, reading the quarterback's intentions, and helping teammates by offering support over the top. In many cases, the FS is the last player between the ball carrier and the end zone, so decision-making and anticipation are key.

The FS is also the final layer of defense when it comes to deep routes. If a wide receiver manages to get past the free safety, the defense is essentially beaten, which often means a touchdown. That reality brings a lot of pressure to this position, especially since, depending on the coverage, the FS may find themselves in less-than-ideal situations. Covering the deepest part of the field means they're often asked to track multiple routes from sideline to sideline.

However, one big advantage the FS has is time and perspective. Positioned deeper than any other defender, they have a broader view of the play as it develops and more time to react. Since the ball takes longer to arrive on deep throws, and receivers must cover more ground to reach the FS's zone, the FS has the opportunity to read the quarterback, break on the ball, and either shut down the pass or come away with a game-changing interception.

What the free safety does

The FS is a roaming defender who's responsible for the deep middle and, at times, the deep sidelines depending on the coverage. They provide coverage help against vertical threats, jump in to contest deep passes, and are often the first responder when a receiver breaks free from a cornerback. In zone coverages, the FS may be responsible for an entire deep third or half of the field. Pre-snap, they must read the offensive formation, watch the QB's eyes and feet, and be ready to react instantly.

But it's more than just deep balls. A smart FS can recognize patterns and motion that hint at trick plays or crossing concepts and adjust coverage on the fly. If the QB stares down one receiver too long, the FS is the one who can punish them with a perfectly timed interception.

The FS must also communicate constantly with the corners and linebackers, calling out formations and adjusting coverage to ensure that no receiver is left uncovered in motion or after a switch.

TIP

Think like a QB. The more you understand how offensive plays develop, the faster you'll recognize where the ball is going. Your goal isn't just to follow the play, it's to beat it there.

Positioning and alignment

The alignment of the free safety depends on the defensive formation being used, but they typically line up 10 - 12 yards away from the line of scrimmage (see Figure 10-3), directly in the center of the field (since they're responsible for protecting the deep part of the field), or shaded toward the strong side of the offense. This positioning allows them to see the full field and respond quickly to deep threats.

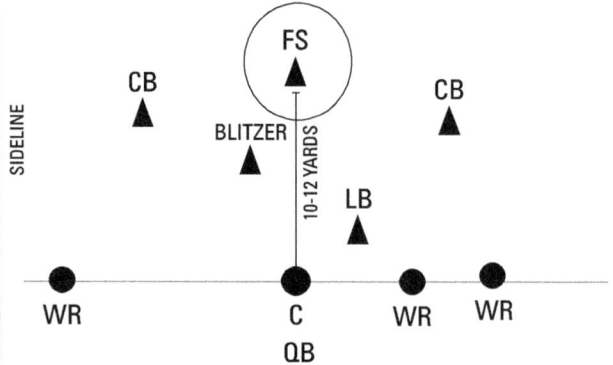

FIGURE 10-3:
The free
safety aligns
approximately
10 to 12 yards
off the line of
scrimmage,
depending on the
defensive
formation
and strategy.

In man coverage, the FS's positioning depends on the defensive system, but like any other player, they will generally line up about 3 yards in front of their assigned receiver (as shown in Figure 10-4). This is the only situation where the FS is not fully responsible for the deep zone, since they're locked into covering one player.

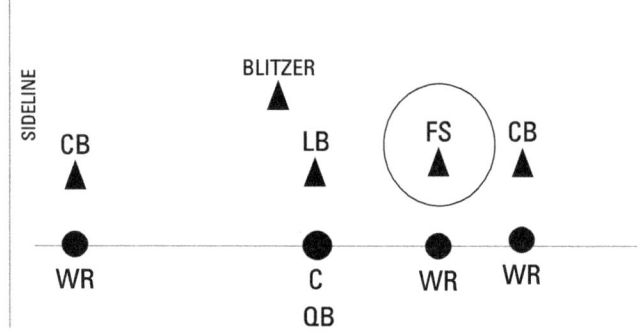

FIGURE 10-4:
The free safety
aligns at least
3 yards away
from the assigned
player to ensure
a quick reaction
when mirroring
the WR.

In zone coverage, the FS must maintain depth and avoid biting on short routes, even if the QB tries to bait them and help over the top to whichever CB draws the fastest or most dangerous WR.

Great FSs keep their feet calm, eyes alert, and mind sharp. They're rarely the first to move, but always the first to arrive when it counts.

DIANA SAYS

Don't just stand in the middle. Shift subtly based on formation and receiver alignment to disguise your intentions. You want the QB to think you're out of position until you show up right on time. Defensive intelligence can beat offensive speed if you know how to use it.

Avoiding Common Mistakes

Even talented defensive backs (DBs) can fall into traps if they rely only on physical ability. Here are some of the most common mental and technical errors:

>> **Biting on fakes or double moves:** Receivers know how to sell a fake. Stay patient and don't commit too early. Trust your hips and your cushion.

>> **Turning too early:** Rotating your hips before the receiver commits can open you up to cuts and create separation.

>> **Ball-watching too long:** While it's tempting to lock in on the QB, you can lose track of your assignment. Balance is key. Scan both the QB and your receiver with peripheral vision.

>> **Forgetting down and distance:** If you're guarding the sticks, play the sticks. A deep drop on third and short gives up easy yards. Positioning has to match the moment.

>> **Panicking when beaten:** Everyone gets beaten sometimes. The key is what happens next. Take a smart angle, don't reach, and go for a clean flag pull.

DIANA SAYS

Don't let one mistake turn into two. Recover, reset, and play the next down with confidence.

4

Building Skills: Key Drills and Plays

Decide which drills can help you.

Perform exercises to get in the right shape for flag football.

Examine plays and strategies to help the offense control the game and score.

Dig into defensive plays and strategies.

IN THIS CHAPTER

» **Mastering key quarterback drills**

» **Developing receiver skills**

» **Building agility and explosiveness for running backs**

» **Sharpening defensive fundamentals for cornerbacks and linebackers**

» **Practicing high-speed flag-pulling and reaction drills**

Chapter **11**

Practicing Drills by Position

"Practice makes perfect." I couldn't agree more with that phrase, not just in sports, but in life. We become what we do consistently. Our physical and mental standards are shaped day by day through our habits and the challenges we decide to face. That's why, before jumping into the drills by position, I want to take a moment to talk about the importance of training habits.

Being the best at your position takes more than just talent, understanding the game, or even love for the sport. Standing out requires a consistent commitment to keep improving and pushing yourself beyond what's expected. It's about doing more, staying after practice, arriving early to work on the details of your position, and setting your own standards. No one will be more responsible for your growth than you. So don't leave your dreams in someone else's hands. Own them. Chase them. Take the lead.

That mindset became a part of me early on. I truly believe one of the things that set me apart as a young athlete was developing the habit of going the extra mile. It started with my dad, who's always been my biggest supporter in this journey. After my practices, even when the whole team had already left, he would stay on the field with me to throw a few more passes. It was our game, just the two of us having fun. But looking back, those extra reps helped me grow faster than I realized.

As I got older, my routines changed. I remember being around 10 years old and showing up to practice at least half an hour before anyone else. My coach would have me do a few reps with a 2.5-kilogram weight to strengthen my arms or hang from a bar to stretch. I thought the bar was just to help me grow taller; after all, I was the smallest player on the team, and every extra centimeter felt like gold. Later, it was running stadium stairs (yes, also my dad's idea) or throwing passes into trash cans after practice in college.

DIANA SAYS

Over time, those little routines became what I now call my *Every Day Drills* (EDD), simple exercises or habits that kept my fundamentals sharp and helped me improve day after day. Some of them weren't flashy or physically intense, but they worked because I did them with intention and consistency. That's where the magic is.

In this chapter, I introduce the concept of EDD so you can build your own routine. These are drills you can add to your training sessions to strengthen your base and keep progressing. Some of them are simple. Some only take a few minutes. But when done consistently and with the right mindset, they'll take you further than you think.

Next comes the fun part: drills by position. There are tons of exercises out there that you can try. I give you a few to start with for various positions, and I encourage you to keep exploring, experimenting, and finding the ones that work best for you.

Quarterbacks

While quarterbacks (QBs) are expected to develop a wide range of skills, this section focuses on some of the most essential ones every quarterback should master: throwing with accuracy, making throws on the move, and escaping pressure from the blitzer. These are the tools that not only define a great QB but also make the difference in critical game situations.

WHY ACCURACY MATTERS TO THE QB

Accuracy is what separates good quarterbacks from great ones. And it's not just about arm strength; it's about balance, ball placement, and throwing mechanics, whether you're standing still, dropping back, or rolling out. Just as important is developing a quick release. On average, a quarterback has about three seconds to get rid of the ball, so every fraction of a second matters. A clean, fast motion can be the difference between a completed pass and a sack.

Accuracy drills

Drill 1: Trash can drop-in (over-the-shoulder accuracy)

1. Place a trash can or tall barrel about 20–25 yards away, simulating a receiver running a deep fade or go route.

2. Throw high-arching passes, aiming to drop the ball directly into the target.

3. Focus on trajectory, timing, and touch.

TIP

You can also place cones on the sides to represent a sideline boundary for added difficulty.

Key focal points: Ball placement, arc control, and deep throw timing.

Drill 2: Precision challenge

1. Set up a net or small target 10–15 yards away.

2. Simulate a drop back with a coach placing a hand or pad in your line of sight at the last second.

3. Deliver the pass around or above the obstacle while keeping your target locked.

Key focal point: Maintaining accuracy despite visual distractions.

Drill 3: Trigger throw (fast release)

1. Have a coach or teammate stand behind you with a hand on your back.

2. As soon as they tap, you drop and throw in rhythm toward a visible target.

This drill builds fast reaction, internal rhythm, and teaches you to fire the ball without delay.

Key focal points: Immediate reaction and clean mechanics under pressure.

Throwing on the go

Drill 4: Rollout touch pass

1. **Start about 10 yards from a target cone or a moving receiver.**

2. **Roll out to the right at 75 percent speed and throw a soft, accurate pass as the target moves laterally across the field.**

3. **Repeat on the left side.**

REMEMBER

The goal is to lead the receiver and control the pace of the throw.

Key focal points: Throwing while moving, hip alignment, and leading the pass

Drill 5: Sprint out + reset and fire

1. **Sprint laterally for 5 yards.**

2. **Plant your back foot and immediately throw toward a midrange target.**

This simulates escaping pressure and needing to throw back across the field or stop and fire.

Key focal points: Footwork, throwing from non-ideal platforms, and game-like recovery.

Evading the blitzer

Drill 1: Cone reaction escape + throw

1. **Place five dome cones in a semi-circle about five yards in front of the quarterback.**

2. **Number the cones from 1 to 5, starting from left to right.**

3. **At the snap, as soon as the QB receives the ball, the coach calls out a number.**

4. **The QB must quickly move toward the indicated cone, square up their shoulders, and throw the ball to a target placed somewhere on the field.**

The drill can be repeated multiple times in a single rep, with the QB returning to their original position in a dropback and preparing for the next call.

Key focal points: Keep your eyes downfield at all times. The QB must move explosively in any direction without losing sight of the receivers. Footwork should be fast, sharp, and controlled.

Drill 2: Tennis ball dodge (peripheral vision & hip movement)

1. **The coach stands 3 to 5 yards in front of the quarterback.**
2. **At the signal to start, the coach begins tossing tennis balls toward the QB's hips, alternating sides.**

   The goal is to simulate a blitzer reaching for the flag.

3. **The QB must keep their eyes downfield — focused on a receiver or target — and use hip rotation to dodge the tennis balls without turning away.**
4. **After each dodge, the QB should quickly return to a strong, balanced throwing position, ready to pass.**

Key focal points: Sometimes there's no time to run. One quick move can buy just enough time to throw. This drill improves peripheral vision, hip mobility, and spatial awareness. Visualize each ball as a blitzer's hand reaching for your flag.

DIANA SAYS

A big part of throwing a good pass starts with how you grip the ball. Some quarterbacks waste valuable seconds trying to find the laces or adjusting their grip. Get one step ahead by becoming so familiar with the ball that you can locate the laces without looking, or better yet, get comfortable throwing without needing to place your fingers on them. That small detail can make a huge difference in speed and consistency.

EDD Drill: Pre-pass footing reset

Take a few minutes each practice to work solely on foot alignment. From your pre-snap stance, simulate the movement you'd use to throw in different directions — left, right, deep, or short. Focus entirely on your lower body. There should be no extra steps, just a quick, deliberate motion into a balanced throwing base. This is where your throw's power and direction truly begin.

Wide Receivers and Centers

Wide receivers bring the offense to life. Their job isn't just about running fast and catching passes; it's about timing, technique, and making sharp, precise movements to create separation. The following drills will help you sharpen the three most essential parts of your game: your hands, your routes, and your footwork.

Catching the ball

Drill: Wall catch reps

1. Stand a few feet away from a wall and rapidly throw a tennis ball at it, catching it as it bounces back.

2. Mix up the height and angles. For added difficulty, use just one hand at a time.

   The small size forces you to focus on hand placement and reaction speed.

Catch with your hands, not your body.

REMEMBER Key focal points: Hand-eye coordination, soft hands, reaction time, one-handed control, and quick recovery.

Running routes

Drill 1: Cone breakdown drill

1. Set up 5 cones in a straight line, 5 yards apart.

2. Sprint to each cone, lowering hips and speed when reaching each one of the cones.

3. At the last cone, break down and cut left or right as if changing route direction.

Focus on staying low and using clean steps to change direction.

TIP Key focal points: Sharp hips, body control, and sudden cuts.

Drill 2: Route ladder

1. Run short routes (slants, outs, hitches) marked with cones.
2. At each route break, exaggerate your foot plant and hip turn to make sure your cuts are sharp.
3. Repeat the sequence without a ball, then add a catch at the end.

Key focal points: Consistent footwork and creating separation.

Agility and footwork

Drill 1: Ladder quick steps

1. Use a speed ladder and practice various foot patterns (two feet in each square, lateral hops, in-and-outs).
2. Keep your arms active and stay on the balls of your feet.

Key focal points: Speed, coordination, and change of direction.

Drill 2: Cone juke & burst

1. Set up 5 cones in a zigzag pattern, 5 yards apart from each other.
2. Approach the first cone, fake a juke to one side, and then explode through the next cone continuously.

This mimics making a defender miss and accelerating after the catch.

Key focal points: Lateral agility, body control, and explosive acceleration.

DIANA SAYS

Becoming a reliable receiver isn't just about catching the ball; it's about how you prepare to catch it. Always bring your hands to the ball, catch with your fingertips, and finish every rep like it matters. Don't wait for a perfect spiral — adjust, adapt, and secure it.

Running Backs

Running backs are known for their explosiveness, agility, and ability to change direction in a split second. Whether you're taking a direct hand-off or catching a pass in the backfield, your ability to burst, move smoothly, and control your body can make all the difference. These drills focus on developing acceleration, footwork, and hip agility.

TIP

As a running back, nothing matters more than getting comfortable with the ball in your hands. Running drills while carrying the ball is essential because it builds confidence, muscle memory, and security under pressure. The more you move, cut, and sprint *with the ball* during practice, the more natural it feels in real game situations.

Acceleration and explosiveness

Drill 1: Cone dash acceleration

1. Place a cone at your starting point and a second cone 10 yards ahead.

2. From a standing start, explode into a sprint with maximum effort and run through the second cone.

3. After reaching it, slow down, reset quickly, and repeat.

4. To increase difficulty, add a third cone 5 yards after the sprint cone and make a sharp lateral cut around it.

Key focal points: Explosive first step, body control, and quick reset after acceleration.

Drill 2: Resistance sprint

1. Attach a resistance band or use a weighted sled (or have a partner provide light resistance with a band around your waist).

2. Sprint 10–15 yards with full effort, focusing on fast leg drive and forward lean.

Key focal points: Explosive drive, acceleration mechanics, and building power.

Footwork and agility

Drill 1: Cone box shuffle

1. Place 4 cones in a square shape, about 3 yards apart each (see Figure 11-1).

2. Start at the front left cone and sprint forward to the front right cone, shuffle sideways to the back right cone, backpedal to the back left cone, then shuffle sideways to return to your starting point.

3. Repeat in both directions.

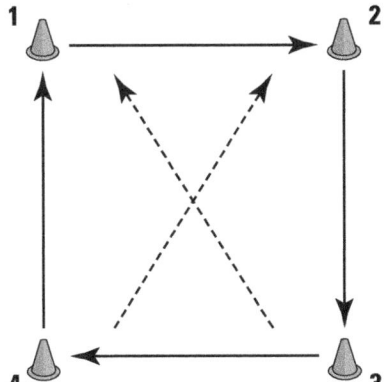

TIP

Switch up the order or direction of the movements to challenge your coordination and reaction.

Key focal points: Sharp directional changes, balanced movement, and controlled footwork while staying low.

Drill 2: Jump cut ladder

1. Lay out a speed ladder on the ground.

2. Begin at one end. Using only one foot at a time, jump into each square.

3. As you land in each square, perform a quick plant and lateral push off, mimicking the cut a running back makes to avoid a defender.

4. Alternate feet as you go down the ladder. Keep your upper body stable and your core engaged to maintain balance.

Key focal points: Foot control, explosive redirection, balance under motion, and fluid reaction.

Hip agility and fluidity

Drill 1: Carioca cone run

1. Place cones in a straight line about 5 yards apart.

2. Sprint forward along the line. Every time you reach a cone, perform a *carioca movement* (grapevine-style step) across the line, exaggerating the hip movement to one side.

3. **Immediately return to the running line and continue.**

4. **Alternate sides at each cone.**

Key focal points: Fluid hip rotation, coordination, and maintaining momentum without stopping.

Drill 2: Figure-8 hips

1. **Set up 2 cones about 3 yards apart.**

2. **With a football in hand, run in a tight figure-8 pattern around the cones.**

REMEMBER

Keep your upper body upright and let your hips lead the turns. Focus on staying balanced and smooth throughout the movement.

Key focal points: Hip mobility, ball control, and body balance.

DIANA SAYS

Great running backs don't just run fast; they run smart. Learn to use your body as a tool. Your hips are your steering wheel. The more flexible and responsive they are, the better you can slip through tight spaces or make a defender miss a flag in the open field.

EDD Drill: Cone skip and cut

1. **Line up 5 cones in a straight line, each 2–3 yards apart.**

2. **Jog through the cones, and as you approach each one, do a quick skip step and explode into a lateral cut.**

   This simulates reacting to a defender in space.

3. **Repeat several times in both directions.**

Key focal points: Rhythm, change of direction, and soft landings with explosive transitions.

Cornerbacks and Free Safeties

Cornerbacks and safeties are the last line of defense and the first line of attack when it comes to shutting down deep passes. These players must have elite footwork, the ability to track and attack the ball in the air, and the discipline to finish plays by pulling flags. The following drills are designed to sharpen those specific areas.

Defensive footwork

Drill 1: Mirror backpedal

1. Set up a line of cones 5 yards apart.
2. Begin at the first cone in a low, athletic stance.
3. On the coach's signal, start backpedaling.
4. When the coach claps or calls out "break," immediately plant your foot and drive forward as if breaking on a pass.

TIP

Add a ball to simulate an interception opportunity.

Key focal points: Smooth backpedal, quick transitions, and breaking with control.

Drill 2: W-backpedal drill

1. Arrange cones in a zigzag or "W" shape about 3 to 4 yards apart.
2. Begin at one end and backpedal at an angle to the next cone, then plant and change direction to the following one.
3. Continue until you finish the shape.

Key focal points: Maintaining balance and vision while changing direction, and simulating downfield receiver coverage.

Attacking the ball

Drill 1: Ball reaction jump

1. Have a coach stand about 10 yards away and hold a football.
2. On the coach's command, sprint toward them.
3. At random, the coach tosses the ball into the air. Your job is to track it, jump, and high point it like you're going for an interception.

Key focal points: Ball tracking, vertical explosion, and making plays on the ball.

Drill 2: Deep ball chase

1. A coach or QB throws a high pass 20–25 yards downfield.
2. Start a few yards behind the WR or alone as a safety, then sprint to close the distance and either deflect or intercept the ball.

Key focal points: Closing speed, timing your jump, and competing for the ball.

Pulling flags

Drill 1: Reaction box flag stop

1. Set up a 10-yard square using 4 cones to mark each corner.

2. Place a small group of offensive players at each side of the square.

3. Assign each group a number or color to identify them. The defender stands in the center of the square.

4. On the coach's signal, one of the groups sprints straight across to the opposite side, trying to cross the square.

5. The defender must quickly identify which group is running, react, and pull the flag of any player before they reach the opposite line.

Key focal points: Reaction time, reading body movement, controlled flag pulls, and breaking toward the ball carrier with urgency.

Drill 2: Chase and pull

1. Set up a 10-yard zone with a touchdown line marked by 2 cones.

2. The defender starts at one of the cones, facing the offensive player. The ball carrier sprints toward the touchdown line and can use as many jukes or changes of direction as they want to try to score.

3. The defender's job is to chase them down and pull the flag while keeping proper hip alignment and staying under control.

Key focal points: Controlled pursuit, maintaining leverage, adjusting angles, and securing the flag without overrunning the play.

DIANA SAYS

Defensive players are like shadows, always there but never caught off guard. Good DBs don't just react, they anticipate. Train your eyes to read hips, your feet to react instantly, and your hands to finish every play by going for the ball or pulling the flag with confidence.

EDD Drill: Cone backpedal & break

1. Set up 3 cones in a line, each 3 yards apart.

2. Start by backpedaling to the second cone, then on a clap or verbal cue, plant and sprint forward to the third.

3. Repeat facing different directions to simulate multiple coverages.

Key focal points: Backpedal form, quick plant, and rapid forward break.

Linebackers

Linebackers must read plays quickly, move laterally with control, shoot gaps when needed, and most importantly, be ready to pull flags in open space. These drills focus on improving quick reaction, lateral movement, forward explosion, and efficient flag pulling.

Reacting

Drill 1: Side to side reaction

1. Place 3 cones in a line, each 5 yards apart.

2. The linebacker starts in the middle; a coach points left or right at random, and the player must explode laterally to that cone, touch it, and then sprint forward for 5 yards as if chasing a ball carrier.

3. Reset at center after each rep.

Key focal points: Fast lateral burst, quick change of direction, and forward transition.

Drill 2: Tennis ball sprint and return

1. Place 3 cones in a line, each 5 yards apart.

2. The linebacker starts at the middle cone in a two-point stance with their weight slightly forward over the toes, ready to sprint.

3. A coach stands behind the cones with several tennis balls and randomly tosses one toward any of the 3 cones.

4. The linebacker must react quickly, sprint to catch the ball before it hits the ground, and then return to the middle cone to reset for the next toss.

Key focal points: Explosive first step, sprint mechanics, and reaction timing while maintaining balance and readiness.

Drill 3: Coverage reaction read

1. Set up 2 cones about 7 to 10 yards apart with a wide receiver at each cone.

2. The linebacker lines up halfway between both receivers, facing a quarterback or coach.

3. On the signal, the QB uses eye movement and body language to fake or throw to one of the receivers, who remains stationary.

4. The linebacker must read the QB and break toward the correct receiver to either cover or pull the flag.

5. As the linebacker improves, the receivers can run short routes, such as slant-outs, double stops to simulate offensive combinations aiming to overload the short zone.

    This helps the linebacker practice anticipating decisions and recovering quickly to defend the play.

Key focal points: Eye discipline, quick reaction, and efficient movement in coverage.

Pulling flags

Drill 1: Flag pull challenge

1. Set up 2 cones 10 yards apart to represent a scoring line.

2. Place the linebacker at the midpoint between the cones, 7 yards back, directly facing the middle of the line.

3. Two offensive players line up opposite the linebacker, side by side, and take turns running full speed toward either side of the scoring line.

4. The linebacker is not allowed to block or shift into the runners' path but must stay balanced and focused to pull the flag cleanly as each runner goes by.

    Each runner starts 2–3 seconds after the previous one to force quick recovery and readiness.

Key focal points: Attacking flags with both hands, fast resets, hand-eye coordination, and focus under pressure.

Great linebackers don't wait; they diagnose and go. Trust your instincts, react without hesitation, and attack the play with controlled aggression.

DIANA SAYS

Blitzers

The blitzer is the spark of pressure in a flag football defense. Speed, discipline, and reaction define success in this role. These drills focus on pulling flags after closing space fast, changing direction on the fly, and adjusting when the quarterback moves or the ball is handed off.

Drill 1: Sprint and redirect flag pull

1. Set up a cone 10 yards in front of the blitzer.

2. Place one offensive player directly at the cone and two more offensive players positioned 7 yards to each side of the cone, all standing with flags ready.

3. On the coach's signal, the blitzer sprints at full speed toward the player in the center, pulling the flag.

4. As soon as the flag is pulled, the coach yells "right" or "left."

5. The blitzer must immediately plant, redirect explosively to the indicated side, and pull the flag from the player positioned there.

   This drill mimics reacting to a last-second quarterback sprint-out or ball handoff.

Key focal points: Speed to the point of attack; sudden redirection; awareness; and clean, aggressive flag pulls while maintaining balance and control.

Drill 2: Forward blitz, backward drop

1. Place the blitzer 7 yards away from an offensive player, with a coach standing behind the offensive player holding a ball, simulating the quarterback.

2. On the signal, the blitzer rushes forward aggressively for 5 yards as if executing a blitz.

3. The coach then simulates a quick pass and signals the blitzer to drop back.

4. At that moment, the offensive player sprints forward to simulate a pass route.

5. The blitzer must quickly flip their hips and transition into coverage, tracking the offensive player.

6. The coach finishes the drill by throwing the ball to the offensive player, challenging the blitzer to react quickly and attempt to intercept or deflect the pass.

Key focal points: Explosive rush, fast hip transition, one-on-one coverage recovery, and ball awareness under pressure.

DIANA SAYS

Blitzing isn't just about speed; it's about timing, angles, and control. Don't aim for the quarterback's center; aim for the flag. Always take smart angles and be ready to adjust mid-sprint. One wrong step can take you out of the play, but a smart read can lead to a game-changing flag pull or even a sack.

MAKE THESE DRILLS YOUR OWN

The drills in this chapter are just the foundation — the kind of focused, position-specific work that every great flag football player builds on. Whether you're a quarterback improving your timing, a receiver sharpening your routes, or a blitzer dialing in your speed and angles, each drill can help you get better at the core skills your position demands. As you grow more confident, feel free to add your own creative twists. Progressions don't always mean making things harder, they can be as simple as adding a visual cue, introducing a tennis ball to improve grip and tracking, or changing a cone layout to boost reaction time. Just make sure you've mastered the basics first. Do every rep with purpose, stay explosive, stay in control, and keep chasing the next level of your game.

Chapter **12**

Getting into Flag Football Shape

lag football is a sport that thrives on speed, precision, and the ability to move with intention. To compete at a high level, players need more than just heart and hustle; they need a body prepared for the physical demands of the game. That means training with purpose, not just lifting weights or running laps, but building specific athletic qualities like speed, agility, explosiveness, and endurance that directly translate to performance on the field.

In this chapter, I break down what it means to be in "flag football shape," shifting the focus depending on whether you're lining up as a wide receiver, quarterback, defensive back, or blitzer/rusher (because each position has unique responsibilities). I also give you examples of drills and exercises tailored to the key traits of each role so you can put that knowledge into action right away.

Understanding the X Factor of Flag Football

As I note throughout the book, flag football is a game of split-second decisions and rapid-fire movement. Every play demands acceleration, deceleration, lateral cuts, and bursts of effort, sometimes within a single second. Because the game is noncontact, you're not relying on brute force to gain yards or stop opponents. What makes the difference is your ability to move faster, make smarter cuts, and keep your energy up longer than the person across from you.

That's where athleticism becomes the X factor:

>> **Speed** is necessary because plays develop fast, space closes quickly, and you need to react in the blink of an eye.

>> **Agility** is key because it's not just about running straight; it's about stopping, cutting, spinning, and moving in every direction without losing control.

>> **Explosiveness** gives you that first-step burst to get open, rush the quarterback, or jump for a tipped pass.

>> **Endurance** is what allows you to keep playing at a high level until the last play of the game, repeating those explosive efforts over and over without losing sharpness.

The speed to run a clean route and break away from a defender. The agility to shift direction mid-stride and still reach full acceleration. The body control to pull a flag without committing a foul. The core strength to throw with velocity and accuracy on the move. These are the building blocks of great flag football players.

Conditioning by Position

Each position in flag football asks something slightly different from your body. All positions should aim to build a solid athletic base across speed, agility, explosiveness, and endurance. These core skills benefit every player on the field. However, I'm splitting each section here because some positions rely more heavily on certain qualities than others.

To build a strong and effective training plan, it's important to work hand-in-hand with an athletic performance coach. They'll help you define your goals, monitor your progress, and adjust your training depending on the time of season, your current performance needs, and your recovery status.

REMEMBER

The following exercises can help you develop the key athletic skills needed for each position, but the volume, intensity, and timing of these drills should always be considered in the context of your personal program and your team's training schedule.

DIANA SAYS

From my experience, becoming a 360 athlete makes a big difference on the field. No matter what position you play, it's worth investing time into building up your skills and athletic performance across the board. I really believe that every flag football player should know the basics of each position. When you do, you become a more complete, all-around athlete, and that's what sets you apart in game situations.

Wide receivers, cornerbacks, linebackers, and safeties

These are the players who log the most miles in a game. Whether you're sprinting downfield for a deep pass or reacting to a cut in coverage, your body must be ready for high-volume, high-intensity movement. At this level, it's not enough to just be fast. You need to sustain that speed, recover between plays, and move with body control in every direction.

Speed

These exercises are designed to help you increase your speed:

» **Flying 10s** (4–6 reps): Set up a 20-yard sprint and time just the last 10 yards. After each sprint, take 2–3 minutes to rest so your legs are fresh and you can give your best effort on every run.

These sprints help you get faster by pushing your top speed, improving the way your brain and body work together when you move at full speed. They also teach your body to move more efficiently: longer strides, quicker turnover, and sharper form, without burning out too early.

» **Resisted sprints** (3 sets of 10–15 yards): Use a sled or resistance band to add resistance as you sprint forward. Rest about 1–2 minutes between sprints to recover fully so you can hit each one with high intensity.

These sprints help you build explosive strength in your legs and improve your ability to take off fast from a still position, something that's key for flag football. Training with resistance makes your regular sprinting feel easier and helps you develop the power to beat defenders off the line or close gaps quickly on defense.

>> **Overspeed runs** (3–5 reps): This drill involves running with a light assist, either using a resistance band that gently pulls you forward or by sprinting down a very slight downhill slope. The goal is to get your legs moving faster than they normally do on flat ground. That extra speed helps your body learn how to increase stride frequency and improve running mechanics. After each rep, rest for about 2–3 minutes so you can fully recover and give max effort on the next one.

These sprints help your brain and muscles get used to faster turnover, making you feel smoother and quicker when running at full speed during a game.

Focus on your running form in every rep. Sometimes it helps to slightly exaggerate the movement so your brain and body can learn the correct technique. Don't forget to fuel up properly before these sessions; your body needs energy to perform at its best and recover afterward.

Endurance

The following exercises involve more running to build up your endurance rather than your speed:

>> **Tempo runs** (6–10 × 100 yards at 70–80 percent max speed): Builds aerobic base while minimizing fatigue. Rest 45–60 seconds between reps to allow partial recovery while maintaining a conditioning effect.

Helps athletes develop efficient pacing and recovery capacity while reducing the risk of overuse injuries.

>> **30-30s** (6–8 rounds): This drill is all about high effort and quick recovery. You run as hard as you can for 30 seconds, then rest for 30 seconds, and repeat. The key is to keep that intensity up in every round, so try to cover the same distance each time.

This helps build endurance by teaching your body how to recover fast and get ready for the next play — just like in a real game. It also pushes your heart and lungs to work more efficiently under pressure. Over time, you'll notice you can move faster for longer without getting as tired.

>> **Shuttle drills (10-20-30)** (2–3 sets): Set up cones at 10, 20, and 30 yards. Start at the baseline, sprint to the 10-yard cone and back, then to 20 and back, and then to 30 and back. Rest 60–90 seconds between sets.

This drill mimics the quick acceleration, deceleration, and directional changes that happen throughout a flag football game. It builds anaerobic endurance, improves foot control, and helps athletes sharpen their ability to stop and go with efficiency and control under fatigue.

Agility (footwork)

If you don't feel light on your feet, don't worry — these agility drills can help you do that fancy footwork:

>> **Ladder drills** (2–3 drills per session): Set up an agility ladder on a flat surface and work through a series of footwork patterns like one-foot-in, two-feet-in, icky shuffle, or lateral steps. These quick patterns train your brain and feet to move together with precision. Rest 30–45 seconds between each drill so you can stay sharp and avoid sloppy steps.

Ladder drills are excellent for improving foot speed, coordination, and rhythm, which all translate into cleaner cuts, faster reactions, and better control during the game. They're a fun way to build fast feet and keep your movement crisp and confident. These drills work best when added at the beginning of your training session as part of your warm-up or activation routine. That way, your body is primed for speed and movement right from the start.

>> **Cone Z-drills** (4–5 reps): Set up cones in a zig-zag (Z-shaped) pattern, about 5 to 7 yards apart. Start by sprinting to the first cone, then plant your foot and cut toward the next one at an angle, continuing through the full Z pattern. Focus on quick, controlled changes of direction while keeping your body low and balanced. Rest about 60 seconds between reps to stay sharp and explosive on each effort.

This drill helps you improve your ability to shift directions efficiently and stay in control, which is key for covering opponents, dodging defenders, or responding to sudden movement during plays. It's a great way to work on foot placement, body control, and acceleration out of breaks, all essential for real game situations.

>> **Mirror drills with a partner** (4 rounds of 30 seconds): Stand facing a partner, about 3–4 yards apart. One person leads with fast, unpredictable lateral and short forward/backward movements, while the other mirrors them as closely and quickly as possible. After 30 seconds, switch roles. Rest about 60 seconds between rounds.

This drill helps you react faster, stay low and balanced, and stay locked in on your opponent's hips, a key skill for defensive players trying to stay in front of their matchup. It's also a fun and competitive way to build reactive agility and sharpen your focus during quick movement changes.

Explosiveness

Build your explosiveness with these jumps and bounds:

>> **Depth jumps** (3 sets of 3–5 reps): Stand on a sturdy box, step off — not jump off — and as soon as your feet hit the ground, immediately jump as high as

you can. This drill is great to add to your gym routine, especially on lower body or explosive power days. Rest about 60–90 seconds between each rep to let your legs recover properly so you can give full effort every time.

Depth jumps help build explosiveness by training your muscles to react quickly and powerfully after landing, just like you would when planting your feet and exploding into a sprint, jump, or quick direction change on the field.

» **Broad jumps** (3–4 sets of 3 reps): This drill is simple but powerful. Stand with your feet shoulder-width apart, swing your arms back, and jump forward as far as you can, landing with control. Broad jumps are great to add to your gym routine, especially on explosive training days.

They help you build horizontal power, which is the kind of strength you use when pushing off to sprint forward or break away from a defender. Rest about 60–90 seconds between sets so your legs can recover and stay explosive for every jump. Doing this consistently will make your first step more powerful and help you move forward with speed and control on the field.

» **Single-leg bounds** (3 sets per leg): This drill is a great way to build power one leg at a time. Start by pushing off with one foot and jumping forward as far as you can, landing on the same leg with control. Repeat for the full set before switching legs. Rest 60–90 seconds between sets to let your legs recover and stay powerful.

This movement trains your legs to be explosive on their own, just like when you're sprinting or cutting during a play. It also improves balance, coordination, and control, all key for flag football athletes who rely on quick footwork and powerful strides in every direction.

Quarterbacks

What really makes a great QB is the ability to move efficiently, generate force from the ground up, and stay mobile through the hips and shoulders to throw accurately from any angle. These athletic skills may not stand out right away, but they're vital for creating time, making throws under pressure, and adjusting to unpredictable situations. Balance, core control, shoulder stability, and hip mobility aren't just nice to have; they're must-haves for anyone serious about excelling at quarterback.

A great QB also needs to master all of these physical tools in addition to their throwing mechanics and game knowledge. And conditioning plays a big part in a QB's preparation; it allows you to stay mentally sharp and make good decisions late in the game when fatigue kicks in. The best quarterbacks don't let exhaustion become an excuse; they stay locked in and consistent, from the first drive to the final whistle.

Core stability

Strengthen your core with these three exercises:

>> **Dead bugs with resistance band** (3 sets of 8–10 reps): This core exercise may look simple, but it's super effective for building stability and control. Lie on your back with your arms extended toward the ceiling and your knees bent at 90 degrees. Loop a resistance band around your feet or hold it taut in your hands. Slowly lower one leg and the opposite arm toward the floor while keeping your lower back pressed flat against the ground. Then return to the starting position and repeat on the other side. Rest 30–45 seconds between sets.

This drill helps strengthen the deep core muscles that stabilize your spine and pelvis, which are key for balance, throwing, and quick transitions. The main thing to focus on is keeping your back flat on the ground the entire time; if it starts to arch, reset and go slower. Quality over speed is what makes this movement so valuable for quarterbacks.

>> **Pallof press** (3 sets of 10 reps each side): This exercise is one of the best ways to train your core to stay strong and stable, especially during movements where your body wants to twist. You'll need a resistance band anchored at chest height. Stand sideways to the anchor, hold the band close to your chest, then slowly press it straight out in front of you and hold for a second before bringing it back in. The band will try to pull you to the side, and your job is to keep your body from rotating. That's what makes this an anti-rotation exercise. Rest 30–60 seconds between sets.

The key is to stay tall, keep your hips and shoulders square, and focus on tightening your core the whole time. This kind of stability is crucial for quarterbacks who need to throw accurately under pressure without losing their balance or posture.

>> **Side planks with reach-through** (3 × 30 seconds each side): This is a great core stability exercise that targets your obliques, shoulders, and deep abdominal muscles. Start in a side plank position with your elbow under your shoulder and your body in a straight line. Extend your top arm toward the ceiling, then slowly reach that arm under your torso in a controlled twisting motion, as if threading it through a space beneath you. Return to the starting position and repeat for the full 30 seconds before switching sides. Rest for about 30–60 seconds between sets.

This movement strengthens your ability to resist unwanted rotation, which is key for staying balanced and in control when throwing on the move or absorbing contact. Focus on keeping your hips lifted, your core tight, and the movement slow and steady to get the most out of each rep.

Hip mobility

Keeping your hips flexible and strong helps a QB prevent LBs and safeties from grabbing their flags; these drills can help:

» **90-90 hip switches** (3 sets of 10 reps): This is a simple but powerful mobility drill that targets both internal and external rotation of the hips. Sit on the ground with your knees bent at 90 degrees, one leg in front and one behind, then rotate your hips to switch sides in a controlled motion. You can use your hands behind you for support if needed. Rest 30–45 seconds between sets.

This exercise helps unlock tight hips, which is crucial for quarterbacks when they need to rotate during throws or shift direction quickly. Focus on keeping your movements smooth and controlled, and sit tall through your spine to get the most benefit out of each rep.

» **Pigeon exercise** (3 sets of 30 seconds each side): This stretch is excellent for improving hip mobility and releasing tight glutes and hip flexors. Start by bringing one leg in front of you, bent at a 90-degree angle, and extend the other leg straight behind you. Lean forward gently over your front leg to deepen the stretch. Rest for about 30–45 seconds between sides.

This exercise helps quarterbacks open up their hips, which is key for rotation and movement efficiency when throwing or evading pressure. Focus on keeping your hips square and breathing deeply to relax into the stretch. It's a great addition to your cooldown or mobility routine.

» **Banded hip openers** (2 sets of 15 reps): This drill is great to include in your warm-up or mobility routine, especially before practice or a workout. Loop a resistance band just above your knees, get into an athletic stance with your feet shoulder-width apart, and slowly step laterally while keeping tension in the band. You can also do forward and backward steps to activate your glutes and hips from different angles. Rest 30–45 seconds between sets.

This movement helps activate your glutes and loosen up your hip muscles, which improves joint mobility and prepares your body for movement. A strong and mobile hip area is key to maintaining good posture, avoiding injury, and creating stability during throwing, cutting, and sprinting. Focus on controlled steps, keeping your knees slightly bent and your hips level to get the most out of each rep.

Shoulder mobility

All players would benefit from increased shoulder mobility, but it's especially important for the quarterback (and their throwing arm):

- » **Band pull-apart** (3 sets of 15 reps): Grab a resistance band with both hands and extend your arms straight out in front of you. Pull the band apart by squeezing your shoulder blades together, keeping your arms straight the whole time, until your arms form a "T" shape. Then return to the starting position with control. Rest 30–45 seconds between sets.

  This exercise helps strengthen the upper back and small stabilizing muscles around your shoulder blades, which are key for shoulder health and posture. For quarterbacks, it helps improve shoulder control and stability, especially when throwing repeatedly. Focus on slow, controlled movement and don't let the band snap back. Keep your core tight and your shoulders away from your ears for the best results.

- » **Wall slides** (3 sets of 10 reps): This mobility drill focuses on improving shoulder range of motion and scapular control, two key components for a strong and healthy throwing arm. A simple version is to stand with your back flat against the wall, arms bent at 90 degrees like goalposts. Slowly slide your arms up the wall while keeping contact with your elbows, hands, and back, then bring them back down. Move slowly and stay focused on form.

  Another variation is the kneeling wall slide. Position yourself with one knee on the ground and the other bent in front of you at 90 degrees, facing a wall. Keep your front shin vertical and your chest tall. Now, place both forearms and hands flat on the wall. Slide your arms upward while trying to open your chest and rotate slightly so that your face changes sides. This version also opens the thoracic spine and hips while challenging shoulder control.

  Rest about 30–45 seconds between sets. Wall slides help quarterbacks (and all players) keep their shoulders healthy, mobile, and stable, especially important when throwing, reaching, or recovering quickly during plays. Focus on keeping your ribs tucked, spine long, and arms moving smoothly without shrugging your shoulders up toward your ears.

- » **Overhead band pass-throughs** (3 sets of 10–12 reps): Hold a resistance band with both hands, arms extended straight in front of you at shoulder height. With control, raise the band over your head and back behind you, keeping your arms straight the whole time. Then bring it back over to the front. The wider your grip, the easier it will be, so adjust hand placement as needed.

  This drill helps improve shoulder flexibility and stability, which are key to a smooth and pain-free throwing motion. It's a great way to activate your shoulders before practice or add to a mobility circuit. Focus on staying tall, keeping tension in the band, and moving slowly and evenly through the full range.

DIANA SAYS

I try to include hip and shoulder mobility every day as part of my EDDs (everyday drills), even on rest days. These small routines don't take much time, but they go a long way. Keeping those areas mobile helps me move better, recover faster, and perform at my best. Trust me, the little things add up. Paying attention to the details can really set you apart.

Balance and agility

If you've wondered how quarterbacks stay on their feet and grounded while the blitzers rush them, it's because they do these drills:

>> **Single-leg hops with stick** (3 sets of 5 reps each leg): Stand on one leg, hop forward, and land on the same leg, trying to stick the landing without wobbling. Pause for a second to lock in your balance before resetting.

This drill improves body awareness, landing control, and overall balance — all of which help quarterbacks stay grounded when throwing on the move or adjusting to sudden changes in play. Rest about 45–60 seconds between sets. Focus on landing softly, keeping your knee in line with your toes, and staying balanced without rushing the movement.

TIP

To add variation and target lateral stability, you can also perform lateral single-leg hops. In this version, you hop sideways off one foot and land on the same foot, then reset and repeat. This works the muscles around the hip and knee in a different plane, which is essential for cuts, rollouts, and quick lateral shifts during a play. Lateral hops help strengthen stabilizing muscles and improve coordination, giving you more confidence and control when you move side to side. It's a small drill that builds big stability, especially when things get chaotic on the field.

>> **Lateral bounds into throw** (3–4 sets): Start by standing on one leg; then bound laterally onto the opposite leg, landing with control. As soon as you land, transition into a throwing motion, either with a football or using a light medicine ball to simulate the throw. Rest 45–60 seconds between reps.

This drill helps quarterbacks practice throwing on the move while also training lateral explosiveness and balance. It mimics real-game situations where you need to reset your feet quickly and throw after rolling out or escaping pressure. Focus on landing with stability, staying low through the hips, and making the throw smooth and accurate immediately after the movement. It's a great way to connect movement with decision making and passing mechanics.

>> **Circle cone reaction drill** (4–6 reps, 2x/week): Set up 4–6 cones in a circle, each about 2–3 yards apart. Stand in the center and have a coach or partner randomly call out the color or number of a cone. Sled to that cone on a

throwing position and return to the center as quickly as possible, ready for the next call. Rest 60–90 seconds between rounds.

This drill improves reaction time, change of direction, and spatial awareness, exactly what a quarterback needs when scanning the field and adjusting on the fly. It also keeps you sharp mentally, helping develop decision-making speed while your body is in motion.

Blitzers

Blitzers are constantly chasing the quarterback and sprinting at full speed over and over again. To excel as a rusher, you need elite first-step quickness, the endurance to do it all game, and the ability to recover and explode again on the next down.

Speed

You have to be super-fast to be an elite blitzer; these drills can help:

>> **Three-point sprint starts** (4–6 reps): This drill helps develop powerful take-offs and sharper acceleration. Start in a low three-point stance, one hand down, knees bent, chest low. From that position, explode forward into a 10–15-yard sprint. Rest for 1–2 minutes between each sprint to stay fresh and explosive.

Practicing this regularly improves your first step quickness, a key advantage when rushing the quarterback or bursting off the line. It also reinforces good sprinting posture and teaches your body how to generate speed from a low, athletic position, which translates directly to game-day performance.

>> **Hill sprints** (6–8 sprints of 10–15 yards): Find a hill with a moderate incline and sprint up at full effort for 10 to 15 yards. Walk back down slowly to recover and rest for 1–2 minutes between sprints.

This drill builds strong, explosive legs and reinforces proper sprinting mechanics, especially that powerful forward lean you need at the start of a play. Hill sprints help you drive through your hips and legs with more force, making your acceleration sharper and your first step more dangerous.

>> **Sled pushes** (3–5 sets of 10–15 yards): Load a sled with moderate resistance and drive it forward explosively for 10–15 yards, keeping your body low and your core tight. Rest 90 seconds to 2 minutes between sets.

This exercise builds powerful legs, improves sprinting form, and reinforces a strong forward lean, exactly what you need for explosive starts and acceleration in flag football.

Explosiveness

Wide receivers, cornerbacks, linebackers, and safeties, as noted earlier in the chapter, train for explosiveness, too, but the drills are different for blitzers:

» **Depth-to-lateral bounds** (3 sets of 3 bounds per side): Start by standing on a box or elevated surface. Step off the box and land softly with your knees bent and chest up. The moment you land, immediately bound laterally off one leg to the side, then stick the landing and reset. Repeat for 3 bounds on each side. Rest 60–90 seconds between sets.

This drill mimics game situations where a rusher makes contact or adjusts after a quick direction change. It helps develop explosive reaction off the ground, improves lateral agility, and teaches the body to stay balanced while shifting power from a vertical landing into a horizontal movement. Focus on landing soft, staying low, and being quick and controlled with every bound.

» **Med ball scoop toss** (4–5 reps per side): Stand sideways to a wall in an athletic stance, holding a light- to medium-weight medicine ball at hip level. With a quick and powerful motion, rotate your hips and explode through your back leg as you toss the ball into the wall like a scoop or underhand swing. Catch the rebound and repeat. Rest 45–60 seconds between reps.

This drill helps develop explosive hip extension and rotational power, two key elements for sprinting, rushing, and quickly changing direction.

» **Sprint starts with medicine ball** (3–4 sets of 5–6 reps): Start in a low, athletic stance while holding a light medicine ball close to your chest. From this position, explode into a short 5- to 10-yard sprint. Right at the moment you take off, throw the ball forward, and keep sprinting through the finish. Rest about 60–90 seconds between sets.

This drill builds explosive hip extension and reinforces proper sprint mechanics by keeping you low, powerful, and quick off the line. Throwing the ball as you sprint helps train full-body coordination and adds resistance that challenges your core and hips to fire explosively. Focus on staying tall through your chest, driving your knees, and keeping your movement clean and aggressive from the first step.

» **Bounding stair runs** (5–7 stairs, 3–4 rounds): Find a staircase with wide, stable steps and start at the bottom. Begin by bounding up the stairs, skipping one or two steps at a time. Focus on using your arms and legs in sync to drive each jump. Land softly on the balls of your feet and immediately explode into the next bound. Once you reach the top, walk back down carefully and rest for about 60–90 seconds between rounds.

This drill reinforces lower-body power, coordination, and rhythm. It also challenges your balance and helps build single-leg strength and reactivity, key qualities for rushers who need to launch forward quickly and stay in control under pressure.

Endurance

Blitzers rest while their team plays offense, but otherwise, they're on through the whole game and must stay strong and speedy until time runs out. These drills help build that strength and speed:

» **20-yard repeat sprints** (8–12 sprints with 20 seconds rest): Set up a 20-yard sprint distance and run each rep at near-max effort. After each sprint, rest for exactly 20 seconds; then go again. The short recovery time keeps your heart rate high and forces your body to get better at working hard under fatigue.

This drill builds anaerobic capacity, helping you stay explosive even after multiple high-intensity efforts. It mimics how rushers have to reset quickly between downs and still perform with maximum effort. Stay sharp with your form, keep your chest tall, and challenge yourself to stay consistent on every rep, even when you're tired. That's how you build game-ready stamina and mental grit.

» **5-10-5 shuttle repeats** (5–7 rounds): Set up three cones in a straight line, each 5 yards apart. Start at the middle cone, sprint to one end cone, change direction quickly, and sprint to the far cone, then return to the middle. Rest for 45–60 seconds between rounds.

This drill helps build both agility and short-distance endurance. It teaches you how to recover quickly between bursts while keeping your footwork sharp and reactive. It's especially useful for rushers who need to explode, reset, and go again within just a few seconds.

Crossing Over: Multi-Sport Advantage

Some of the best flag football players weren't raised on one sport. They've been shaped by movement patterns from basketball, soccer, softball, and beyond. This is no coincidence. These sports train transferable athletic skills that give you a huge edge in flag football, not just in terms of performance, but also in how fast you can learn, adapt, and grow as an athlete.

This list highlights ways various sports prepare athletes to be great flag football players:

TIP

>> **Football players** already bring a strong foundation to flag because they understand the flow of the game, offensive and defensive strategies, and the timing of plays. Many of the skills they've developed, like route running, hand-eye coordination, and reading coverage, transfer smoothly to the flag football field.

What they should focus on is refining their body control, agility, and spatial awareness, especially since flag football demands quicker lateral movement, precision in space, and clean transitions without contact. Honing these areas helps football players adapt faster and become impact players in the flag format.

>> **Basketball players** are used to making quick cuts, changing direction in tight spaces, and staying low and reactive on defense. They also learn to read the court and anticipate movement, which directly applies to reading coverages and creating separation on routes. Their hand-eye coordination and rotational power also translate well to catching and throwing on the move, making them strong playmakers on both sides of the ball.

>> **Soccer players** develop incredible lower-body coordination, quick footwork, and endurance from constantly running and changing pace. Their ability to scan the field while moving at full speed helps them adjust to fast breaks in offense and defensive coverage in flag.

>> **Baseball and softball players** excel in tracking the ball and reacting quickly with short, explosive movements. Their hand-eye coordination and rotational power are big assets when it comes to catching, throwing, and making plays on the move.

>> **Gymnasts and dancers** bring exceptional body awareness, control, and mobility, skills that help prevent injury and improve foot placement, balance, and flexibility in tight game scenarios.

>> **Track athletes** build a foundation of speed, acceleration, and rhythm. Their sprint mechanics and conditioning carry over directly into game action, especially for receivers and rushers.

Multi-sport athletes tend to be more adaptable, resilient, and coachable. They're used to handling different types of movement, pressure, and coaching styles. For young athletes, playing other sports isn't a distraction; it's a powerful way to become faster, smarter, and more versatile on the flag football field.

Chapter **13**

Offensive Plays and Strategies

U nderstanding the strengths and weaknesses of various defensive coverages helps lay the foundation for building a smart and versatile offensive playbook. Knowing what each defense is designed to take away — and more importantly, what it leaves open — gives you a huge advantage on the field. To that end, in this chapter, I discuss how to observe a team's strengths to implement an effective offensive strategy, including what the goals of an effective strategy are. I introduce offensive formations and describe various defensive coverages and how to play against them. Finally, I end the chapter with a short section on the importance of extra points.

TIP

This chapter focuses on plays that include route running and being able to read man-to-man coverage. Chapter 6 covers both concepts in some detail, so if you're unfamiliar with them, be sure to check out that chapter before diving into the plays discussed here.

Using Strategy to Play to a Team's Strengths

One of the most exciting things about flag football is how much freedom teams have to express their identity through strategy. Even when playing under the same format or rulebook, the way a team executes can look completely different from one opponent to the next. That's the beauty of the sport. Its flexibility opens the door for players and coaches to truly maximize their creativity and strengths.

Some teams lean heavily on raw talent. They live for one-on-one matchups and trust their wide receivers to come down with the ball no matter what. Watching these teams feels like watching a highlight reel; every pass is a chance to make a big play. It's a style that screams confidence: "Throw it up and I'll go get it."

Other teams focus on speed and timing. They execute a fast-paced offense with short, sharp routes designed to get the ball out quickly and let receivers create yards after the catch. In these systems, the rhythm of the play matters just as much as the read.

And then there are the most dangerous teams, the ones that are unpredictable. The teams that mix styles, shift gears, and never stop adapting. Creativity is one of the most powerful tools an offense can have. But it's also one of the hardest to master. It takes the right talent on the field, yes, but more than anything, it takes vision and boldness from both coaches and players.

No matter what system you build, there's no perfect formula. The goal isn't to copy what someone else is doing; it's to build a style that matches your team's personality and enhances its strengths.

DIANA SAYS

One of the most common mistakes I see coaches make is trying to force a system onto players, instead of building a system around their players. It doesn't work. You have to adapt to the tools you have. Get to know your athletes. Observe. Listen. Be creative. Build something unique. The best offenses don't just play, they evolve.

Defining the Goals of an Effective Offense

Sure, the main goal of an offense is obvious: Score as many touchdowns as possible. But in reality, the road to the end zone takes a lot more than just talent. The best offenses have a clear purpose behind every snap. In this section, I describe the five core objectives that set up successful drives and ultimately, wins.

1. Consistency

Consistency is the heartbeat of any unstoppable offense. It's not just about scoring, it's about executing the basics with excellence over and over again. That means

>> The quarterback makes smart reads and delivers accurate passes.

>> Receivers run clean routes with perfect timing.

>> Catches are secured, and the play doesn't stop there — yards after the catch matter.

Consistency is built through repetition, trust, and discipline. When every player does their job right, the defense has no room to breathe.

2. Efficiency

Efficiency means making the most out of every opportunity. Every play call should have a purpose, whether it's to score, gain a first down, manipulate the defense, or set up the next play. Great offenses don't just wing it. They know when to strike and when to be patient. Think of it like chess, not checkers.

3. Adaptability

No matter how much film you watch or how well you prepare, game day will always throw surprises. Weather, matchups, defensive schemes — they change fast. That's why the best offenses are flexible. They can shift gears, adjust routes, and change the game plan on the fly. Adaptability is what separates good teams from great ones.

4. Game control

Offenses don't just respond to pressure; they create it. Controlling the pace of the game means making the defense react to you, not the other way around. You decide the tempo, dictate the rhythm, and force the other team to play on your terms. This kind of command comes from confidence, preparation, and mental toughness.

5. Drive

Scoring takes more than execution; it takes attitude. A great offense is always hungry for points. It doesn't play it safe just to avoid mistakes. It goes for the win.

It keeps the pressure on. The mindset of a scoring offense is aggressive, fearless, and focused on finishing every drive in the end zone. Besides these goals, the general goal for the offense is to gain yards, gain the first-down line, and score a touchdown and the extra points.

Mastering Offensive Formations

Just like everything else in flag football, a successful play starts with something simple: the right formation. Think of it like setting the stage. Where each player lines up, how much space is between them, and how balanced the formation looks directly shapes how the play unfolds and how the defense reacts.

Getting everyone lined up correctly with the right spacing helps make sure that every route has room to develop and ends up in the perfect spot. It's all about creating space and setting up your offense to succeed. (See Chapter 6 for more information about routes and how to run them.)

Switching between different formations during a game keeps things exciting. It forces the defense to constantly adjust and reshuffle their assignments, which can create just enough confusion or mismatch to open up big plays. Knowing when to switch things up and how to use formations to your advantage gives your offense a serious edge.

Throughout this section, I provide a closer look at the basic formations in flag football, along with their pros and cons. This way, you'll know exactly how and when to use each formation when designing your plays.

REMEMBER

Each of these formations can be used to set the tone for your offense. The key is to understand not only how they work, but when to use them based on your personnel, game situation, and the defensive look you're facing. The best offenses don't just choose one — they use all three and keep defenses guessing.

Spread

In the spread formation, receivers line up wide across the field, usually evenly spaced (see Figure 13-1). The idea is to stretch the defense horizontally and create more room for receivers to run their routes.

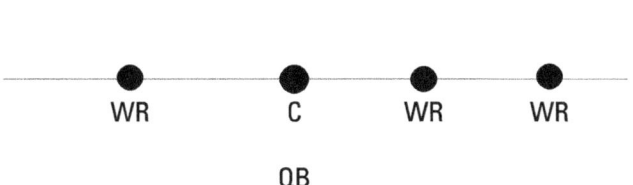

SPREAD

FIGURE 13-1:
For the spread
formation,
players line up
evenly spaced at
the line of
scrimmage.

Advantages of the spread formation include the following:

>> Maximizes spacing and isolates defenders

>> Makes it easier to recognize zone versus man coverage pre-snap

>> Great for quick throws, slants, and outs

>> Opens running lanes for QB keepers or reverses

There's really only one disadvantage to the spread formation: Timing and accuracy must be sharp because mistakes can lead to turnovers.

Trips

Trips line up three receivers on one side of the field, as shown in Figure 13-2. This overloads the defense on that side and forces them to either rotate a safety over or risk not having enough players to cover that zone of the field.

TRIPS

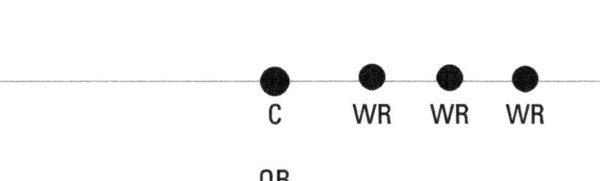

FIGURE 13-2:
For the trips
formation, three
WRs line up on
one side of
the field.

Advantages of the trips formation include the following:

>> Creates confusion in man coverage

>> Easy to overload a zone

>> Offers multiple quick reads for the quarterback on one side

>> If the defense chooses to overload the zone too, it opens opportunity for one-on-one matchups and composed crossing routes

Disadvantages of the trips formation include these:

>> The opposite side of the field is less balanced and easier to defend.

>> If not used with motion or variation, defenses can anticipate the play.

Bunch

The bunch formation places receivers close together. They can be lined up next to the center (see Figure 13-3) or in a triangle formation at one side of the field (see Figure 13-4). This setup is ideal for misdirection and pick routes; with everyone lined up closely together, it becomes much easier to naturally run into defenders or force them to switch coverage mid-play.

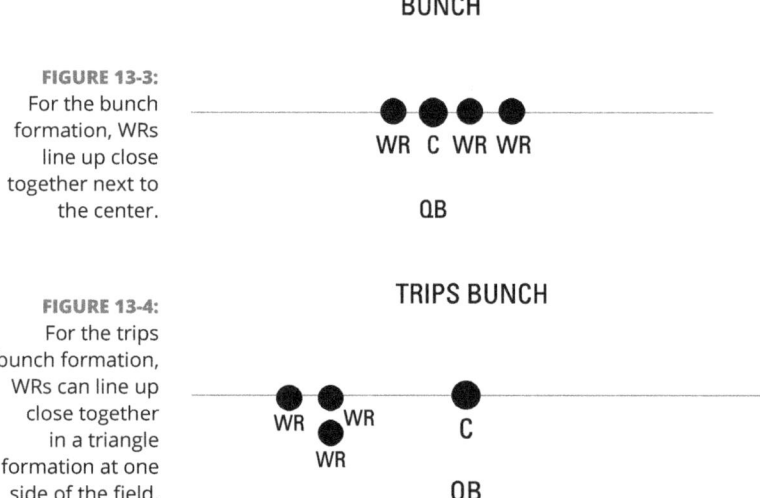

FIGURE 13-3: For the bunch formation, WRs line up close together next to the center.

FIGURE 13-4: For the trips bunch formation, WRs can line up close together in a triangle formation at one side of the field.

Advantages of the bunch formation include the following:

>> Forces the defense to navigate traffic and react quickly

>> Excellent for quick-hitting plays like screens or rub routes

>> Easy to disguise route combinations

Disadvantages of the bunch formation include these:

>> Can feel crowded, limiting space for receivers to operate

>> Requires sharp timing and chemistry between QB and receivers

Beating a Defense

For an offense to really shine, it needs more than just talent and timing. It needs a plan. And a big part of that plan lives inside the playbook. In the earlier section "Using Strategy to Play to a Team's Strengths," I talk about how important it is to build your playbook around your players' strengths, but there's another key piece: building your plays around the defenses you'll face.

A strong offense knows how to break down the most common defensive formations by identifying weak spots, reading alignments before the snap, and attacking vulnerable zones. This section walks you through how to do exactly that.

I look at each major defensive coverage and explain how to recognize the open areas on the field before the snap and key reads. Most importantly, I show you how to beat each coverage using smart route combinations, spacing, and decision making from the quarterback's perspective.

REMEMBER

Defenses can disguise their intentions and switch coverages on the fly. But as long as you stay clear on your offensive strengths and stay ready to take advantage of every yard the defense gives you, you'll always find ways to keep the ball moving and stay ahead of the game.

Beating man-to-man coverage: Cover 1

Cover 1 is one of the most common defensive coverages in flag football.

From an offensive point of view, this formation opens up plenty of exciting opportunities, especially if your players have a speed or athleticism advantage.

The biggest advantage of facing Cover 1 is that every route is essentially a one-on-one battle. That means the offense has a clear opportunity to exploit favorable matchups. If your wide receiver is quicker, faster, taller, or more agile than the defender in front of them, you should be looking to take full advantage of that.

Good timing and trust between the quarterback and receiver become essential here. Quick slants, fades, and comeback routes are great tools to gain separation and make defenders pay for even the smallest mistake. Plays don't have to be fancy, just well executed.

TIP

What happens when the defense also has incredible athletes? That's when your creativity matters even more. Relying purely on athleticism won't be enough. You'll need route combinations, motions, and rub concepts to free up space and help your receivers get open.

Next, I dive into two of the most valuable tools you can use to beat man-to-man defense: understanding matchups and mastering crossing routes. These two concepts go hand-in-hand when it comes to creating separation, gaining yards, and setting your offense up for big plays.

Matchup

When it comes to Cover 1, winning the matchup is everything. The *matchup* is the strategy of assigning each defender to cover an offensive player. Identifying the right matchup pre-snap means spotting where your receiver has a clear edge, whether it's speed, size, route-running, or just confidence.

TIP

If your receiver can beat the defender one-on-one, that's a green light. You don't need to overthink it, just throw it with good timing and give your playmaker the chance to shine.

But matchups go beyond physical ability. Think about who's guarding who. Has a defender been late on breaks? Are they playing with a cushion? Are they showing signs of getting tired or confused? Every little detail helps you make a smarter read.

Here's a great example of how to capitalize on a favorable matchup. Compound routes can be especially useful in helping a wide receiver gain separation from a defender. In Figure 13-5, for example, the center runs a compound route to win the matchup. These routes force defenders to stay locked in. Any misstep, whether it's biting on a fake or losing balance, can turn into a big gain. When run with precise timing and execution, compound routes put defenders in high-pressure situations where even the smallest mistake can be costly. (See Chapter 6 to find out more about compound routes.)

REMEMBER

For diagram purposes, any route that ends with an arrow indicates a player can keep running until they reach the desired open window. On the other hand, routes that end with a flat line indicate the player should stop and settle into the designated spot. Refer to Figure 13-5 for an example of each.

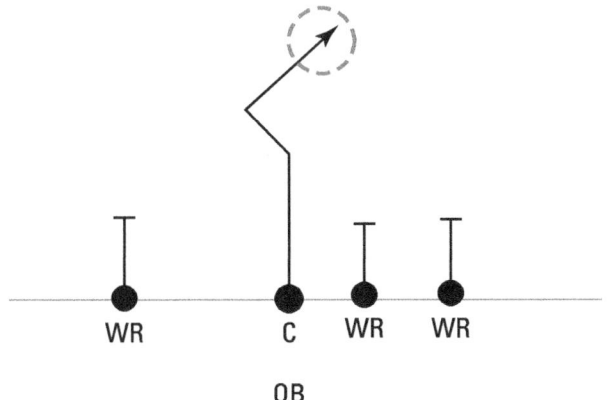

FIGURE 13-5:
An offensive play taking advantage of a favorable matchup through a compound route run by the center.

Another great way to take advantage of matchups is by designing compound route combinations that force defenders to chase receivers across the field while also opening up passing windows. Figure 13-6 shows a play with two compound routes, which can be effective, especially when attempting to gain yards or make it to the red zone. Personally, these are some of my favorite types of plays because they really highlight a wide receiver's skill set: their speed, footwork, and agility. When the timing between the quarterback and receiver is right, all it takes is one or two steps of separation to complete a pass and turn it into a game-changing play.

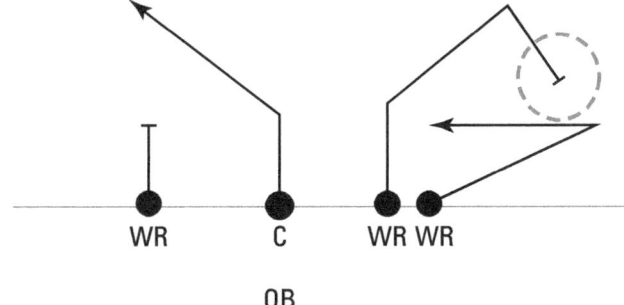

FIGURE 13-6:
An offensive play with two compound routes.

Now, here's where it gets interesting. Even if your best offensive player is facing the defense's top defender, you can still use that to your advantage. Sometimes, putting your star WR in motion or as the primary route can draw extra attention, and that opens up space for someone else. In this case, your "best" player becomes a decoy to help another teammate make the big play. It's all about understanding the defense's focus and flipping it in your favor.

Crossing routes

Crossing routes are routes that receivers run that intersect (or cross) each other's paths. They're one of the most effective ways to beat man-to-man coverage. Why? Because crossing routes force defenders to chase receivers across the field, often through traffic, which creates natural separation and confusion.

When receivers run crossing routes, they're not just trying to get open; they're putting the defenders in a difficult position. If the defender plays too tight on the man-to-man coverage, they risk getting picked off by a teammate's route or a bump from another player. If they play too loose, they give up yards and timing.

Here's an example of how this concept plays out using deep crossing routes. Imagine two receivers running post routes while a third runs a 10-yard in (see Figure 13-7). The goal is to time their breaks so they occur near each other, creating traffic and confusion for defenders. With precise timing, this setup forces the defense to either adjust on the fly, risking blown coverage, or stay so tight that they get lost in the traffic, allowing a receiver to break free for a big gain.

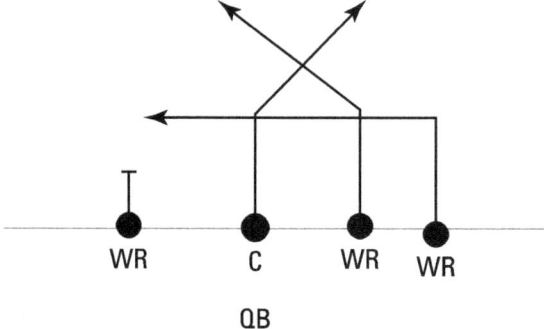

FIGURE 13-7: Offensive play with two crossing posts and a 10 yard in.

Another favorite of mine is the mesh concept (see Figure 13-8), where two receivers run shallow crossing routes in opposite directions. The goal? Force the defenders to fight through the "mesh" at full speed. If just one slips, it's an easy completion with potential for big yards after the catch.

Man-to-man coverage invites competition. Between route combinations, timing, and formation creativity, there are endless ways to outsmart tight coverage.

Now that I've covered how to beat man-to-man, I next dive into zone coverage, where the challenges shift and strategy becomes all about space and reads.

FIGURE 13-8:
An offensive
play using the
"mesh" concept
with two short
crossing routes
in opposite
directions.

WR   C   WR   WR

QB

Beating zone coverage

When a defense plays zone, each defender is responsible for guarding a specific area of the field rather than a specific player. For the offense, this means a completely different strategic approach. Instead of looking to win individual matchups, the focus shifts to finding and attacking open windows in the defense.

Zone defenses are preventive by nature. While they're designed to cover large areas of the field and prevent big plays, their structure also creates natural soft spots, gaps between zones, or behind slower drops. And that's where the offense can strike.

From an offensive perspective, seeing a zone coverage usually signals a more cautious or conservative approach by the defense. That caution gives the offense room to work with timing, spacing, and layered route concepts.

REMEMBER

A *layered route* refers to a passing play in which multiple WRs run routes at different depths, essentially creating layers of potential targets for the quarterback. The defense must decide which routes to cover, which can potentially leave one open.

The advantage for the offense? You don't need to outrun a defender; you just need to get to the open space at the right time. That means the quarterback must read the defense quickly and deliver the ball accurately, while the receivers focus on identifying the holes and settling into them. When executed properly, beating a zone can be just as explosive as beating man coverage, if not more.

Zone defenses leave space; that's the truth. The first and most straightforward strategy is to attack those vulnerable areas right away with routes that are designed to land exactly in those soft spots. But it's rarely that simple. Defenses know their weak areas too, and they'll often use smart positioning and adjustments to protect those zones. That's where key offensive concepts come into play, principles that help split defenders, manipulate coverage, and fully take advantage of how zones are structured. These tools make all the difference when it comes to executing an efficient and dynamic offensive attack.

TIP

The challenge for the offense is to find those soft spots and hit them with precision. Here's a look at the most effective strategies to break down zone coverages:

>> **Zone overload:** This strategy involves sending multiple receivers into one defender's zone, essentially overwhelming their coverage responsibilities. A zone defender can only guard one assignment at a time. If two or more receivers enter their zone simultaneously, they must choose who to cover, leaving the other open.

>> **Levels:** This involves stacking receivers vertically at different depths on the same side of the field. The goal is to stretch defenders front to back and force them to commit to a level.

>> **Clear and replace:** This concept works by having one receiver blaze through a zone at full speed, drawing the defender with them and essentially "clearing" the space. As that defender gets pulled out of position, a second receiver follows behind, slipping into the space just vacated. It's like opening a door and walking through it right as it swings wide — clean, simple, and highly effective when timed right.

>> **Splitting the defender:** This is one of the simplest and most effective principles. The idea is to place a receiver between two zones, right in the gap where the defenders' responsibilities meet. If timed correctly, the quarterback can throw the ball before the defender fully commits to either zone, catching them in a gray area. Zone defenders must cover space, not players. When you run a receiver directly between two zones, you force both defenders to hesitate, each unsure if the responsibility is theirs. That hesitation creates just enough of a window for the QB to deliver a strike.

These concepts are all about patience, timing, and reading the field. Zone coverage dares you to be smart. Mastering these ideas gives your offense the tools to stay one step ahead.

Now that you know the key strategies to beat zone concepts, it's time to put them into action. In the following sections, I break down specific zone coverages like Cover 2, Cover 3, and Cover 4 and show you exactly how to attack each one. From recognizing their structure pre-snap to executing the right plays with confidence, each breakdown gives you the tools to outsmart even the most disciplined defenses.

REMEMBER

The plays included are here to serve as a guide, examples to show you what's possible and how each type of zone can be approached. Don't be afraid to tweak them, combine ideas, or create brand new ones based on your own team's style and strengths. That's part of the fun of flag football: Building plays off the field can be just as exciting and creative as executing them on game day.

Cover 2

Cover 2 is a zone defense where the field is split into halves by two deep safeties, while the remaining defenders cover underneath zones (see Figure 13-9). This setup is designed to prevent deep passes and limit big plays by keeping everything in front of the defense. From an offensive perspective, understanding how this coverage works is key to finding the weak spots and exploiting them.

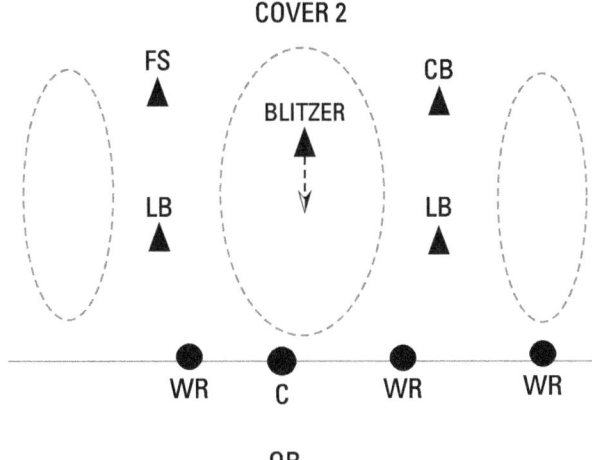

FIGURE 13-9: The middle and side lines zones (circled) can be exploited as they are weaknesses in the coverage.

In Cover 2, the biggest vulnerability lies in the space between the deep safeties and the cornerbacks, especially along the sidelines. There's also an opening down the middle of the field if the safeties don't react quickly enough to deeper inside routes. If you can force defenders to choose between responsibilities, or if you can time your throws just right, you can hit these zones with precision.

Advantages for the offense include the following:

» Opportunities to attack the sideline.

» Soft middle zone can be exploited.

» Underneath defenders are often pulled by short routes, opening space behind them.

» Great for layered plays.

Disadvantages for the offense include these:

>> Deep safeties help prevent big vertical plays.

>> Short to intermediate throws require sharp timing and precision.

>> Isolating defenders for one-on-one matchups is difficult.

DIANA SAYS

I honestly think Cover 2 is one of the easiest coverages to beat, mainly because so many of the offensive principles I've talked about fit perfectly against it. Be patient. This type of defense is designed to limit big gains, so you may not get a huge chunk of yardage on every snap. But if you stay consistent and execute your reads, those completions will stack up fast and take you into the red zone before you know it.

Here's a great example of how to attack Cover 2 using multiple concepts in one play. Figure 13-10 shows a combination that stretches the defense both vertically and horizontally. On the left side, the outside WR runs a quick out route to the flat, attacking the sideline and pulling the LB low. At the same time, the center runs a deep post or seam route right between the two safeties, targeting one of the most vulnerable areas in Cover 2. The inside right WR runs a hitch, anchoring the linebacker and preventing deeper help. Finally, the outside right WR attacks the deep sideline with a comeback route, attacking another area in Cover 2. This creates a layered stretch on both sides of the field, giving the QB multiple high-percentage options depending on how the defense reacts.

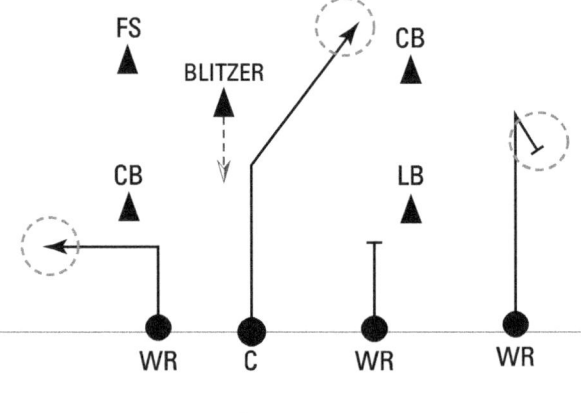

FIGURE 13-10: This play targets Cover 2 by stretching the defense vertically and horizontally.

REMEMBER

A *seam route* is when a receiver runs vertically up the field, exploiting the seam (gap) between defenders.

Figure 13-11 shows another great example of how to attack Cover 2, this time using a combination of timing and spacing to create confusion in the second level of the defense. The left-side WR runs a quick out route to pull the cornerback into the flat. Meanwhile, the slot WR on the right runs a slant route right behind a short hitch by the inside WR, perfectly targeting the soft zone between the linebacker and the CB. This overloads the LB zone and creates a natural "clear and replace" situation where the stop route anchors the linebacker just long enough for the slant to fly right behind. The QB reads the linebacker's reaction and delivers the ball into the opening. It's a quick-hitting concept that doesn't rely on deep throws but still slices through Cover 2 by attacking one of its most vulnerable zones, the space between the shallow and deep zones, while forcing the LB to make a decision that will end up opening a player for the QB to throw the ball.

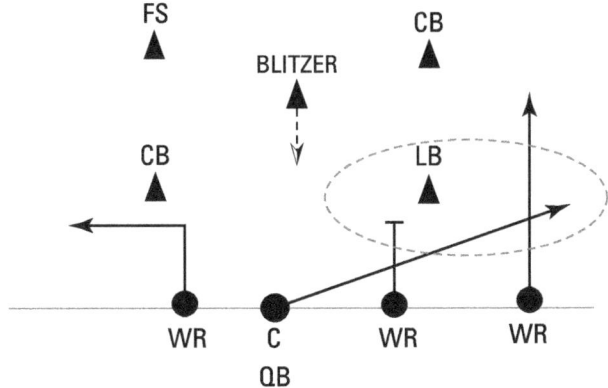

FIGURE 13-11: This play attacks Cover 2 by flooding the right side with three layered routes: short, intermediate, and deep.

REMEMBER

Those were just two examples of how you can attack a Cover 2 defense. Whether you're using concepts like levels, clear and replace, or flooding a zone, the key is always the same: Find the soft spots and be intentional with your route combinations. Cover 2 gives you windows; you just have to design plays that open them wide.

Cover 3

When you're facing a Cover 3 defense, you're looking at a setup with three defenders responsible for the deep thirds of the field, usually two corners and a safety. The LB in this case is underneath to guard the short and intermediate zones. For the offense, this means you're not going to find many openings deep unless you're really good at manipulating defenders. Instead, your focus should be on working the soft spots underneath and just outside the numbers.

From an offensive point of view, Cover 3 presents a unique mix of challenges and opportunities. While it protects well against vertical threats, it often opens up soft areas between the deep and underneath defenders, especially along the sidelines and in the seams.

Advantages for the offense include the following:

» The deep sideline just outside the cornerback's zone is often left vulnerable.

» Seams between the deep third zones can be attacked with speed and timing.

» The flats and short hooks can be exposed with quick reads.

» Great for flood concepts and high-low combinations.

Disadvantages for the offense include these:

» Strong coverage against deep posts and go routes.

» Three deep defenders make it harder to find big yardage through the air.

» Requires excellent timing and anticipation to hit the windows between zones, especially to hit the seams areas.

Cover 3 demands smart play design. The best way to beat it is by layering routes, forcing defenders to choose between covering short and deep, and exploiting the spaces they vacate. The seams between the deep safety and outside zones (see Figure 13-12) are the soft spots to target. Underneath, the flats and hook zones near the numbers also present opportunities.

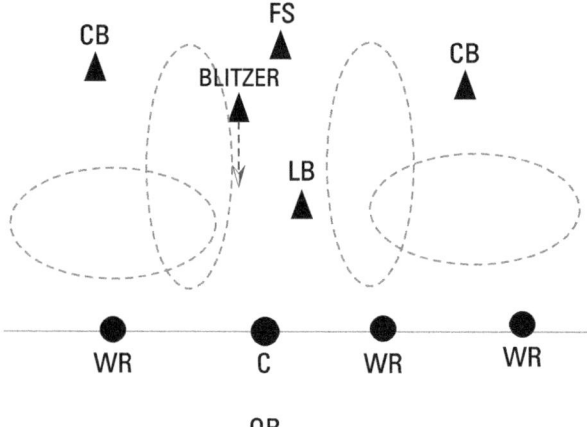

FIGURE 13-12: This diagram highlights the main vulnerable areas in a Cover 3 defense.

Figure 13-13 features a great example of a play designed to beat Cover 3. In this setup, the right outside WR runs a go route to pull the right-side cornerback deep and clear out the zone. Meanwhile, the inside right WR runs a quick slant to the right, while the center also runs a slant to the left. This forces the linebacker to choose because they can't cover both sides at once. The left outside WR runs a 10-yard in route, aiming for the window behind the linebacker and in front of the safety.

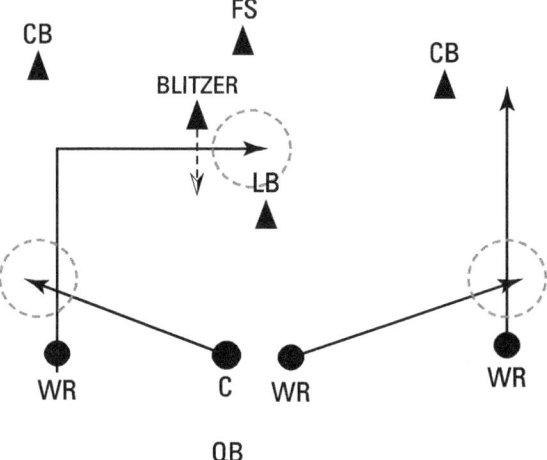

FIGURE 13-13:
This play attacks Cover 3 by overloading the linebacker's short zone with two quick slants, one from the center and one from the inside right WR.

This play works because it overloads the short zone covered by the linebacker while simultaneously challenging the free safety (FS) to decide whether to stay deep or help in the middle. If the FS stays back, the in route is open. If the FS steps forward, the QB may find a deeper opportunity down the seam. It's a simple read with smart route spacing, giving the QB a clean decision and the offense a high-percentage chance to move the ball effectively.

Figure 13-14 shows another example against Cover 3. This play is a great example of how to attack the seam in Cover 3. The inside right WR runs a quick out-and-up into the seam area, which is one of the most vulnerable spots in this coverage. To create space, the left outside WR runs a post route to pull the free safety toward the middle of the field, while the right outside WR runs a go route to stretch the deep cornerback on that side. This clears the top and opens a clean lane in the seam for the inside route.

This play is effective because it isolates the linebacker and forces the FS to pick a side. With the middle cleared and the sideline stretched, the seam becomes a wide open window if the throw is timed right. It's a perfect example of how to manipulate defenders and hit one of Cover 3's softest spots with a vertical concept.

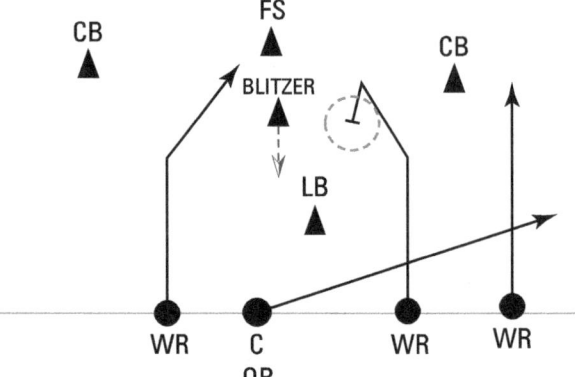

FIGURE 13-14:
This play targets the seam in Cover 3 by clearing out the coverage with a post route from the left WR and a go route from the outside right WR.

No matter which concept you decide to run, whether it's flooding the sideline, stretching the seam, or pulling defenders with smart route combos, the key to beating Cover 3 is patience, timing, and smart play design.

Cover 4

When you line up against a Cover 4 defense in flag football, you're facing a zone setup with four deep defenders covering quarters of the field, usually two safeties and two defenders positioned wide. This makes Cover 4 a very conservative look, typically used in fourth-and-long situations to prevent deep completions or near the red zone.

What this means for the offense is that it will be tough to go deep unless you can pull defenders out of position. But with fewer defenders underneath, the flats, curls, and short sideline zones tend to open up, especially when you can occupy deep coverage with vertical routes, but it also means you need to be smart and patient.

This coverage can also be used in red zone situations, where the defense aligns four defenders right along the goal line to protect against quick scoring routes. In this setup, shown in Figure 13-15, each defender is responsible for a quarter of the front line, ready to jump anything breaking into their zone. From the offense's perspective, this creates a wall of coverage at the most critical area of the field. It forces the QB to either throw into a tight window or use underneath motion and spacing to create enough confusion for someone to slip through. Execution has to be sharp, routes must develop quickly, reads must be instant, and timing has to be on point.

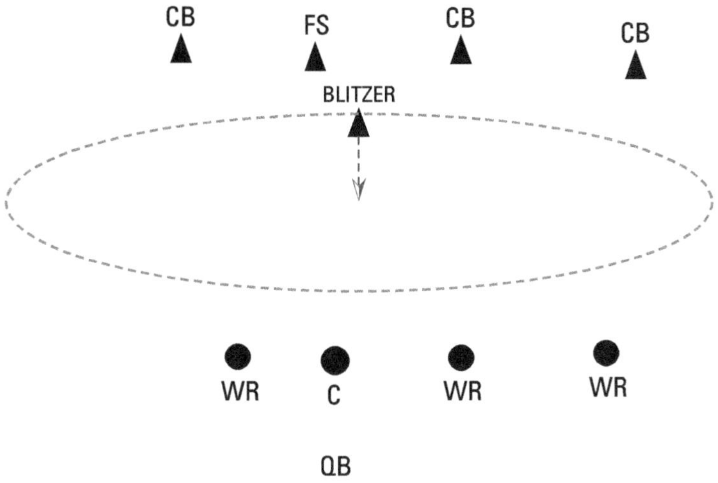

FIGURE 13-15:
With four
defenders
dropping deep,
the short flats
and outside
curls — especially
just beyond
the line of
scrimmage —
are left open.

Advantages for the offense include the following:

>> The short flats and outside curls are usually open.

>> Great opportunities exist to use underneath routes to move the chains.

>> It's an ideal setup for spacing concepts and quick throws.

>> Overloading one quarter of the field at a time can be productive.

Disadvantages for the offense include these:

>> Four-deep structure takes away deep routes, especially posts and corners.

>> Requires patience to work underneath without forcing deep shots.

>> Mistimed throws or bad reads can lead to defenders jumping routes.

>> Limited opportunity for one-on-one mismatches.

Cover 4 is all about limiting risk on defense, so the offense needs to stay disciplined, take what's available, and use timing and spacing to create openings. Following are some example plays that take advantage of this structure.

In the example shown in Figure 13-16, the offense takes advantage of the short outside zones once again. The left WR runs a stop route right into one of the soft spots left open underneath the deep quarters, giving the QB a reliable and quick option. The center runs a slant to the right, attacking the short sideline area and putting pressure on the lone underneath defender. Meanwhile, the right WRs run a post and a go route, pushing both the corner and the safety deep. This clears out space underneath for the slant to develop and potentially gain yards after the catch.

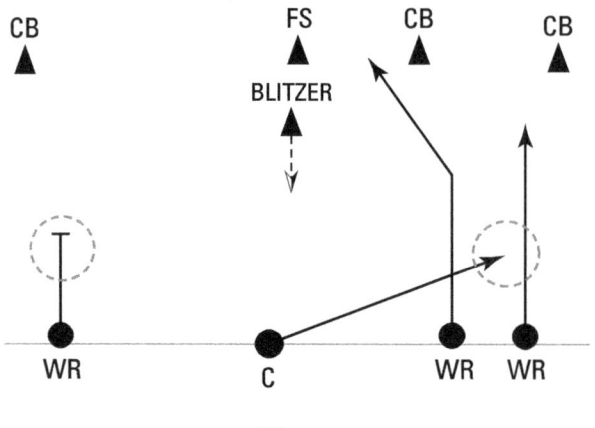

FIGURE 13-16:
This play attacks Cover 4 by stretching the coverage vertically and horizontally.

What happens when a defense plays Cover 4 at the red zone? Figure 13-17 highlights a great red zone play designed to beat Cover 4 by overloading both outside quarters. On the right side, the outside WR runs a stop route right at the first line, aiming to sit in the soft space just beneath the deep coverage. Inside of him, the next WR runs a sharp corner route, targeting the space just behind the CB in that same outside quarter. This puts immediate pressure on the deep defender to choose between the short or deep threat. On the left side, the outside WR runs a go route to stretch the deep coverage vertically, while the center runs a quick slant to the left underneath. This slant targets the short sideline and forces the left corner to decide: Either jump the slant or stay back on the go.

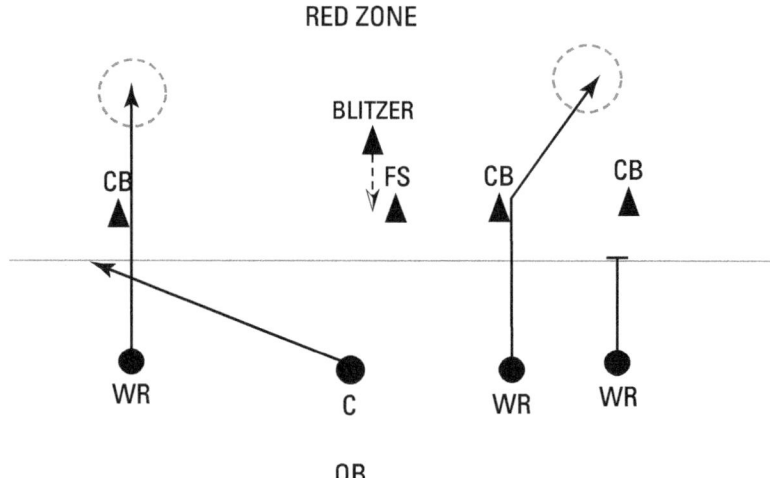

FIGURE 13-17:
This red zone play attacks Cover 4 by overloading each outside quarter.

This play works because it forces both outside defenders into a high-low dilemma, effectively overloading each quarter of the field. It's especially effective in the red zone, where quick reads and precise route spacing can break through even the most disciplined Cover 4 shell.

No matter which look the defense gives you, Cover 4 is all about patience and precision. With the deep routes taken away, the offense has to be willing to work underneath, use timing to its advantage, and layer routes smartly to stress each deep quarter.

REMEMBER

These examples show how you can overload zones, manipulate defenders, and open up space even against a conservative setup. When executed well, your offense can stay efficient and explosive without ever forcing the deep ball.

Cover 31

Cover 31 is a hybrid zone coverage used in flag football that places three defenders underneath and one defender deep, typically on the strong side, while the fifth defender is the blitzer (see Figure 13-18). From the offense's point of view, this creates an aggressive setup that tries to limit short completions while still protecting the deep field. But here's the catch: only one deep safety is responsible for covering the entire backfield. This leaves the defense vulnerable to deep throws, especially if the offense can stretch the field and isolate the safety with multiple vertical threats.

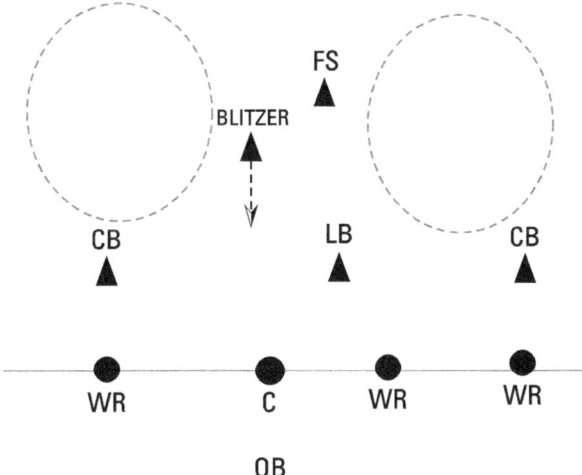

FIGURE 13-18: With only one deep defender in Cover 31, the deep middle and sidelines are exposed.

This coverage is often used to disguise intentions or apply more pressure underneath. It requires sharp communication and quick reactions from the defense, and just one mistake can open up a big play.

Advantages for the offense include the following:

>> Deep middle and outside zones can be exploited with vertical concepts.

>> One single deep defender creates isolation mismatches.

>> Overloading the deep defender with crossing or layered routes can create confusion and open windows.

>> Three short defenders may leave gaps on the opposite side of the field, especially with motion or quick swings.

>> A clear pre-snap read allows the QB to adjust protection and target weak spots instantly.

Disadvantages for the offense include these:

>> Short zones on the strong side may be covered tightly.

>> The QB must quickly recognize the hybrid look and react.

>> Misreads can lead to defenders jumping short routes.

Facing a Cover 31 means the offense needs to be alert and aggressive, look to stretch the field, attack the deep one-on-one matchups, and use layered routes to test the single deep safety.

Here's a strong example of how to take advantage of Cover 31 using vertical pressure and route layering. In this play, shown in Figure 13-19, the center and the tight WR on the right both run corner routes, aiming to divide the deep safety and force a decision. This stresses the one deep defender, who can't effectively cover both breaking routes. Meanwhile, the two outside WRs run short stop routes near the sidelines, keeping the cornerbacks shallow and occupied. This clears space behind them for the corners to develop and gives the QB a clear read based on the safety's reaction.

This play is effective because it isolates the deep safety while keeping the short defenders pinned low, creating a wide-open window for at least one of the corners to break free.

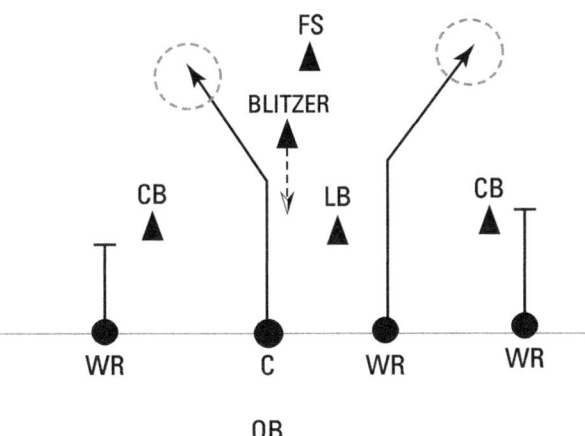

Double QB

This aspect is part of what makes flag football so dynamic and different from tackle football. It opens up endless creative possibilities and gives the offense another dimension to attack from. In certain situations, especially when more than one player is lined up behind the line of scrimmage, a second player, not just the quarterback, can legally throw or run the ball. This ability to rotate roles mid-play makes defenses hesitate and creates mismatches all over the field.

In this section, I describe how the double QB system works and look at a few play examples that show how dangerous this strategy can be when used correctly. Once you understand the basics, you'll be ready to get creative and start drawing up your own plays using two QBs, or two passers on the field. Personally, this style of play is one of my favorites; being a QB who can also run the ball, it adds more ways to enjoy the game and create explosive plays from anywhere on the field.

Figure 13-20 shows an example of this play, where a second player (QB2) lines up behind the line of scrimmage to the left of the quarterback. At the snap, the QB quickly pitches or passes the ball to QB2, who now becomes the passer. The original QB sprints toward the left sideline, attacking the space vacated by the left WR, who runs a deep go route. The center runs a slant to the right to pull defenders away from the left side, clearing room for the QB to become a receiver. Meanwhile, the right WR runs a deep in route, offering a secondary option, especially if the cornerback follows him across the field.

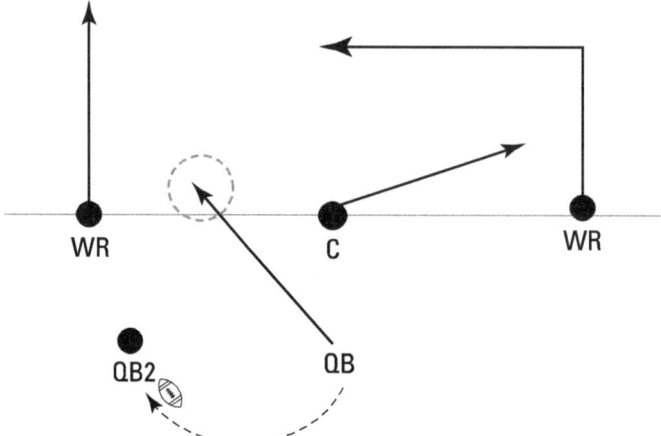

FIGURE 13-20:
In this example of the double QB play, the QB pitches to QB2 while sprinting left.

This play is effective because it stretches the defense laterally and vertically, while shifting traditional roles and responsibilities. It forces the defense to adjust on the fly and opens up space by moving players out of position. Plays like this show how versatile flag football can be and how dangerous a double QB setup becomes when executed with timing and precision.

Another variation of the double QB play is shown in Figure 13-21. This time, the center runs a slant to the left, crossing in front of QB2. The play starts with the QB tossing the ball to QB2, then immediately running a bubble route to the right. The design here plays off the defense's reaction. If the linebacker bites on QB2, the slant by the center is likely to be wide open. If the cornerback crashes on QB2, the linebacker takes away the slant, the free safety covers the go route, and the other corner follows the deep in route. Then the original QB ends up in a one-on-one matchup against the rusher with wide open space on the right side. This setup creates multiple reads and forces the defense to commit early, opening up opportunities across the field depending on their choice.

The double QB strategy is one of the most exciting tools in your offensive playbook. It's not just about adding another player downfield; it's about forcing the defense to hesitate and overthink. Whether you're using it to create confusion, mismatches, or simply to have fun experimenting, the double QB adds a new layer of versatility to the game.

TIP

Keep exploring, keep designing, and never be afraid to get creative. Sometimes the most unexpected play can be the one that changes the game — that's how dangerous the double QB strategy can be when used correctly.

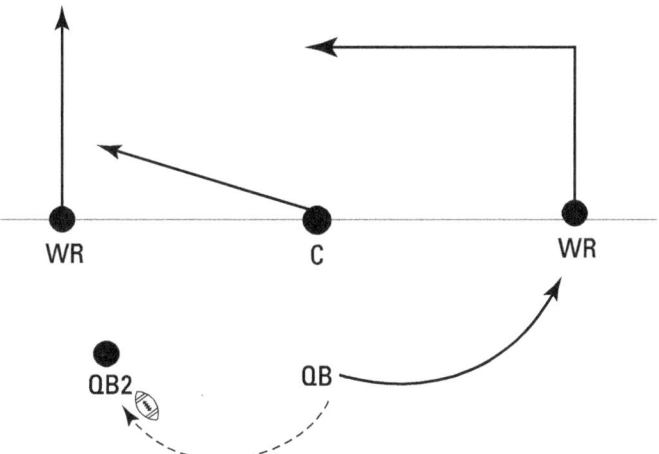

FIGURE 13-21:
This play uses
a double QB
setup to create
layered reads.

Nailing One- and Two-Point Conversions

Extra points in flag football may seem small, but they can decide the outcome of an entire game. After every touchdown, teams get to choose between two conversion options:

>> Going for one point from the 5-yard line

>> Going for two points from the 10-yard line

On paper, the closer 1-point play may sound easier, but in reality, things aren't always that simple.

From the 5-yard line, defenses have less space to cover, which can actually make it harder for receivers to get open or for route combinations to fully develop. On the flip side, a 2-point attempt from the 10-yard line gives the offense more room to get creative. There's space for deeper cuts, better timing, and even the chance to run the ball.

**DIANA
SAYS**

Choosing between the two isn't just about distance. It's about momentum, game strategy, and reading the defense in front of you. In tight matchups, these decisions become game changers. Knowing your team's strengths, understanding what the defense is giving up, and calling a play that fits the moment is what separates good teams from great ones.

There's no perfect answer when it comes to conversions. What matters most is knowing your offense and understanding what the defense is showing you. Every team is different, and so is every game situation. Use the concepts covered earlier in this chapter, like stretching zones, high-low reads, crossing routes, and double QB, to build your best version of a 1- or 2-point play.

REMEMBER

What makes a play successful is not where it starts, but how it attacks the weak spots of the defense.

Chapter **14**

Defensive Plays and Strategies

The defense's job goes beyond simply stopping the offense from scoring — it's about keeping the opponent guessing, disrupting their rhythm, and forcing mistakes. To do that, defenses rely on strategy, smart coverages, and deception. In this chapter, I introduce the goals of an effective defense, describe how different defensive formations and coverages work, and explore the mindset that turns a group of players into a dominant unit. By the end, you'll see how great defenses don't just react, they dictate the game.

Defining the Goals for Effective Defense Formations

A great defense doesn't just react, it dictates. The goal is simple: Stop the offense from scoring. But achieving that requires discipline, communication, and the ability to adapt in the blink of an eye.

In flag football, defensive success relies on smart positioning and anticipation. As I mention elsewhere in this book, there's no tackling, so defenders must rely on footwork, angles, and flag-pulling technique to stop plays in space. Every inch matters.

The defense is the ultimate line to prevent a team from scoring points. Their job is not only to force incomplete passes, pull flags, and stop big plays, but also to contain the other team from gaining confidence and becoming a real threat. This is where communication, strategy, and athleticism take center stage.

There's a popular saying: "Offense scores points, but defense wins championships." While technically the team with the most points wins, I've seen firsthand how elite defenses make the difference between a good team and a great one.

One of the best examples I've ever experienced was at the 2022 World Games in Birmingham, Alabama. That tournament was historic for my team, not just because our offense scored over 30 points in every game, but because our defense allowed only one touchdown or fewer across the entire tournament. In the gold medal game, before our offense even stepped on the field, our defense had already put 8 points on the board with a pick-six and a sack. We won that game 39–6 against the United States, a true team effort from start to finish.

From my experience, a solid defense doesn't just hold the scoreboard steady; it boosts morale, brings calm to the offense, and creates momentum. It allows the offense to focus on execution without the pressure of constantly playing catch-up. A strong defense builds the foundation for championship runs.

An effective defense focuses on

>> Limiting big plays

>> Forcing turnovers or incompletions

>> Applying pressure on the quarterback

>> Winning matchups in the red zone

>> Adjusting to different offensive formations and tempos

It's about creating doubt. When the offense starts second-guessing, the defense is in control.

REMEMBER

Mastering Defensive Formations

As discussed in earlier chapters, there are several defensive formations in flag football. Each one comes with its own alignment and purpose. Some are built to aggressively challenge short passes, while others are more conservative, focused on protecting the deep zones. But calling a great defense takes more than just picking the right look; it takes strategy.

How do you choose between each type of defense? When is it better to play aggressively and when should you play safe? That's when the game gets even more fun. This is where flag football starts to feel like chess. You need to consider game situations, field position, and the clock to make smart decisions.

DIANA SAYS

Great defenses don't just stop completions; they get ahead of the offense. They anticipate, confuse, and take the ball away, breaking the offense's rhythm and forcing them to second-guess every move.

Defensive formations can apply pressure or slow the tempo. I break down the key factors to consider when making a defensive call and how to mentally prepare your players for each scenario.

Game situation

Who's ahead on the scoreboard? How much time is left? Which team is controlling the pace? The answers to these questions define the *game situation.*

If your team is winning by two touchdowns and time is running out, the offense will likely go for big plays. In this case, playing a more preventive defense makes sense. On the flip side, if you're trailing by a touchdown with little time left, it may be time to dial up the pressure and gamble on a turnover.

And what if you're only down by 1 or 2 points with under two minutes remaining? That's when things get really interesting. You may want to go all-in with an aggressive defense, trying to snag an interception and give your offense a final shot. Even if the opponent scores, it gives your offense a chance to answer with enough time on the clock. That's strategic risk-taking.

REMEMBER

Defense isn't about perfection; it's about playing two steps ahead and shifting momentum.

Field position

Where the offense is on the field plays a huge role in what kind of defense to run. First down on their own 5-yard line? They'll likely run a quick, safe play to avoid a safety. This is a great time to call a Cover 1 (man-to-man), Cover 2, or even a more aggressive Cover 31 to tighten up short throws.

In long-yardage situations (10+ yards to go), playing a Cover 3 or Cover 4 can help protect against deep throws. No matter what the yard line is, defenses must decide which zones to protect and which to leave open based on the situation.

Time management

While the offense typically controls the pace of the game, smart defensive strategy can influence time, too.

If your team is up and there's plenty of time on the clock, playing a soft zone like Cover 3 or 4 can encourage the offense to make short, slow gains. The goal is to let the clock run while keeping everything in front of you.

But when time is tight, especially under two minutes, the offense will try to stop the clock with sideline passes. This is where a Cover 2 comes in handy. It leaves the middle open but locks up the edges, forcing the offense to use the middle of the field where the clock keeps ticking.

Being aware of the clock and making the right defensive call can be the difference between closing a win or giving up a last-minute score.

Providing Defensive Coverage

Once you understand the situation, it's time to choose the right coverage. Defensive coverages are the foundation of how a team protects different areas of the field. The two main categories are *man-to-man* and *zone*. Each one requires different levels of athleticism, communication, and game awareness.

Some teams stick to one or the other, while others switch between both depending on the opponent. Great defenses know how to disguise coverages and force offenses into uncomfortable decisions.

Man versus zone coverages

Both approaches are effective depending on the factors I discuss previously in the chapter (game situation, field position, and time management), but you must consider the advantages and disadvantages that each of them has.

Table 14-1 compares man and zone coverages to help you understand the differences between the two.

TABLE 14-1 ## Man versus Zone Coverages

	Man-to-Man	Zone
Responsibility	Guard a specific player	Guard a specific area
Strengths	When you're physically more athletic than the opponent, it's great against short passes and quick throws	Limits big plays, good for confusing the QB
Weaknesses	Can be beat by fast or tricky routes (like double moves)	Vulnerable to short completions if defenders react late
Physical Demand	High: Requires speed, footwork, and stamina	Moderate: More about positioning, reading plays, and working together
Communication	Less pre-snap, more individual effort	Requires strong communication and awareness
Best Used When	Facing a team with one or two key targets	Against balanced offenses or deep threats

Most elite teams know how to work with both. You can start with man-to-man to apply pressure and then rotate into a zone to bait a mistake. Versatility is everything.

Man-to-man coverage

In man-to-man coverage, every defender is responsible for locking down a specific offensive player, with one deep safety sitting back to help over the top. This safety becomes a crucial safety net in case a defender gets beaten.

Man-to-man works best when your defenders are athletic, disciplined, and able to stay with their matchup across the field. It's aggressive, straightforward, and puts pressure on the offense to make tight throws in tight windows.

This list highlights key traits of man-to-man coverage:

>> One defender per offensive player (plus the QB)

>> One safety in the deep middle

>> Great against short, quick passes and slants

>> Weakness: Can be vulnerable to double moves or rub routes if communication isn't sharp

This is a high-risk, high-reward defense. If every player does their job, it forces the offense into low-percentage throws.

Locking someone down one-on-one requires more than just raw speed. The following traits are what make a great man-to-man defender:

>> **Quick feet:** Allows fast reactions to sudden cuts and fakes

>> **Body control:** Helps maintain balance and adjust while shadowing routes

>> **Strong eyes:** Knowing when to look at the QB versus staying glued to the receiver

>> **Anticipation:** Recognizing route concepts and jumping in front of passes

>> **Flag pulling under pressure:** Staying composed in open space and finishing the play

DIANA SAYS

If you love challenges and hate being bored on the field, Cover 1 is your best friend. It's the closest thing to one-on-one combat in flag football. Just remember, it only takes one slip to give up a touchdown, so focus is everything.

Cover 2

Cover 2 is one of the most balanced and symmetrical coverages in flag football. Its structure divides the field into four clear zones, two short zones and two deep zones, with one defender positioned in the center of each quadrant. This proportional setup makes it both simple and effective.

While each defender is responsible for a specific zone, the key challenge in Cover 2 is managing who to cover when multiple receivers cross into your space, especially on double moves or crossing routes. Because the areas are evenly distributed, they're not too large to defend, but fast-paced plays can still create confusion.

In this scheme, shown in Figure 14-1, communication is everything. Each defensive player is positioned in the center of their assigned quadrant, responsible for everything that enters their zone. If a receiver moves from one zone to another, the defensive assignment naturally shifts. Passing off players cleanly requires defenders to stay vocal and alert.

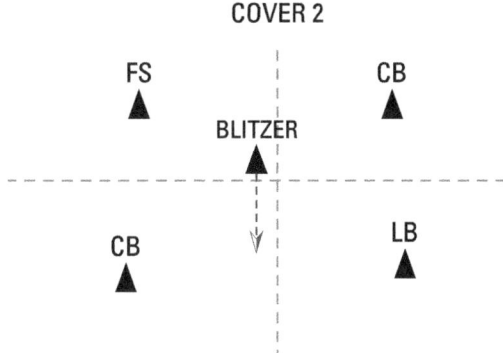

FIGURE 14-1: In Cover 2, the field is divided into four equal zones, two deep and two short.

Here's what makes Cover 2 particularly effective:

>> Strong control of the short middle and sideline zones

>> Two deep defenders to reduce the risk of long completions

>> Great against balanced offensive attacks that don't rely too heavily on one player

However, it can become vulnerable against plays that overload a single zone or send multiple routes through the same space. That's where anticipation and zone discipline become crucial.

DIANA SAYS

Cover 2 may seem basic, but when executed right, it's a headache for any offense. It brings order and structure to the field and lets you focus on being in the right place at the right time. Communication makes or breaks this coverage, so talk, point, and adjust constantly.

Cover 3

Cover 3 divides the width of the field into three vertical zones. The free safety is responsible for the deep middle, while the two cornerbacks each take care of the deep sideline thirds. This setup creates a solid shell of deep coverage that forces the offense to keep its game underneath.

There's also an imaginary horizontal line through the middle of the field that defines the short zone (see Figure 14-2). That entire area belongs to the linebacker, making this one of the most demanding roles in the formation. The LB must read the QB, track short crossing routes, and often react to multiple targets at once.

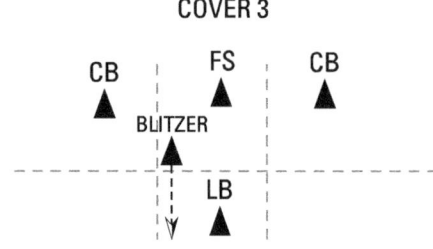

COVER 3

FIGURE 14-2:
In Cover 3,
the field is split
into three
vertical zones.

This coverage is ideal in long-yardage situations or when the defense wants to take away deep threats. It's designed to force the offense into shorter passes and rely on execution rather than big plays.

Key to minimizing damage from short routes is smart support from the corners. If a CB reads that no deep route is coming their way, they may drop down to help the short zones, but only if communication with the free safety is crystal clear. One misstep, and the deep sideline could be left wide open.

Here's what makes Cover 3 effective:

>> Provides strong protection against deep throws

>> Forces the offense to work the short field

>> Is an excellent option for 3rd-and-long situations

Here's what you need to watch out for with Cover 3:

>> The short zones can get flooded with routes if the linebacker is stretched too thin.

>> Overeager corners may abandon their deep third too early.

DIANA SAYS

I love how strategic Cover 3 can be. It puts your instincts and communication to the test. If you're a linebacker, this is your moment to shine, trust your reads, stay balanced, and fly to the flag. If done right, this coverage turns explosive offenses into conservative ones.

Cover 4

Cover 4, often referred to as *quarters coverage*, splits the deep field into four equal parts. It can also be used effectively in the red zone, where space is tighter. Each defender is responsible for one of those quarters, creating a shell that blankets deep routes and helps neutralize explosive plays. This makes Cover 4 one of the best for any situation where giving up big yardage is not an option, or for red zone defense, where defending the first line becomes priority.

Typically, the two safeties cover the inner quarters, while the cornerbacks are responsible for the outer quarters, as shown in Figure 14-3. This coverage is especially useful in 4th-and-long situations or when the offense is looking to strike deep.

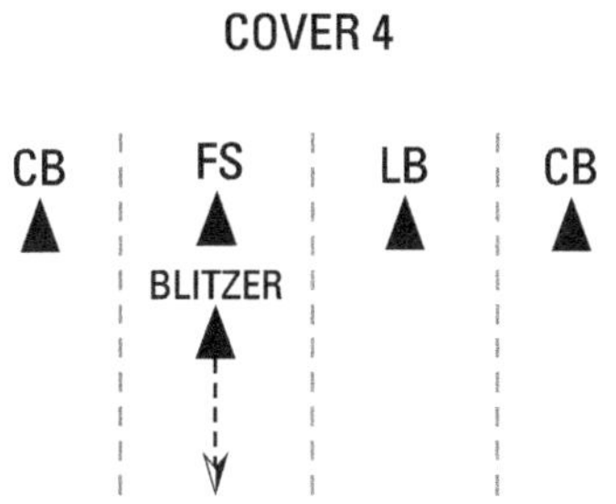

COVER 4

FIGURE 14-3:
In Cover 4, the field is divided into four deep zones.

```
CB  ¦   FS   ¦  LB  ¦  CB
▲   ¦   ▲    ¦  ▲   ¦  ▲
    ¦ BLITZER ¦     ¦
    ¦   ▲    ¦      ¦
    ¦   ¦    ¦      ¦
    ¦   ¦    ¦      ¦
    ¦   V    ¦      ¦
```

Communication between defenders is critical here, especially when receivers run crossing routes that transition through multiple zones. Players must be clear about who's passing off and who's taking over.

This list shows why Cover 4 works:

» Provides excellent deep field protection

» Forces the offense to complete multiple short passes

» Is great against offenses that rely on deep posts and corners

These are the challenges to watch out for with Cover 4:

» Can be vulnerable to short-yardage gains.

» Requires disciplined reads from all defenders.

» Defenders must stay back and avoid biting on underneath fakes.

DIANA SAYS

When the pressure is on and the offense is going for it all, Cover 4 is your safety net. It gives your team the best chance to shut down long passes and regroup. Trust your teammates, hold your zone, and make sure nothing gets behind you.

Cover 31

Cover 31 brings an aggressive, pressing mentality to the field. It mixes man and zone elements to throw off the quarterback's timing and force rushed decisions. This coverage is designed for moments when the defense needs to make something happen, either a turnover or a quick stop.

In Cover 31, shown in Figure 14-4, the defense lines up with three defenders in the short zone and one responsible for the deep area. This alignment brings a pressing and aggressive energy to the field with the specific goal of neutralizing first-read passes. By crowding the short zones, this coverage disrupts quick throws and forces the quarterback to hold the ball longer, creating opportunities for sacks, mistakes, or turnovers.

FIGURE 14-4: In Cover 31, three defenders line up in the short zone, and the FS is the only player responsible for the deep area.

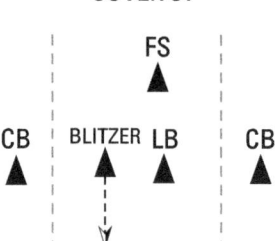

This formation is often referred to as "all or nothing" because of the risks involved. If the communication breaks down or the press is mistimed, the offense could strike quickly with a big play. But when executed well, it disrupts the quarterback's rhythm and puts pressure on the offense to adjust.

Here's what makes Cover 31 unique:

>> Combines deep coverage with aggressive press technique

>> Great for disrupting quick routes and forcing turnovers

>> Useful in must-stop situations or when the defense wants to shift momentum

When using Cover 31 as a strategy, be careful of the following:

>> Vulnerable to deep shots if press defenders miss their jam

>> Requires high-level communication

>> Risky if the offense has multiple deep threats

DIANA SAYS

Cover 31 is a statement. You're telling the offense: We're coming after you. It's not for the faint of heart, but it's the kind of defense that can flip a game in one play.

Building the Wall: Core Elements of an Unstoppable Defense

A great defense isn't just about Xs and Os; it's about execution, chemistry, and mindset. *Building the wall* means creating a defense that holds its ground through discipline, communication, and effort. When each player knows their role and commits to it with confidence, that's when defense becomes dominant.

In this list, I break down the pillars of a truly effective unit:

>> **Discipline:** Every coverage and every call depend on defenders doing their job. Whether it's staying in your zone or sticking to your matchup, success comes from not trying to do too much. Trust the system. One wrong step or decision can create gaps that the offense will exploit instantly.

>> **Communication:** Talk before the snap, during the play, and after the whistle. Adjustments happen fast, whether it's passing off a receiver, recognizing motion, or calling out bunch formations. Defense is a team effort, and communication is what glues it together.

>> **Mentality:** Defensive success is rooted in confidence. Whether you just gave up a touchdown or made a huge stop, your mindset should stay the same: next play. Stay hungry, stay focused, and bring the energy that lifts your team.

>> **Fundamentals:** The flashy plays get the highlights, but the basics win games. Clean footwork, solid flag pulling, proper angles, and good reaction time all add up. Drill the fundamentals until they become second nature.

DIANA SAYS

Defense is a mindset. It's taking pride in being the reason the other team doesn't score. You don't need to be the fastest or strongest to be great on defense; you need to be smart, committed, and ready to fight for every inch.

Playing Mind Games: Outsmarting the Offense

Once the fundamentals are in place, the next step is discovering how to disguise your intentions and keep the offense guessing. Advanced defenses don't just line up and play; they use strategy and deception to gain the upper hand.

TIP

The key concept here is disguising your coverage. This means showing one alignment during the quarterback's pre-snap read, and then switching to a different coverage the moment the ball is snapped. It adds a layer of dynamism to your defense, forcing the offense to adjust in real time.

For example, defenders may line up as if they're playing Cover 1 but immediately rotate into a Cover 3 shell after the snap. Or a defense may show man press at the line, only to drop into a zone. These sudden shifts mess with timing, route decisions, and quarterback confidence.

Defenses that master this art

>> Delay the quarterback's read, giving rushers more time to apply pressure.

>> Force throws into tight windows.

>> Cause hesitation or even force timeouts from the offense.

Pulling this off requires communication, chemistry, and commitment from the whole unit. Every player needs to sell the look and shift with precision.

DIANA SAYS

This is where defense becomes fun. It's not just about stopping plays; it's about getting inside the offense's head. Make them second-guess everything. When you start controlling what they do, you know your defense is winning.

5
From Youth Leagues to the International Stage

IN THIS PART . . .

Tour the many varieties of flag football.

Check out how flag football is becoming more popular in high schools and colleges.

Overview international competitions.

Dig into the World Games.

See what it takes to get to the Olympics.

Chapter **15**

One Sport, Many Styles

The beauty of flag football is how easily it adapts. Whether you're playing at the highest level in an international competition, college, or a pick-up game at your local park, the energy, excitement, and creativity stay the same. In this chapter, I discuss variations of flag football, including beach and coed, and give an overview of NFL FLAG, an influential youth flag football program.

Exploring Varieties of the Game

Over time, different styles of flag football have evolved or adapted, giving each version of it its own flavor — but at the core, they all celebrate speed, skill, and inclusion. In this section, I cover 5-on-5, 7-on-7, beach, and coed flag football.

5-on-5

This is the official format used in international competitions sanctioned by the International Federation of Flag Football (IFAF) and the most popular worldwide, being the main style for most countries. It's impressive to think that, unlike in places like the United States or Mexico, where the sport has been played in different formats, many players around the world only know 5-on-5 as *the* version of flag football.

It's fast-paced, strategic, and played on a smaller field than traditional tackle football. The smaller fields create small windows of opportunity, making precision of the utmost importance. Each player on the field has a clear role, and there's a strong focus on agility, awareness, and quick decision-making. It's also the format being pushed for the Olympic Games in LA 2028.

7-on-7

This version of flag football is probably one of the original ones, since it mirrors tackle football a bit more in spacing and route design — just without the contact. Back in the day, it was the most popular style of the game (it's the style I started playing!) before 5-on-5 became the dominant version.

It's still common in high school and college leagues, especially in Mexico, Canada, Panama, and the United States. But here's the thing — there's no single rulebook for 7-on-7. Almost every league has its own spin on it.

In many places, it's played on a full field (100 yards × 53 yards, or sometimes 100 × 40) with four 15-minute quarters and a halftime. One major difference is that this format allows for kicking — meaning games start with a kickoff, touchdowns are followed by kick attempts for extra points, and the flow includes kick returns just like in tackle football.

There are several versions of 7-on-7, and one worth highlighting is the format played in National Association of Intercollegiate Athletics (NAIA) college competitions in the United States, which I explain more in Chapter 16.

According to IFAF guidelines, 7-on-7 also includes the following specific features:

>> It's played 7-on-7 with team rosters of up to 20 players.

>> Field width is increased to 30 yards × 50 yards long.

>> Field size can vary depending on game site or age group, ranging from 40 to 60 yards in length and 25 to 35 yards in width.

>> End zones may be shortened to a minimum of 8 yards.

>> Field proportions should stay balanced — each half of the field should keep roughly a square or rectangular shape, depending on the format.

These adaptations allow flexibility in how and where 7-on-7 is played, making it ideal for both formal and recreational purposes. It also makes a great development space for athletes transitioning between flag and tackle or looking to sharpen their field IQ.

Beach

A more casual, yet increasingly popular, format. Played on sand, this version demands strong footwork, balance, and a different kind of stamina. You'll often find it at festivals, coastal tournaments, or community events — and even though the vibe is relaxed, the competition gets real.

Beach flag football has its own twist on the rules. While it follows the general principles of flag football, here are some key differences:

>> Played 4-on-4 instead of 5-on-5, with team rosters capped at 10 players.

>> The field is smaller — just 25 yards long with no midfield line.

>> No shoes allowed! All players must play barefoot.

>> Games start from the team's own 1-yard line, not the 5.

>> Two 15-minute halves make up the 30-minute game.

>> Timeouts are shortened to 30 seconds.

>> The quarterback must throw within 5 seconds.

>> Blitzers start from only 5 yards away.

>> After a score, the ball is placed at the opposing team's 1-yard line — no kickoffs.

These adjustments create a faster, physically demanding experience, making beach flag both a fun challenge and a unique variation of the sport.

Coed (or mixed)

Flag football is one of the few sports where mixed-gender teams are not only common but celebrated. In coed formats, men and women compete side by side — and often, leagues include rules that encourage balance, like awarding more points when a female player scores.

TIP

This format can be played in any of the styles mentioned previously: 5-on-5, 7-on-7, and even beach flag. It's a powerful way to break stereotypes and promote gender inclusion in sport, and it's just as popular in youth leagues as it is in adult competitions.

Introducing NFL FLAG Football

NFL FLAG (nflflag.com) is one of the biggest and most influential youth flag football programs in the world. Backed by the National Football League (NFL), it was launched in 1994 with the goal of making flag football more accessible and inclusive for kids of all skill levels. Since then, it has grown into a massive movement that has not only shaped the game at the youth level in the United States but has also expanded internationally.

NFL FLAG leagues are available for kids between the ages of 5 and 17 in all girls, boys, and coed formats. The divisions are usually broken down by age group to ensure fair competition and skill development. Throughout the rest of this section, I take a closer look at how NFL FLAG is structured and where it's making an impact.

WHAT NFL FLAG MEANS TO ME

Personally, the NFL FLAG program has a special place in my heart. Even though my international experience started years before I was introduced to NFL FLAG, being part of it was one of the most memorable chapters of my athletic career. I started playing NFL FLAG in Mexico City at age 14, as the only girl in an all-boys league. (Flag just wasn't that popular back then. Not many girls were playing the game yet.)

After competing in the national championship in 2011 with my team in Mexico, I was invited to join a team from Philadelphia for the NFL FLAG Regional Championships in Baltimore. It was the first time I got to play in an all-girls league — and with girls my own age! We won and earned a spot at the national championship in New Orleans months later.

That experience was truly life changing. It opened a world of possibilities and showed me how powerful sport can be in breaking down cultural and language barriers. Through that journey, I found not only competition, but also connection — a new family in my teammates and coaches.

Finding where it's played

NFL FLAG started in the United States but now reaches athletes in over 13 countries through NFL FLAG International, including Mexico, Canada, Australia, China, Germany, Ghana, and the United Kingdom. Its presence continues to grow through partnerships and global tournaments that promote the sport around the world.

Understanding the rules

NFL FLAG follows a 5-on-5 noncontact format, designed to prioritize speed, safety, and inclusiveness. Here are some of its key rules and game characteristics:

- **Field dimensions:** 25 yards wide by 70 yards long with 10-yard end zones (or 64 yards with 7-yard end zones). Midfield marks the first down line. No-run zones exist 5 yards before midfield and the end zone, where only passing plays are allowed.

- **Game format:** Two 24-minute halves with a continuous clock in regular season. Tournament play uses two 12-minute halves with a running clock.

- **Starting position:** Each possession starts at the team's own 5-yard line. Teams have four downs to reach midfield, then three downs to score.

- **Scoring:** A touchdown earns 6 points. Extra points can earn 1 or 2 points:
  - 1-point attempts are played from the 5-yard line and must consist of pass-only plays.
  - 2-point attempts have to be made from the 10-yard line, but this time with the option to run or pass during the play.

- **Safety:** A safety earns 2 points for the defense when the offense is stopped in its own end zone.

- **Passing:** Only one forward pass is allowed per play, thrown behind the line of scrimmage. The quarterback has a 7-second pass clock unless the ball has been handed off or lateraled.

- **Running:** No running in no-run zones (the first 5 yards of the field, middle field, and end zone). The QB cannot run past the line of scrimmage (LOS) unless the ball has been handed off first.

- **Rushing the passer:** One or two defenders can rush from 7 yards back. All defenders can rush once the ball has been handed off or lateraled behind the LOS.

>> **Flag pulling:** Defenders must pull a flag to stop a ball carrier. No tackling or blocking is allowed. Flag guarding (using hands or body to block the flag) carries a penalty.

NFL FLAG rules are designed to teach fundamentals while keeping players safe and engaged. The structure also helps younger athletes transition into more advanced levels of the sport. You'll find many similarities between the rules and regulations for IFAF and NFL FLAG.

Looking at its international intention

NFL FLAG International was created to help grow the game beyond U.S. borders. It gives international athletes the chance to compete at elite levels — including the NFL FLAG International Championships, held annually in the United States as part of Pro Bowl or Super Bowl week. This global tournament brings together youth teams from around the world to celebrate the sport and represent their countries on a big stage.

REMEMBER

NFL FLAG isn't just a league — it's a launchpad. Many athletes who start with NFL FLAG go on to represent their national teams in international competitions or earn scholarships to play in college programs. The impact it has had on globalizing the sport is undeniable.

Chapter **16**

Homing in on High School and College Flag Football

Flag football isn't just one of the fastest-growing sports in the world; it's becoming a vehicle for young athletes to chase their dreams. Whether it's playing in their local communities, competing internationally, or representing their countries, the opportunities in flag football now go far beyond the field.

As the sport grows in popularity, high schools and universities have started keeping up with the pace, adding flag football to their athletic programs and even offering scholarships at both the high school and college levels.

REMEMBER

While scholarship programs are still expanding, the biggest opportunities today are found in Mexico and the United States. But by the time the next edition of this book comes out, that list will probably be a lot longer!

This chapter gives you a clear look at how flag football is evolving in high schools and colleges, with a spotlight on the two countries leading the charge: Mexico and the United States.

Becoming a Sanctioned High School Sport in the United States

Flag football is rapidly gaining traction across the United States, particularly at the high school level. As of early 2025, 14 states have officially sanctioned girls' flag football as a varsity sport, including Florida, California, Pennsylvania, and New York, among others. These states have integrated the sport into their high school athletic programs, allowing for official state championships and providing increased resources for female athletes.

Sanctioning a sport at the high school level means it is formally recognized by the state's high school athletic association. This recognition brings several benefits:

>> **Official recognition:** Athletes can earn varsity letters, and the sport is included in official school records.

>> **Access to resources:** Schools allocate funding for equipment, coaching staff, and facilities.

>> **Structured competition:** Teams participate in regulated seasons, culminating in state championships.

>> **Pathways to higher opportunities:** Sanctioned sports often have clearer pathways to collegiate athletics and scholarships.

The importance of sanctioning extends beyond the field. It provides legitimacy to the sport, encourages broader participation, and opens doors for athletes to pursue the sport at higher levels, including college and potentially international competition.

Exploring Flag Football in College

Flag football is more than a game; now it's a bridge to education, opportunity, and lifelong impact. As the sport grows, colleges are stepping up, too, offering young athletes a chance to pursue both their academic and athletic dreams.

Right now, Mexico and the United States are leading the way when it comes to flag football at the college level. Interestingly, Mexico was ahead of the curve, offering athletic scholarships for flag football over a decade ago. I know this firsthand because when I started college, I was part of one of the first generations of athletes to earn a scholarship for flag football at Tecnológico de Monterrey.

DIANA SAYS

I know what just one opportunity can do because it changed my life completely. That college scholarship for flag football? It opened doors I never imagined. I graduated top of my class in Marketing and Communication from one of the most prestigious universities in Latin America. And later, I got my master's degree thanks to that same opportunity.

That's the power of sport. It opens doors, yes, but more than anything, it gives you the confidence to walk through them. I've always believed that education and sports should go hand in hand. Together, they shape who we are. They teach us how to lead, how to solve problems, and how to keep going when things get tough. And honestly, that's what makes us unstoppable on and off the field.

Throughout the rest of this section, I give a brief overview of how flag football has evolved in colleges and universities in Mexico and the United States.

Mexico

Mexico has been a trailblazer when it comes to flag football at the college level. Athletic scholarships for the sport have been around for over a decade, and both independent and state-funded universities have embraced the game, creating real opportunities for student-athletes to grow both on the field and in the classroom.

Independent universities

Several independent universities across the country have strong flag football programs and offer athletic scholarships. Among them are

>> Tecnológico de Monterrey (ITESM)

>> Universidad del Valle de México (UVM)

>> Universidad de las Américas Puebla (UDLAP)

>> Universidad Anáhuac

>> Universidad La Salle

>> Universidad Iberoamericana (IBERO)

These schools compete in national events organized by CONADEIP (the national collegiate sports commission for private institutions), such as the *Campeonato Nacional de Flag Football de Primera Fuerza*, one of the top college-level flag football tournaments in the country.

DIANA SAYS

While I was playing college flag football, my team and I held the national title from 2017 to 2020, right before the world hit pause due to the COVID-19 pandemic. It was an unforgettable run filled with passion, hard work, and memories that will last a lifetime.

State-funded universities

On the state-funded side, schools like the Instituto Politecnico Nacional (IPN) and Universidad Nacional Autónoma de México (UNAM), among others, have developed competitive programs as well. In addition, the Mexican Federation of American Football (FMFA; fmfa.mx) organizes the *Universiada Federada*, bringing together university teams from across the country to compete in high-level flag football competition.

United States

While Mexico may have been the first to embrace flag football at the college level, the United States isn't staying behind. In recent years, the sport has started gaining serious ground on American campuses too. As flag football continues to grow, more colleges are jumping on board, not just to create space for competition, but to offer academic and athletic opportunities. From official varsity programs to fast-growing club teams, college flag football in the United States is becoming a legitimate path for student-athletes who want to play at a high level while pursuing a degree.

The two main organizations shaping this space are the NAIA and the NCAA, each with its own timeline, reach, and opportunities for the future.

NAIA

The National Association of Intercollegiate Athletics (NAIA; www.naia.org/landing/index) was the first college-level organization in the United States to officially recognize women's flag football as a varsity sport. In 2020, in partnership with the NFL and RCX Sports, NAIA made history by launching the first sanctioned college flag football programs in the country.

Since then, more than a dozen NAIA colleges have added flag football to their athletic programs, with many of them offering athletic scholarships. The official season runs in the spring and includes regular season play, conference championships, and a national invitational. These are not just recreational teams — these are competitive programs with structure, coaching, and real stakes.

Here's the full list of NAIA colleges with flag football programs:

>> Baker University

>> Bethel University

>> Campbellsville University

>> Cottey College (Missouri)

>> Florida Memorial University

>> Graceland University

>> Kansas Wesleyan University

>> Keiser University (Florida)

>> Life University

>> Midland University (Nebraska)

>> Milligan University

>> Missouri Valley University

>> Ottawa University (Kansas)

>> Point University

>> Reinhardt University

>> Saint Thomas University (Florida)

>> Southwestern University

>> Talladega University

>> Thomas University (Georgia)

>> Tougaloo College

>> University of Saint Mary's

>> Warner University (Florida)

>> Webber International University

NJCAA FLAG FOOTBALL

The National Junior College Athletic Association (NJCAA) officially recognizes a women's flag football program: It's a 5-on-5 version, played primarily by women at the two-year college level. The following NJCAA schools have programs:

- Bryant & Stratton College (Wisconsin)
- College of DuPage
- Daytona State College
- Florida Gateway College
- Harford Community College
- Hesston College
- Hocking College
- Howard Community College
- Nassau Community College
- Pasco-Hernando State College
- Pratt Community College
- Wallace State Community College

By getting ahead of the curve, the NAIA has set the tone for what's possible when academic institutions take flag football seriously. They've created a platform where young women can chase their dreams, develop their game, and earn a degree at the same time.

It's a major win for the sport and a clear sign that flag football is here to stay at the collegiate level.

NCAA

The National Collegiate Athletic Association (NCAA), home to many of the biggest and most competitive college sports in the United States, has started laying the foundation for flag football's next big leap. While it hasn't yet fully sanctioned flag football as an official sport, the movement is well underway, and the momentum is building fast.

What's especially exciting is the push to make women's flag football a Division I sport. When that happens, it will mark a major turning point. NCAA Division I (D1) status means greater investment, more scholarships, higher visibility, and the kind of infrastructure that can take the sport to the next level. From media coverage to athletic funding, the D1 label changes everything. It turns potential into long-term sustainability.

Right now, flag football programs exist at the club level across a growing number of NCAA schools. These programs often operate with the same drive and competitive spirit as varsity teams and serve as a key proving ground for what a full NCAA-sanctioned structure could look like.

The NCAA schools currently offering flag football at the club level include:

>> Alabama State University

>> Benedictine University (Illinois)

>> Bluefield State University

>> Bowie State University

>> Centenary University (New Jersey)

>> Claflin University

>> College of Staten Island

>> Emmanuel University (Georgia)

>> Fayetteville State University

>> Holy Family University

>> Huntingdon College

>> Immaculata University

>> Johnson C. Smith University

>> LaGrange College

>> Marymount University (Virginia)

>> Neumann University

>> Rockford University

>> St. Joseph's University – NY, Brooklyn

- St. Joseph's University – NY, Long Island

- SUNY – Brockport

- SUNY – Cortland

- SUNY – Geneseo

- Virginia Union University

- Winston-Salem State University

The growing involvement of the NCAA is not just a step forward; it's a signal. It tells athletes, schools, sponsors, and fans that flag football isn't just a side activity anymore. It's a real sport with a real future, and the NCAA may just be the next big player to help elevate it to where it belongs.

Reviewing the Rules

One of the most interesting contrasts in college flag football is the difference in game format and rules between Mexico and the United States. For instance, in NAIA college flag football, players can actually block, something you almost never see in international 5-on-5 flag football!

In Mexico, college flag football follows the IFAF 5-on-5 format, which includes smaller fields, no-contact rules, and a fast-paced, high-skill style of play. As discussed in earlier chapters, the IFAF rules prioritize agility, precision, and creativity. This version is widely used across the country and has become the standard for university competitions.

Meanwhile, in the United States, college flag football, especially at the NAIA level, is played in a 7-on-7 format, and the differences go far beyond just the number of players. As I explain in Chapter 4, the field is wider and longer, allowing for more spread-out formations and strategic depth. And here's where it gets really wild: Blocking is permitted. Yes, even for someone who has played flag football for years, that's a bit of a surprise. But in the NAIA rulebook, blocking within certain guidelines is allowed, adding a unique layer of physicality and play design to the game.

Another key difference? Kicks are also permitted in the NAIA game style. This changes game strategy completely, offering more variety in play-calling and scoring opportunities.

These variations don't just reflect different rulebooks; they represent how flexible and diverse the sport can be across countries and competitions. Whether it's 5-on-5 or 7-on-7, flag football continues to adapt and evolve, opening even more doors for athletes around the world.

To make it easier to compare, I created the chart in Table 16-1 showing the main differences between college flag football rules in Mexico and the United States.

TABLE 16-1   College Rules: Mexico versus the United States

Feature	Mexico (5-on-5)	U.S. (7-on-7 NAIA)
Number of players on field	5	7
Field size	Smaller	Larger
Blocking	Not allowed	Allowed
Kicking	Not allowed	Allowed
Governing rules	IFAF	NAIA/NFL guidelines

Chapter **17**

Investigating IFAF International Competitions

When the national anthem plays and a player stands tall with a flag over their heart, something changes. This isn't just about the game anymore. This is about legacy, pride, and representing something far bigger than yourself. That's the magic of international flag football.

At the highest level of the sport, where passion and preparation meet opportunity, the International Federation of American Football (IFAF; www.americanfootball.sport) runs the show. IFAF is the global governing body for flag and tackle football, and under its wing, international competitions have become the ultimate stage for athletes dreaming of wearing their country's colors.

These aren't just tournaments. They're a showcase of speed, strategy, and national pride. They define who's leading the sport and how the game is evolving worldwide. With 72 member nations across five continents, flag football is experiencing remarkable growth in every direction: from powerhouse programs in the Americas to rising stars in Africa and Asia.

International flag football under IFAF is divided into two major formats:

» **Continental Championships**, which bring together the best teams from each region.

» **World Championships**, where the top countries face off for global dominance.

These events are more than a competition. They are windows into culture, grit, and unity. For many young athletes, they are the dream. A dream to one day not just play for a club or a school, but to represent a nation, to hear their name called in the World Cup roster, to fight for a gold medal, and to prove themselves on a field where the world is watching.

Whether you're already dreaming of playing on the world stage or just discovering the thrill of the game, diving into IFAF competitions is like unlocking a front row ticket to flag football's most electrifying world: a global movement where nations clash not with hits, but with heart, and where the dream to wear your country's name on your back burns brighter than ever.

In this chapter, I dive into the structure, the stories, and the significance of IFAF international play, the heart of flag football's highest level.

Citing Continental Championships

Before players chase global glory, they fight for regional supremacy. IFAF's Continental Championships are the proving-ground tournaments held every two years, nestled between World Championships, that determine the elite from each continent. In 2023, the Championships reached new heights, with major events staged across three continents: North America (Charlotte, United States), Europe (Limerick, Ireland), and Asia (Kuala Lumpur, Malaysia). It was the biggest year yet for the Continental circuit, proof that the sport isn't just growing, it's thriving on a truly global scale. For athletes, winning here is more than a trophy; it's proof you belong on the world stage.

Each region reflects its own flavor of flag football excellence, which I explore throughout the rest of this section.

The Americas

This region includes powerhouses like the United States, Mexico, Panama, and Brazil. It's often one of the most competitive zones, not just because of the talent, but because of the sport's explosive growth in both North and South America. The rivalry between Mexico and the United States has become one of the sport's defining narratives, with packed stadiums, highlight-reel plays, and some of the fiercest flag football ever played.

These same countries, along with 16 other federations under IFAF Americas, were part of a historic moment in 2023 when Charlotte, North Carolina, hosted the first-ever Americas Continental Championship. That tournament marked a turning point in the region, officially launching a new era of international flag football in the Americas. With both men's and women's national teams competing, it set the tone for what future championships and World Cup qualifications would look like moving forward.

Europe

A powerhouse region featuring countries like Austria, Spain, Italy, Germany, the United Kingdom, France, and Denmark, Europe brings a rich mix of rapid growth and emerging strength to the field. Its championship cycles offer a snapshot of how much the sport has evolved across the continent.

According to the current IFAF World Rankings, Austria holds the No. 2 position in men's flag football globally, and Italy ranks among the top five in the women's division. These standings reflect the consistency and competitive rise of European programs as they continue to push the global standard forward.

Asia

With leagues in Japan, South Korea, Thailand, and more, Asia's championship features lightning-fast, disciplined play. It's a showcase of speed and strategy, setting the scene for future global contenders. Japan leads the charge in this region and currently ranks No. 6 in both the men's and women's IFAF World Rankings, positioning itself as a legitimate threat to the podium at future world events and more.

Africa

Flag football is thriving in Africa. In 2025, history was made as Cairo, Egypt, hosted the first-ever African Continental Championship, marking a groundbreaking moment for the sport on the continent. Nations like Nigeria, Morocco, and South Africa took the field, but it was Nigeria that stole the spotlight. With dominant performances in both divisions, Nigeria claimed gold in both the men's and women's tournaments.

Their victories didn't just earn them regional glory; they also became the first African teams to qualify for the 2026 IFAF Flag Football World Championships, where they'll proudly represent the continent among 16 competing nations.

Whirling through World Cups

When a player steps onto the field at a World Championship, they're not just competing, they're becoming part of history. The IFAF Flag Football World Championships are the pinnacle of the sport, where the best of the best go head-to-head for the ultimate prize. Representing your country on this stage means everything: national pride, years of preparation, and the dream of leaving a mark that lasts far beyond the final whistle.

Every two years, countries from every continent send their top athletes to compete. And while medals are handed out, what players and fans remember most are the moments: a game-saving flag pull, a trick play that stuns the crowd, a national anthem playing after a hard-fought win. These tournaments are electric, and they're where the sport's future is constantly being shaped.

DIANA SAYS

I still remember the first time I wore the national team jersey at just 16 years old during the World Championship in Grosseto, Italy. The feeling of representing my country on that stage is something I still can't fully explain, even after more than 12 years with Mexico's national team. It was a moment of pure pride and emotion, but also one of deep responsibility. Wearing your country's name across your chest isn't just a dream come true; it's a commitment to give everything you've got, every single play.

The history of the IFAF Flag Football World Championships reflects how fast the sport has grown on the global stage. Since the first edition in Vienna in 2002, these championships have gone from a small international gathering to a highly competitive, emotionally charged tournament that brings together the best flag football nations in the world.

From the mid-2000s, countries began cementing their legacies. Austria's men's team emerged as an early powerhouse, taking gold back-to-back in 2004 and 2006, while France and Canada were right on their heels. On the women's side, Mexico took the world by storm early on, claiming gold in 2004 and again in 2008 and 2012, setting the stage for a legacy of fierce competition.

The 2010s were marked by the USA's rise to dominance. The U.S. men's team began collecting golds, starting in 2010 in Ottawa, Ontario (the host of the IFAF World Championship), turning themselves into the team to beat. By 2014, the U.S.

women's team joined the party too, showing off depth, strategy, and athleticism that raised the level of the competition.

But it wasn't all one-sided. Teams like Panama, Denmark, and Canada consistently stayed in the medal conversation. Mexico's women remained a global force, adding medals in nearly every edition. Austria, never far from the podium, continued to be a giant in both men's and women's divisions.

As the championship moved into the 2020s, new stories started to unfold. In 2021, the United States reclaimed the gold in the women's division, with Mexico taking silver and Japan earning its first-ever bronze. On the men's side, the U.S. also topped the podium, followed by Mexico and Austria. Then, in 2024, something exciting happened: Nations like Japan (women's bronze) and Switzerland (men's bronze) climbed the podium once again, signaling a shift in the competitive landscape.

What once seemed like a small movement now lives in the hearts of thousands of fans across continents.

REMEMBER

The evolution of the game can be seen not just in how many teams now compete, but in how diverse the medal tables have become. The dominance of a few nations is being challenged by new, exciting programs.

Figure 17-1 shows the full list of medal winners from every World Championship. It's a great way to look back and understand how the game has evolved and how new nations are starting to shake up the podium.

Year and Location	Men's Gold	Men's Silver	Men's Bronze	Women's Gold	Women's Silver	Women's Bronze
2002 - Vienna	Austria	Germany	France	Sweden	France	--
2004 - Thonon-les-Bains	Austria	Germany	France	Mexico	Finland	Sweden
2006 - Daegu	France	Denmark	Thailandia	France	Japan	Finland
2008 - St-Jean-Sur-Richelieu	Canada	Denmark	France	Mexico	Canada	France
2010 - Ottawa	USA	Denmark	Italy	Canada	USA	Austria
2012 - Gothenburg	Austria	USA	Denmark	Mexico	USA	France
2014 - Grosseto	USA	Mexico	Italy	Canada	USA	Austria
2016 - Miami	USA	Denmark	Mexico	Panama	Austria	Mexico
2018 - Panama City	USA	Austria	Denmark	USA	Panama	Canada
2021 - Jerusalem	USA	Mexico	Panama	USA	Mexico	Austria
2024 - Lahti	USA	Austria	Switzerland	USA	Mexico	Japan

FIGURE 17-1:
World Championship medal winners.

Reviewing World Rankings

The latest IFAF World Rankings reflect the growing global landscape of flag football, based on recent performances at continental and world-level competitions. Here's how the top programs stand today:

Women's Rankings (Top 5):

1. United States

2. Mexico

3. Austria

4. Japan

5. Panama

Men's Rankings (Top 5):

1. United States

2. Mexico

3. Germany

4. Austria

5. France

These rankings don't just celebrate success, they track momentum. New nations are climbing fast, proving that in flag football, today's dreamers can become tomorrow's champions.

Chapter 18

Diving into The World Games

For many athletes, representing their country is already a dream come true. But doing so in a global multi-sport event, surrounded by some of the world's best in countless disciplines, takes things to a whole new level. That's exactly what the World Games represent for the flag football community. In this chapter, I provide a brief overview of the history of the World Games and end the chapter with a quick comparison of the World Games and IFAF World Championships.

Exploring The World Games History

The World Games are an international multi-sport event organized by the International World Games Association (IWGA; www.theworldgames.org), featuring sports and disciplines not yet included in the Olympic Games. They take place every four years, one year after the Summer Olympics.

The idea of The World Games was born out of a need to give visibility to sports that were not included in the Olympic Games. In 1980, the IWGA was officially founded by 12 international sports federations. Just one year later, in 1981, the very first edition of The World Games took place in Santa Clara, California. From the beginning, the Games were created with the goal of supporting emerging sports, offering them a platform to showcase their athletes and reach wider audiences. Since then, The World Games have been held every four years, always one year after the Summer Olympics. Over time, they've grown into a prestigious and meaningful international event where high-performance and innovation collide.

Flag football was officially added to this prestigious stage for the first time in 2022, during the 11th edition of The World Games in Birmingham, Alabama. That moment was historic. For the first time, our sport stood alongside dozens of others in an Olympic-style environment. Athletes shared the village, the ceremonies, and the nerves. The energy was electric. And the games? Some of the highest-level flag football the world has ever seen.

This World Games edition featured eight men's and eight women's teams from around the world. These countries earned their place through a qualification system tied to their performance at the IFAF World Championships and regional competitions.

On the women's side, the podium featured Mexico, the United States, and Panama. The final was a thrilling showdown between Team USA and Mexico, an intense match that had everything: speed, strategy, and passion. Mexico ended up dominating the game with a 39–6 score, sealing a historic gold medal victory. The bronze medal match saw Panama claim third place with a solid performance, showing just how much the level of play across the Americas has grown.

In the men's bracket, the United States took gold, followed by Italy with the silver, and Austria securing bronze. Each game highlighted how much the sport has matured worldwide. The tempo, the decision making, the athleticism — none of it looked like a sport making its debut. It looked like it belonged.

DIANA SAYS

I had the honor of being part of that historic moment. It was my fifth time representing Mexico in an international tournament, but the World Games were something completely different. From the moment we arrived at the athlete's village, it felt special. Waking up early and heading to the dining hall, seeing it packed with some of the world's greatest athletes from all kinds of disciplines, all chasing the same goal, was surreal. One of my favorite parts was running into athletes from other sports during breakfast, getting to know their journeys, learning about their events, and sharing that quiet excitement before a day of competition. It reminded me that even though our sports may be different, the love and passion for what we do connect us deeply.

But once you step onto the field, everything changes. The pressure is different. You face the best of the best. Every single game feels like a playoff. There's no time to warm up or settle in; if you blink, you're out.

I'll never forget that championship run with my team, the songs we sang on the bus or in the locker room before a match, and our late-night recovery sessions after a long day of games, scouting, and studying. We made history together, defeating Team USA in the final with a dominant 39–6 win. What made that team special wasn't just talent. It was the connection, the unity, the joy of playing together. That's what pushed us past the limits and helped us bring home the gold medal in flag football's first-ever appearance at the World Games.

This edition of the World Games was intense and full of emotion, not just for the women's division but for the men's as well. Figure 18-1 shows the final standings in both brackets.

FIGURE 18-1: The final standings of the 2022 World Games held in Birmingham, Alabama.

Year and Location	Women's Gold	Women's Silver	Women's Bronze	Men's Gold	Men's Silver	Men's Bronze
2022 - Birmingham, Alabama	Mexico	United States	Panama	United States	Italy	Mexico

Comparing The World Games to the IFAF World Championships

Both The World Games and the IFAF World Championships are elite-level tournaments, and both bring together top national teams. But the format, context, and ambitions are different.

The IFAF World Championships are standalone events dedicated exclusively to flag football. They are run by the International Federation of American Football (IFAF), and all the member federations participate, making it the most globally inclusive competition for the sport. The full attention is on the sport.

The World Games, on the other hand, place flag football within a much wider sports ecosystem. These games receive more international exposure and are perhaps one of the toughest competitions in the sport, since only the top national teams in the world earn a spot to compete. As they are governed by the IWGA under the umbrella of the International Olympic Committee, it's a powerful platform for any sport aspiring to join the Olympic program, like flag football was back then.

Being part of The World Games sent a powerful message: Flag football isn't just growing. It's thriving.

Unlike the World Championships, which are open to a larger number of teams, The World Games allow only the top eight national teams per division to participate. That means every snap, every play, and every game in the qualification process matters.

Qualification typically happens through regional IFAF championships and World Championship rankings, but the exact process can vary depending on the cycle. For example, for the 2022 edition, the United States earned automatic qualification as the host nation, and the other seven spots were awarded based on performances at the previous IFAF World Championships and continental tournaments.

It's a system designed to ensure that only the very best earn their place, but also one that constantly invites new contenders to rise. The competition is fierce, and that's part of what makes The World Games so special.

IN THIS CHAPTER

» Understanding what led flag football to become an Olympic sport

» Seeing how the NFL and IFAF played vital roles in global development

» Breaking down the expected qualification process for LA 2028

» Exploring how Olympic recognition will impact players, countries, and the sport

Chapter **19**

Becoming an Olympic Sport: LA 2028

When the news broke that flag football had officially been included in the Los Angeles 2028 Olympic Games, it felt like the world shifted, at least for the flag football community around the world. For years, the dream felt far away. Now it's a reality. This chapter takes you through flag football's journey to becoming an Olympic sport.

Dreaming the Dream: From Grassroots to Olympic Bid

The journey to LA 2028 wasn't just about convincing the International Olympic Committee (IOC; www.olympics.com/ioc); it was about showing the world that flag football belongs. To do that, the sport needed more than medals and games. It needed a movement.

DO NOT UNDERESTIMATE THE POWER OF A DREAM

DIANA SAYS

Work hard and stay true to yourself. Playing flag football has taken me around the world. Being part of the movement that made flag football an Olympic sport and having the opportunity to represent my country in LA28 takes me to another level. I still get chills thinking about what it will feel like to walk into that stadium in LA, knowing this sport finally made it to where it belongs.

Inclusion in the Olympic Games is one of the highest recognitions a sport can earn. The process involves years of evaluation and strategy. For flag football, the campaign focused on everything that makes the sport unique: accessibility, inclusion, fast-paced action, low barriers to entry, and global reach.

The International Federation of American Football (IFAF) led the formal bid process, while the NFL brought star power, resources, and global momentum. The sport's visibility exploded thanks to international competitions, grassroots programs, and high-profile activations like the Pro Bowl Games (`www.nfl.com/pro-bowl-games/`). Flag wasn't just growing, it was thriving.

DIANA SAYS

I was blessed with the opportunity of being part of these efforts, representing the athletes' voice alongside IFAF and the NFL. I had the honor of working closely with the IOC to help make this dream a reality. This is one of the biggest achievements of my life, something I'm incredibly proud of and grateful to have been part of. As a girl, I grew up watching the Olympic Games every four years, dreaming of one day stepping onto that stage. The Olympics are the pinnacle of any athlete's career. To know that now I and so many other flag athletes around the world will have the opportunity to live that dream is nothing short of magical.

One of the biggest turning points came in 2022 during The World Games in Birmingham. It was the first time flag football was featured as an invitational sport on a major multi-sport stage, and it delivered in every way. Athletes from across continents played with passion, skill, and purpose. The stands were packed, the games were intense, and the Olympic world was watching . . . the IOC took notice. That week in Alabama made one thing clear: Flag football wasn't a maybe; it was a must.

Identifying the Power Players: IFAF and NFL's Global Push

IFAF has been the backbone of flag football's international growth. It oversees member federations, standardizes the rules, runs competitions, and ensures the sport keeps expanding in the right direction. But it wasn't until the NFL joined the mission full force that things really accelerated.

The NFL didn't just support the Olympic bid; it helped fuel it. Through initiatives like NFL FLAG, global ambassador programs, and events in Mexico, Brazil, the United Kingdom, Germany, and beyond, the league brought the game to new countries, new fans, and new fields. They put flag on some of the biggest stages: halftime shows, Pro Bowl formats, and youth tournaments alongside Super Bowl week.

The message was loud and clear: This sport is the future.

Together, IFAF and the NFL built a powerful alliance, one focused on growing the sport in a sustainable, inclusive, and Olympic-minded way. From youth leagues to elite competitions, the pathway from "backyard" to "Olympic" was starting to take shape.

Getting on the Road to LA: How Teams Will Qualify

I'm sure the big question on every athlete's mind is: How does my team get to the Olympic Games?

While some details are still being finalized, the qualification process is expected to follow a clear and fair path. It will likely mirror what already happens at the international level through IFAF, with World Cups and continental championships playing a major role.

Here's what's expected:

>> **Host country advantage:** The United States will likely receive automatic qualification for both men's and women's teams.

>> **World Cup results:** Placements at IFAF World Cup in 2026 may impact rankings and seedings for LA 2028.

>> **Continental representation:** Top finishers from regional championships in the Americas, Europe, Asia, Africa, and Oceania will be able to compete for a spot at the Olympics through repechage in 2027. (*Repechage* is a French term describing a system in sports where teams that lose in early rounds have a chance to qualify if they meet certain criteria.)

>> **Federation eligibility:** Only teams governed by official IFAF member federations can qualify. This ensures integrity and global coordination.

Each country will decide its own national team selections, but one thing's for sure: The path to LA will be competitive, elite, and unforgettable.

Exploring What This Means for the Sport

Olympic inclusion changes everything. It brings visibility, resources, and legitimacy, but most importantly, it brings opportunity:

>> For young athletes, the idea of competing on the world's biggest stage wearing your country's colors is no longer a fantasy. It's a goal worth chasing. This is the moment to dream bigger.

>> For countries, being in the Olympics unlocks government support, national recognition, and funding. Programs that were once struggling to stay afloat now have reason to grow, invest, and believe.

>> For the sport itself, this is a launchpad. Flag football will now be introduced to millions of new fans, shown on prime-time TV, celebrated in opening ceremonies and embraced as part of the Olympic family.

And it couldn't be happening at a better time. This sport is about speed, strategy, and skill, but it's also about values. Gender equality. Inclusion. Accessibility. Flag football reflects what the future of sport should look like.

6

The Part of Tens

IN THIS PART . . .

Explore skills needed to start playing flag football.

Discover reasons to play flag football.

IN THIS CHAPTER

» **Becoming a good listener and teammate**

» **Being resilient**

» **Building up your agility, speed, and coordination**

» **Having endurance**

» **Staying positive and curious while believing in yourself**

Chapter **20**

Ten Essential Skills to Get Started

You don't need to be the fastest, strongest, or most athletic person to play flag football. In fact, many of the most important skills don't come from the gym; they come from how you listen, how you move, how you think, and how you treat others. That's part of what makes flag football so special. It's a sport that meets you where you are and helps you grow from there.

If you're brand new and wondering where to begin, these ten skills can help you step onto the field with confidence.

Listening and Learning

Flag football can feel like a whole new world at first. You encounter movement in every direction, fast decisions, and unfamiliar terms flying around. The best way to jump in is to stay open and eager to learn. Listening carefully to your coach, your teammates, or even players on the sidelines, give you clues to improve. In flag football, things happen fast, and those who are quick to listen are the ones who grow fastest. Everyone starts somewhere, and those first steps are made clearer when you're tuned in.

Being a Good Teammate

You don't need to be a star to make a big impact. Being a great teammate means celebrating others, encouraging effort, and bringing good energy to the huddle, especially when things get tough. In flag football, there are many circumstances where a player, or even two, is used as a decoy to confuse the defenders and help another player to be open to catch a pass and make a play. Embracing that role shows real teamwork and proves the game isn't just about one player. Flag football is full of quick decisions and high emotions, so having someone who lifts others up can shift the entire vibe of the team. Whether you're on the field or cheering from the sideline, your attitude matters more than you think.

Having the Courage to Try (and Try Again)

Everyone makes mistakes. The difference between a player who grows and one who gives up is simple: One keeps showing up. Courage in flag football doesn't mean never feeling nervous; it means pushing past that feeling. Trying a new position, raising your hand to join a team, going for the ball even when you may drop it — all of that takes guts. And each brave try helps you get better. Resilience is built by giving yourself permission to not be perfect.

Being Agile

Agility is what lets you change direction in an instant. It's how you cut across the field, dodge a defender, or react to a last-second move. In flag football, plays don't go in straight lines; they twist, curve, and shift on the fly. That's why agility is key. When your feet, hips, and brain move in sync, you become hard to catch and fun to watch. Agility turns you into a playmaker, helping you move smarter, not just faster.

Being Fast (If Not the Fastest)

Speed shows up everywhere in flag football. It helps you sprint down the sideline for a touchdown, chase down a runner from behind, or get into position before the ball is snapped. You don't need to be the fastest person alive, but quickness in short bursts is a huge advantage.

TIP

Speed gives you space, surprises your opponents, and helps turn a simple play into something electric. Whether you're running with the ball or racing to make a flag pull, speed keeps you in the action.

Maintaining Coordination and Balance

Your hands, eyes, feet, and brain all have to work together on the field. Whether you're catching a ball, pivoting around a defender, or reaching for a flag, coordination is what keeps it smooth. Balance keeps you upright and in control during sharp turns, quick stops, and fast moves. Without these skills, even the fastest players can get tripped up. With them, you stay centered, stable, and ready to make things happen.

REMEMBER

Many movements in flag football aren't traditional. Training your body and muscles to frequently be able to repeat these movements is a challenge. You may find yourself working muscles in an area (around your knees, for example) that you normally wouldn't think about.

Building Endurance

Flag football is quick, but it keeps going. Between plays, sprints, and moments that demand full focus, having endurance means you can bring the same energy in the last drive as you did in the first. It helps you stay locked in and ready, even after a long game. Endurance isn't just physical; it's mental too. It helps you think clearly, communicate, and keep competing all the way through.

Staying Positive, Even When It's Hard

Sometimes you'll drop a pass. Sometimes your team will lose. And sometimes things just won't go as planned. But flag football, like life, rewards those who bounce back. Positivity isn't about pretending everything's great. It's about finding the good, learning from mistakes, and keeping your head up.

Your teammates feel your energy, and your own confidence grows when you stay focused on what's next instead of what went wrong.

REMEMBER

Being Curious About the Game

The more curious you are, the faster you'll grow. Want to know what a quarterback looks for before a throw? Ask. Wonder why a defense lines up a certain way? Watch and learn. Flag football is full of small details and smart strategies, and exploring them makes the game more fun. Curiosity turns players into students of the game, and students into leaders.

Believing You Belong on the Field

This game is for everyone, no matter your size, background, or skill level. The moment you step onto the field, you're part of the team. Believing you belong helps you stand taller, speak louder, and play freer. Confidence doesn't come from being perfect. It comes from showing up and giving your best.

Flag football is full of players who started just like you, unsure but excited. And now? They're leading, scoring, and shining. You can too.

DIANA
SAYS

IN THIS CHAPTER

» **Strengthening your mental toughness**

» **Exploring new opportunities and feeling empowered**

» **Taking your place as part of a team — and having fun while doing it!**

» **Believing in yourself**

» **Making lifelong friends**

Chapter **21**

Ten Reasons to Play Flag Football

lag football is more than just a sport; it's a doorway to growth, to connection, to self-discovery. It invites you to move your body, challenge your mind, and trust your heart. Whether you're stepping onto the field for the first time or chasing bigger dreams with every snap, this game has something to offer you. It teaches lessons that stick — about resilience, teamwork, leadership, and belief. This chapter offers ten powerful reasons why flag football is worth your time, your energy, and your heart.

You'll Build Mental Toughness

Flag football is a playground to experience life's challenges. It won't always be easy or fun. You'll fail and lose, many, many times. But that's the beauty of it. Every setback teaches you to rise, to trust your fight, and to be resilient — a skill I discuss in Chapter 20 and bring up again because it's that important.

This sport challenges you to try again and again, even when it hurts. Just like in life, you'll miss a flag here and there, you may drop the ball in a key moment, or simply run out of time. But flag football teaches you that there's always another play, another shot. And that you must keep going until the very last whistle, because sometimes, miracles happen. All it takes is faith, heart, and a little belief in that one Hail Mary to change everything.

You'll Find New Opportunities

Flag football is more than just a sport; it's now a path forward for boys and girls, especially for girls and women who can now dream bigger than ever. The explosion of opportunities is rewriting what's possible. Today, flag football players can compete on the biggest international stages, representing their country at a World Cup or even the Olympic Games.

REMEMBER

The opportunities don't stop at the sideline. Through scholarships and academic programs, flag football is also opening doors off the field, helping athletes achieve their educational and professional goals. It's no longer a dream; it's a real path to make it happen.

You'll Feel Empowered

Flag football allows you to be your true self on the field and get to know your potential in ways you never imagined. It gives you a platform to lead, to challenge yourself, and to grow. It breaks stereotypes, especially for girls and women, and teaches you to believe in your strength and potential. Every practice, every game is a reminder that you're capable, competitive, and in control of your own narrative.

DIANA SAYS

That feeling of confidence? It sticks with you long after the final whistle and transcends the field.

You'll Find Your Place

Flag football is for everyone. No matter your size, background, or experience level, there's a role for you. Flag football celebrates diversity, not just in who plays, but in *how* they play. You may be the shifty runner, the strategic thinker, the explosive blitzer, or the go-to receiver. In this game, everyone matters. You won't have to change who you are to belong. You already do.

You'll Discover the Power of Teamwork

That's how dreams come true, not alone, but side by side with your teammates. Flag football reminds you that no great moment happens without the people around you. Success isn't built on one standout performance, but on unity. Every touchdown, every flag pulled, every smart decision is born from trust and collaboration. You learn to listen, to lift each other, to stay strong in tough moments, and to celebrate the little wins together.

That team spirit becomes something bigger. It teaches you how to show up for others in life, just like you do on the field. The power of teamwork goes beyond the game. It builds habits that shape how you connect, support, and lead in everyday life. Together, you grow, fall, rise, sometimes lose, and win.

You'll Have Fun (and It's Easy to Learn)

Flag football is just plain fun. It's fast, creative, and full of highlights, and every play has the potential to be game-changing. Whether you're scoring touchdowns, making flag pulls, or throwing that perfect pass, the thrill is real. Even on the sidelines or watching from a screen, it's exciting, easy to follow, and full of surprises.

TIP

It's also one of the most accessible sports out there. You don't need fancy equipment: just a football, a pair of flags, and a place to play. It can be played almost anywhere: parks, school fields, beaches, or even the street.

And the best part? You don't need to be an athlete or have previous experience. The game is simple, welcoming, and easy to pick up for anyone.

You'll Grow to Believe in Yourself

This sport stretches your limits and reveals what you're truly made of. Every sprint, every drop of sweat, every missed play is part of the journey. With each step forward, you start trusting yourself more. You begin to realize that you are capable of more than you thought — not just on the field, but in life. Flag football teaches you that believing in yourself is the first step to greatness. And when you believe in the power of your dreams, everything begins to shift. Progress builds confidence, confidence builds courage, and courage turns effort into transformation. That belief in your skills, in your heart, in your dreams can change your game — and it can change your life.

You'll Create Lasting Connections

Flag football unites people by heart. We are tied together by the same passion for the game, and that kind of bond is unbreakable. Team sports build strong bonds, but flag football takes it a step further. The nature of the game, being fast-paced, inclusive, and team-centered, brings people together quickly. You learn to trust one another, celebrate together, and lift each other through wins and losses. Whether it's a casual recreational league or a national team, the people you meet through flag often become lifelong friends.

You'll Build Leadership Skills

Flag football creates leaders, on and off the field. From calling plays to helping a teammate bounce back from a tough moment, the sport teaches you how to guide others, stay accountable, and step up when it counts. You don't need to be the loudest voice. In flag, leadership comes in all styles, and every team needs different types of leaders to succeed.

You'll Develop a Healthier Body

Flag football is a full-body workout in disguise. The sport demands quick sprints, sudden stops, directional changes, hand-eye coordination, and explosive movements, all of which improve cardiovascular health, agility, endurance, and muscle tone. Since you're constantly on the move and immersed in the game, it doesn't feel like a typical workout. It's play, but your body will thank you.

Glossary

1-point conversion: A scoring play after a touchdown where the offense runs a play from the 5-yard line for one extra point.

2-point conversion: A scoring play after a touchdown where the offense runs a play from the 10-yard line for two extra points.

5-on-5: A style of flag football where each team has five players on the field at a time. It's the official format used in international competitions sanctioned by the International Federation of Flag Football (IFAF).

7-on-7: A style of flag football where each team has seven players on the field at a time. Common in high school and college leagues.

7-yard chain: A chain that connects two indicators signaling where the blitzer is positioned before a play starts.

audible: A change in the play called at the line of scrimmage, usually by the quarterback, after reading the defense.

back judge: Focused on deep passes and defensive coverage, the back judge is a referee watching for holding, illegal contact, and defensive fouls.

backfield: The area behind the line of scrimmage where the quarterback and running backs usually line up.

ball carrier: The player holding the ball and advancing it forward during a play.

ball possession: The period when one team has its offensive players on the field, with control of the ball.

beach flag: A 4-on-4 style of flag football that's played on sand.

blitz/blitzer: A defensive player who rushes the quarterback right after the snap, coming from at least 7 yards behind the line. Also known as the rusher.

center: An offensive player who starts the play at the line of scrimmage and snaps the ball (passes it backward) to the quarterback.

cleats: Shoes with molded or detachable studs on the bottom that provide traction on the field.

coed flag: A mixed-gender style of flag football; this style can be 5-on-5, 7-on-7, and even beach flag.

completion: A legal forward pass caught by a receiver in bounds.

conversion: The extra point(s) attempted after a touchdown — either 1-point (from the 5-yard line) or 2-point (from the 10).

cornerback (CB): A defensive player responsible for covering wide receivers, typically playing near the sidelines. Sometimes referred to as corner.

coverage (defensive): A strategy used by the defense to guard against passing plays, either through man-to-man or zone schemes.

dead ball: A ball that is no longer in play, usually after a flag pull, incomplete pass, touchdown, or the ball going out of bounds.

defense: A team is the defense when their opponent has the ball (the offense); the defense does everything in their power to stop the offense from scoring.

defensive line: The front line of the defense, usually where the rusher lines up.

dive/jump: An illegal move where the ball carrier jumps or lunges forward, typically to avoid a flag pull.

double stop: A route where a receiver runs and then abruptly stops and plants their feet to be an easy target for the quarterback.

down: A play or attempt. The offense has four downs to reach the midline or score.

down indicator: A visual marker that shows the current down (first, second, third, or fourth) during a series of plays, typically displayed on a pole or a digital device held by an official on the sideline.

drive: A series of offensive plays until the team scores, turns the ball over, or runs out of downs.

drill: A repetitive practice activity used to develop specific skills.

dropback: When a quarterback takes some steps backward after receiving the snapped ball; they do this to see what's happening on the field before making a pass.

end zone: The scoring area at each end of the field. A touchdown is scored when the ball is carried into or caught in this zone.

Every Day Drills (EDD): Simple exercises that, when done consistently, can help an athlete keep fundamentals sharp and make improvements day after day.

extra point: The bonus scoring attempt after a touchdown. (*See also:* conversion.)

false start: A penalty when an offensive player moves illegally before the snap.

field dimensions: In 5-on-5 flag football, a standard field is 50 yards long and 25 yards wide, with 10-yard end zones.

field judge: A referee on the sidelines watching for penalties, out-of-bounds calls, and scoring plays.

first down: When the offense advances the ball past the midfield line within their set of downs, earning a new set of four downs.

flag: A strip of fabric, usually nylon, attached to a flag football player's belt.

flag belt: A belt with two or three attached flags that each player wears. The goal on defense is to pull these flags.

flag guarding: An illegal move where a runner blocks defenders from pulling their flag using their hands, ball, or body.

flag pull: The action of removing the flag from the belt of the ball carrier to stop the play. Also called *deflagging*.

formation: The specific arrangement of offensive or defensive players before the snap.

forward pass: A pass thrown in the direction of the opponent's end zone.

free safety (FS): A member of the secondary (defensive backs responsible for covering receivers and defending passes) and the last line of defense when it comes to deep routes. Also referred to as the safety.

game clock official: This referee is positioned on the sideline and ensures that time is managed correctly.

hand-off: A legal exchange where the ball is handed from one player to another without passing it.

hash marks: Small lines marked on the field to indicate key yardage points, often used to align plays or set formations.

head referee: The main official who oversees the entire game and makes final rulings on plays.

hitch route: A route where the receiver runs a short distance and then stops to turn back, facing the quarterback to catch a pass.

holding: An illegal action where a player grabs or holds an opponent or their equipment to slow them down or gain advantage.

incompletion/incomplete pass: A forward pass that touches the ground before being caught, or one that is caught out of bounds.

interception: A defensive player catching a pass intended for the offense.

International Federation of American Football (IFAF): The governing organization overseeing American football, including flag football.

International Olympic Committee (IOC): The international organization overseeing the modern Olympic Games.

International World Games Association (IWGA): The organizer of The World Games, an international multi-sport event that features sports and disciplines not yet included in the Olympic Games.

jersey: The official shirt a player wears during the game, often with a number on the back.

juke: A quick and deceptive change of direction to evade defenders without making physical contact; typically, the player fakes going one way and instead goes another way.

jump/dive: Jumping or diving to avoid a flag pull is considered illegal in most rule sets.

linebacker (LB): A versatile defensive player who lines up behind the rusher and covers the middle of the field.

line of scrimmage (LOS): The imaginary line where the play starts, drawn across the field where the ball is placed.

loss of down (LOD): A penalty that causes the offense to lose the right to repeat the down.

man-to-man coverage: A defensive scheme where each defender is responsible for one offensive player. Often referred to simply as man coverage.

middle line: The line at the exact middle of the field. Teams must cross it for a new first down.

mouthguard/mouthpiece: A protective device worn in the mouth to reduce the risk of dental injuries.

no-run zone: A marked zone (usually 5 yards before the end zone or midfield) where running plays are not allowed.

offense: A team is the offense when they have possession of the ball and are moving the ball down the field, attempting to score touchdowns.

out route: A route where the receiver runs straight and then cuts sharply toward the sideline.

pass interference: An illegal act by a defender or receiver that prevents the opponent from making a fair attempt to catch the ball.

running back (RB): An offensive player who receives hand-offs from the quarterback and runs the ball downfield, attempting to move the ball closer to the goal and eventually score touchdowns.

rusher: A defensive player tasked with pressuring the quarterback. (Often the same as a blitzer; sometimes called pass rusher.)

penalty: A rule violation that results in a loss of yards, a loss of down, or a repeat of the play.

pick: Slang term for an interception.

pick six: When an interception is returned for a touchdown.

post route: A route where the receiver runs straight and cuts toward the center of the field at a 45-degree angle.

pylon: A small marker placed at the corners of the end zones.

quarterback (QB): The leader of the offense who receives the snap and makes the decision to pass, hand off, or run the ball.

red zone: The area within 20 yards of the opponent's end zone. It's a critical scoring area.

reverse: A running play where the ball is handed to one player, who then hands it to another running in the opposite direction.

route: The path a receiver runs to get open for a pass. (*See also:* route tree.)

route tree: A diagram showing the various routes a receiver can run, usually numbered from 0–9.

rusher: A defensive player who applies pressure to the quarterback after the snap. Also known as the *blitzer*.

sack: When the rusher pulls the quarterback's flag before a forward pass is thrown.

safety: A scoring play for the defense (worth 2 points) when the offense is stopped in its own end zone.

secondary: The group of defensive backs responsible for covering receivers and defending passes.

shorts (game shorts): Part of the uniform, worn without pockets to avoid flag interference.

sidelines: The boundary lines along each side of the field. Players or coaches must remain outside of them when not in play.

slant route: A route where the receiver takes a few steps forward and cuts at a diagonal angle across the field.

snap: The action that starts the play; the ball is passed backward to the quarterback by the snapper (or center).

spin/spinning: A legal move where the runner rotates their body to evade a flag pull, as long as it doesn't raise the flag's level.

sprint: A short burst of fast running used during plays or drills.

stance: The starting position of a player before the snap.

stop route: A route where the receiver runs forward and abruptly stops to turn and face the quarterback.

team area: Space located 3 yards behind the sidelines that's 20 yards long (18.2 meters). It's where the coaches and team staff stand with players who aren't currently on the field.

timeout: A pause requested by a team to stop the clock or regroup. Each team gets two per half.

touchback: When the ball is declared dead in the end zone and possession is given to the defending team at the 5-yard line.

touchdown: When a player crosses the opponent's goal line with the ball or catches a pass in the end zone. Worth 6 points.

wide receiver (WR): An offensive player who specializes in catching passes.

zone coverage: A defensive strategy where players guard a specific area of the field instead of one assigned player.

Index

A

acceleration, 144
accuracy drills, 139
agility and footwork, 143

B

backfield, 47, 68, 71, 89, 94, 101–105, 107–109, 111, 120–121, 143, 187
back judge, 36
ball, 26–27
  attacking the ball, 147
  catching the ball, 142
ball carrier, 45, 53, 91, 118–120, 130, 148, 149, 212
ball possession, 38
banded hip openers, 160
baseball and softball players, 166
basketball players, 166
beach flag, 18, 209, 210
beating a defense
  cover 2 defense, 179–181
  cover 3 defense, 181–184
  cover 4 defense, 184–187
  cover 31 defense, 187–189
  crossing routes, 176–177
  double QB system, 189–191
  man-to-man coverage, 173–174
  matchup, 174–175
  seam route, 180
  zone coverage, 177–178
beating man-to-man coverage, 86
blitz/blitzer, 23, 51, 52, 67–69, 93, 102, 103, 106, 140–141, 163–165, 187, 209
  body control, 115
  coverage, 121
  crouched and ready, 117
  defending a crowded backfield, 120–121
  linebacker, 118
  lining up, 115–116
  practicing drills by position, 150–151
  reaction, 114–115

reading hand-offs, 118–120
role and responsibilities, 111–113
speed, 114, 163
stance, 116–117
three-point stance, 117
two-point stance, 117

C

catching the ball
  beating man-to-man coverage, 86
  body positioning, 85
  eyes on the ball, 84
  field awareness, 87
  finishing the play, 85–86
  gaining yards, 86
  hands ready, 85
  hips and dips, 87
  no contact/blocking, 87
  quick feet, 87
center
  field vision and awareness, 81
  quick release, 81
  red zone, 80
  stance and snap, 80–81
cleats, 24–26, 37
clock management, 58
coaches
  athletic trainers, 35
  beyond the game, 34
  building team culture, 31–32
  coach's resume, 30
  defensive players, 39
  flag football player, 39–40
  game strategy and preparation, 31
  handling challenges and setbacks, 32
  leadership, 30–31
  managers, 35
  mentorship, 31
  motivation and earning players' trust, 32–33
  offensive players, 37–39

coaches *(continued)*
  the players, 37
  power of motivation, 33–34
  referees and officials, 35–36
coed flag, 209–210
compound routes, 83–84
Continental Championships
  Africa, 225–226
  America, 224–225
  Asia, 225
  Europe, 225
cornerbacks (CBs), 69–71, 102, 105, 120, 124, 126–130, 146–148, 155–150, 189, 190, 199, 201
crash course, 40

D

dead ball, 22
defensive backs, 123
defensive coverage
  cover 2 zone, 198–199
  cover 3 zone, 199–200
  cover 4 zone, 201–202
  cover 31 zone, 202–203
  man-to-man coverage, 197–198
  man *vs.* zone coverages, 197
defensive footwork, 147
defensive formations
  field position, 196
  game situation, 195
  goals, 193–194
  time management, 196
discipline, 203
double QB system, 189–191
double quarterback, 103
double stop, 150
down indicator, 22–23, 37, 48, 126
drive, 33, 44, 169–170
dropback, 64

E

effective offense
  adaptability, 169
  consistency, 169
  drive, 169–170
  efficiency, 169
  game control, 169
end zone, 18, 20, 22, 44, 209, 211
Every Day Drills (EDD), 138, 146, 148, 162
explosiveness, 144, 164–165
extra point, 46, 191, 211

F

false start, 51, 52, 80, 117
federation eligibility, 236
the field
  competitive play, 17
  field dimensions, 18
  marks on the field, 19–20
  playing surface, 18
field dimensions, 18, 211
field judge, 36, 47, 48
first down, 20, 22, 23, 41, 51, 53, 73, 88, 112, 113, 117, 126
5-on-5, 14, 41, 42, 44, 47, 70, 72, 89, 90, 208, 210, 211, 218, 220, 221
5-yard penalties, 52–53
flag belt, 10
flag football
  adult leagues, 14
  basic facts, 9–10
  in college, 214–220
  discovering, 8–9
  game rules, 10
  high school sport in United States, 214
  International competitions, 15–16
  levels of play, 13–16
  in NFL, 14–15
  overview, 7–8
  reasons to play, 243–246
  reviewing the rules, 220–221
  start young and grow, 11–12
  stereotypes, 10
  tracking history, 12
  World cups, 13
flag football shape
  agility (footwork), 157
  blitzers, 163

conditioning by position, 154–155
crossing over, 165–166
endurance, 156, 165
explosiveness, 157–158, 164–165
quarterbacks (QBs), 158–163
speed, 155–156
X factor, 154
flag guarding, 52, 53, 97–98, 212
flag pull, 25, 52, 86, 95, 97–98, 113, 125, 150, 151, 198, 212, 245
football players, 166
footwork and agility, 144–145
forward pass, 53, 54, 90–92, 211
free safeties, 146–148
free safety (FS), 69, 74, 128, 130–132, 146–148, 183, 190, 199, 200
fundamentals
  ball positioning, 66
  dropping back, 64
  good grip, 64–65
  power and efficiency, 65
  quick feet, 64
  stance, 63
  timing and accuracy, 65–66

G

game-changing flag pull, 151
game clock official, 36
game varieties
  beach, 209
  coed (or mixed), 209–210
  5-on-5, 208
  7-on-7, 208–209
gymnasts and dancers, 166

H

hand-eye coordination, 115
hand-off, 92–94, 96, 118–121
head referee, 36
hip agility and fluidity, 145–146
hitch route, 70
holding, 42, 125
hybrid players, 91

I

IFAF 5-on-5 Flag Football rulebook, 90
incompletion/incomplete pass, 51, 65, 104, 106, 126, 194
Instituto Politecnico Nacional (IPN), 216
interception, 20, 104, 124, 128, 131, 147, 195
International Federation of American Football (IFAF), 9
  Continental Championships, 224–225
  overview, 223–224
  World Championships, 224, 226–227
  World Rankings, 228
International Federation of Flag Football (IFAF), 208
International Olympic Committee (IOC), 231, 233, 234
International World Games Association (IWGA), 229, 231

J

jersey, 10, 23–24, 36, 53, 226
juke, 87, 96, 98, 114, 143, 148
jump/dive, 52, 53

L

linebacker (LB), 69, 118–120, 155–158, 183
  backfield, 103–105
  communication, 107
  filling a hybrid role, 102
  instinct, 107
  is positioned, 105–106
  overview, 101–102
  playing downfield, 103–105
  practicing drills by position, 149–150
  pulling flags, 150
  quickness, 106–107
  reacting, 149–150
  reading the offense, 108–109
  stance, 108
  vision, 107
Los Angeles 2028 Olympic Games
  global ambassador programs, 235
  grassroots to Olympic bid, 233–234
  Olympic inclusion changes, 236
  teams qualification, 235–236
loss of down (LOD), 51, 53–54

M

mastering offensive formations
  bunch formation, 172–173
  spread formation, 170–171
  trips formation, 171–172
med ball scoop toss, 164
mental game (reading the qb), 115
mentality to precision
  accuracy (and timing), 61
  agility, 62
  arm strength and release, 61
  competitiveness, 61–62
  emotional intelligence, 62
  intelligence, 62
  positive leadership, 61
  strategy, 62
  vision, 63
Mexico
  independent universities, 215–216
  state-funded universities, 216
mind games, 204
mouthguard/mouthpiece, 24–26

N

nailing one-and two-point conversions, 191–192
National Association of Intercollegiate Athletics
  (NAIA), 216–218
National Collegiate Athletic Association
  (NCAA), 218–220
National Football League (NFL), 9
National Junior College Athletic Association
  (NJCAA), 218
NFL FLAG football
  international intention, 212
  overview, 210
  rules, 211–212
90-90 hip switches, 160
no-run zone, 20, 45, 46, 90, 91, 211

O

offensive plays and strategies
  beating a defense, 173–190
  effective offense, 168–170
  mastering offensive formations, 170–173
  nailing one-and two-point conversions, 191–192
  team's strengths, 168
Olympic movement, 16
1-point conversion, 46, 191–192
out route, 83, 170, 180, 181

P

pass interference, 48, 51, 53, 125
penalties and violations
  automatic first down, 53
  disqualification, 54
  5-yard penalties, 52–53
  loss of down, 54
  10-yard penalties, 53
penalty, 36, 37, 42, 51–52, 81, 90, 92, 97, 98, 113, 115,
  117, 119, 212
pigeon exercise, 160
playmaker
  competitiveness, 79
  consistency, 79
  field awareness, 78
  hands, 78
  speed and endurance, 78
  timing, 79
post route, 83, 176, 183, 184
practicing drills by position
  blitzers, 150–151
  cornerbacks and safeties, 146–148
  Every Day Drills (EDD), 138
  linebackers, 149–150
  overview, 137–138
  quarterbacks (QBs), 138–141
  running backs, 143–146
  wide receivers and centers, 142–143
Pro Bowl Games, 234
pulling flags, 148
pylon, 22

Q

quarterbacks (QBs)
  accuracy drills, 139–140
  balance and agility, 162–163
  blitzers, 140–141
  core stability, 159

fundamentals, 63–66
hip mobility, 160
from mentality to precision, 60–63
pre-pass footing reset, 141
reading the defense, 66–75
role of the offense, 57–58
shoulder mobility, 160–162
size matter, 60
strong throwing arm, 59
throwing on the go, 140

R

reading the defense
7-second rule, 67–68
coverages, 68–74
pre-snap read, 66–67
in red zone, 75
reasons to play, flag football
create lasting connections, 246
feeling empowered, 244
find new opportunities, 244
to find your place, 244–245
grow to believe in yourself, 245–246
having fun, 245
healthier body, 246
leadership skills, 246
mental toughness, 243–244
teamwork, 245
red zone, 75, 80, 127, 175, 180, 184, 186, 187
referee's iconic look, 36–37
referees' signals
game management signals, 49–50
penalty signals, 51–52
scoring and possession signals, 51
reverse, 92–93, 108, 118
roles of the officials
down judge (DJ), 48
field judge, 48
game management signals, 49–50
penalties and violations, 52–54
penalty signals, 51–52
referee, 47
responsibilities, 48–49
scoring and possession signals, 51

side judge (SJ), 48
route tree, 81–83
rules
check out coin toss, 43–44
downs and yards, 44–45
golden rule, 41–42
ins and outs of game clock, 42–43
roles of the officials, 46–54
scoring points, 45–46
running back (RB), 89, 91, 92, 97, 118, 143–146
acceleration and explosiveness, 144
EDD drill, 146
footwork and agility, 144–145
hip agility and fluidity, 145–146
running game
acceleration, 96
being agile, 97
field awareness, 97
flag guarding, 97–98
hand-offs, 92
hybrid players, 91
receiving hand-off, 96
reverse, 92–93
running back (RB), 91
running play, 90–91
run the ball, 91–92
skills, 95–98
variations on running formations, 93–95
running routes, 142–143

S

sack, 46, 67, 113, 114
scoring points
extra points, 46
safeties, 46
touchdowns, 45
secondary, 117–127
secondary players
body control (non-contact) and reaction, 125
common mistakes, 133
cornerbacks, 127–130
flag pulling, 125–126
free safety, 130–132
game situation, 126–127

secondary players *(continued)*
  hands, 124
  overview, 123
  speed and quickness, 124
  vision, 124
7-on-7, 41, 208–210, 220, 221
7-yard chain, 23
situational awareness
  adjusting the situation, 127
  forcing them to stay in bounds, 127
  know the down and distance, 126
skills
  being agile, 240
  being curious, 242
  being fast, 241
  being good teammate, 240
  believing you belong on field, 242
  building endurance, 241
  courage to try, 240
  listening and learning, 239–240
  maintain coordination and balance, 241
  stay positive, 242
slant route, 104, 181
soccer players, 166
spin/spinning, 7, 26, 27, 64, 98, 113, 154, 208
stance, 63, 80–81, 108, 116–117
stop route, 181, 185, 186, 188

T

team area, 23
team's backbone, 35
10-yard penalties, 53
thinking smart, 88
touchdown, 22, 30, 45, 51, 130, 160, 191, 195, 211, 245
track athletes, 166
2-point conversion, 191–192

U

uniforms
  cleats, 24–25
  flags, 25

jersey, 23–24
mouthpiece, 25–26
not permitted, 26
pants, 24
United States
  high school sport, 214
  NAIA, 216–218
  NCAA, 218–220
Universidad Nacional Autónoma de México (UNAM), 216
unstoppable defense, 203

W

wide receivers
  lining up, 79
  motions, 80
  release, 80
  stance, 80
World Championship, 13
World Games
  history of, 229–231
  IFAF World Championships, 231–232

Y

yard lines
  7-yard chain, 23
  down indicator, 22–23
  goal lines, 22
  marks painted, 22
  out of bounds, 22
  team areas, 23

Z

zone coverage, 69, 80, 102, 127, 129–132, 177, 178, 197

About the Author

Diana Flores is the captain and quarterback of Mexico's World Champion National Flag Football team. Flores is also a highly sought-after game analyst and sports broadcaster for major networks, like FOX Deportes and Univision, and has covered some of their biggest events, including Super Bowl LVIII. As the sport's Global Ambassador for both the NFL and the International Federation of American Football (IFAF), Flores is dedicated to advancing flag football's reach worldwide.

A flag football superstar, Flores has competed in numerous national and international tournaments, representing Mexico on the world stage. Her career highlights include four National Titles since 2017, a Bronze Medal in the 2016 World Cup, a Silver Medal in the 2021 World Cup, and recognition as the Best Offensive Player at the 2018 World Flag Football Championship. In 2022, she was named the Most Valuable Player (MVP) at the World Games, where she led her team to a Gold Medal. Most recently, Flores again led Mexico to another championship and back-to-back Gold Medal victories at the 2025 World Games.

Off the field, Flores continues to break barriers and to inspire. She is being honored as the 2025 Game Changer Award recipient by the Women's Sports Foundation and was recognized by Forbes in its prestigious "30 Under 30" Class of 2024. In 2023, she was the featured star in the NFL's Super Bowl LVII advertisement, "Run With It," which won an Emmy and further cemented her as one of the most recognizable faces in flag football and a global champion of the sport's historic growth.

Author's Acknowledgments

This project means the world to me. It's one of the biggest and most special milestones in my career; the chance to share what I love most with new audiences around the world. Writing this book challenged me in ways I never expected, but every late night, every edit, and every memory poured into these pages was worth it. Seeing it become a reality fills me with immense pride and gratitude.

I'm deeply thankful to every person who believed in me when opportunities were few, to every coach and teammate who pushed me to grow, and to every young girl who reminds me why this work matters. You are the reason I keep fighting for this sport, for the chance to play, to lead, and to dream.

To my family, thank you for your endless love, patience, and strength. Especially to my brother, Jaime, thank you for sharing this passion for flag football with me like no one else, for being my partner in every new challenge, on and off the field. You've been my teammate in life since day one.

Dreams like this one don't come true alone. To the incredible *For Dummies* team and my editors Jennifer Yee, Nicole Sholly, and Matt Reimel, thank you for working on this project with so much dedication, care, and enthusiasm. And to my entire management team, thank you for believing in this vision and helping me bring it to life.

And finally, to every reader holding this book: I hope you find a piece of inspiration in these pages, to grab a flag, take the field, and discover how this game can change your life, just like it changed mine.

Publisher's Acknowledgments

Senior Acquisitions Editor: Jennifer Yee
Project Manager: Nicole Sholly
Copy Editor: Christine Pingleton
Technical Editor: Matt Reimel

Senior Managing Editor: Kristie Pyles
Production Editor: Bharaneedharan Murthy
Cover Image: Courtesy of Andy Keith